RABBI DOVID MEISELS

Rosh Hashanah & Yom Kippur Secrets

The Mysteries Revealed

Translated by Rabbi Avraham Y. Finkel

ROSH HASHANAH AND YOM KIPPUR SECRETS

First Published 2004
Copyright © 2004 by
RABBI DOVID D. MEISELS

ISBN 1-931681-61-9

Other books by the author:
Shabbos Secrets
The Radiance of Rosh Hashanah 1&2
The Radiance of Yom Kippur
Perspectives on Pesach
The Ten Wondrous Makkos
Seder Talk Haggadah
Bar Mitzvah and Tefillin Secrets

Distributed By:
ISRAEL BOOK SHOP
501 Prospect Street
Lakewood NJ 08701
Tel: (732) 901-3009
Fax: (732) 901-4012
Email: isrbkshp @ aol.com

Printed in the U.S.A.

This book is dedicated
to be a source of merit
in restoring the health
and in strengthening

יששכר דוב בן תמר נ"י

May Hashem send him from
heaven a speedy and complete
recovery of spirit and body
among the other sick people of
Israel.

In the *Zechus* of being
Mezakeh es Harabbim
may his parents
merit to have much
nachas from him and
from the entire family.

Rabbi Y. Belsky
506 East 7th Street
Brooklyn, NY 11218

ישראל הלוי בעלסקי

Rabbi Dovid Meisels has once again demonstrated his masterful talent for presenting a basic tenet of Torah Judaism in full color, in a manner which both attract and inforces, teaches and inspires and inflames the desire to return to the sources from when this treasurehouse of knowledge, derived. This book is about Bar Mitzvah. Our sages teach us that at the Bar Mitzvah one's mind mature to a level known as Da'as. Prior to that age a great amount of accumulated knowledge may have been acquired. The process of chinuch can often achieve incredible results with some youngsters surpassing many of their elders who have long celebrated their Bar Mitzvah. Yet the da'as of maturation will not arrive until the day of his Bar Mitzvah. At that moment a new level of insight and analytic ability will begin to seep into the child's thinking. This must then be nurtured and nourished for it to develop properly, and to achieve its potential.

Rabbi Meisels has given an extra ordinary gift to these youths and their mentors culling from the holy sources the choicest material to guide them in understanding the many aspects of Bar Mitzvah in full depth.

In some instance he has taken Torah gems of great complexity and presented their essence in a manner digestible to young and old alike without losing a grain of their profundity and deeper meaning.

May Hashem Yisborach grant him the wherewithal to carry on his wonderful work as a guide to his flock and as an inspiring educator of young men.

Signed this 4th day of Adar 5764.

Rabbi Yisroel Belsky

This haskamah was written for the book "Bar Mitzvah and Tefillin Secrets" published by the same author

אגודת הרבנים דארצות הברית וקנדה

**THE UNION OF ORTHODOX RABBIS
OF THE UNITED STATES AND CANADA
235 EAST BROADWAY
NEW YORK, N.Y. 10002**

964-6337
964-6338

13 Shevat, 5764/2004

Rabbi Dovid Dov Meisels, the son of the revered Rebbe of Seagate, NY, showed me the sefer he wrote, entitled *Pe'er David*, a superb anthology on the subject of bar mitzvah with a detailed discussion of the laws and customs of the mitzvah of *tefillin*. The sefer will be of great benefit to boys who are about to become bar mitzvah, their fathers and teachers, and to anyone seeding a better understanding of *kiyum hamitzvos*.

I am delighted to note that the sefer *Pe'er David* is now available in an easy-to-read English translation, making it accessible to the widest circle of readers.

The Gemara in *Sanhedrin* 69b tells us that Betzalel was thirteen years old when he made the *Mishkan*. How are we to understand that a thirteen year-old boy was given the task of building the abode where the *Shechinah* would dwell? This teaches us that every bar mitzvah boy has the potential of growing up to build a home worthy of having the *Shechinah* rest on it.

In the same vein, the Sages tell us that Yaakov's sons, Shimon and Levi, were only thirteen years old when single-handedly they rescued their sister Dinah form captivity in Shechem. With selfless dedication the young boys fought for the sake of Jewish *kedushah* and morality, setting an example for every bar mitzvah boy to do his best to preserve the eternal values of *kedushas Yisrael*.'

My *berachah* is that the author's "springs may spread outward," and in the merit of the mitzvah of tefillin may we be worthy to see the coming of Mashiach and the *geulah sheleimah*, speedily in our days.

With Torah greeting,

צבי מאיר גינסבורג
Chairman and Director
The Union of Orthodox Rabbis
Of the United States and Canada

★★★This haskamah was written for the book "Bar Mitzvah and Tefillin Secrets" published by the same author★★★

Table of Contents

Preface

The days of Elul approach. The month of mercy gives us time, days of preparation to greet the great and awesome day of Hashem—Rosh Hashanah. Every Jewish soul tries to connect with the Creator, to fan the spark of *teshuvah* that is found within every heart. For we know that our lives hang in the balance on the Day of Judgment.

How do we allow the fire to ignite? How can we give it the proper fuel to burn? How do we awaken our fear of Hashem, so that the outcome for the New Year will be only good?

"*Zechor yemos olam, binu shnos dor va'dor.* Remember the days of world, understand the years of every generation."

Our fathers and teachers recall the holy service of righteous individuals in the previous generation. In their day, we are told, you could see on their faces that the days of *teshuvah* had arrived. You could see the fire that burned inside; it was evident in every footstep.

Every individual made great preparations for the Days of Awe. He dug deep into the depths of his soul, carefully accounting where his service of Hashem was lacking. He sincerely tried to determine where he strayed, how to correct what went wrong. Some committed themselves to extra study of Torah. Others worked to improve their character traits, or undertook acts of kindness to help their fellow man. Still others uplifted their *davening* so it could fly on wings to the Throne of Glory.

In those days, even the plain folk prepared themselves before *davening*. They prayed slowly, trying with all their might to have the proper *kavanah*. These simple workers, who usually rushed every morning to their stores and businesses, remained in the *beis medrash* until noon during Elul. They were busy with Torah and *avodah*, focusing their hearts on their Father in Heaven. They concentrated on repairing the shortcomings of their souls, preparing to be worthy of greeting their King and Creator during the Days of Awe that were quickly approaching.

We acknowledge that it is a different world today. We sigh for what we have lost and not regained.

Yet it is not only in our times that the descent of the generations has been so obvious. In the previous generation, too, people ruefully recalled what used to be. Jews who were completely submerged in the service of Hashem—even they bemoaned the descent of the generations. They, too, would recall with longing the days of their youth.

"*Rosh Chodesh* Elul of yesteryear!" This was the refrain on the lips of every generation. With great emotion, they would recollect the fiery enthusiasm and inspiration of the righteous during the High Holy Days. They would envision the service of sincere Jews during earlier days, when all were possessed by the fear and trepidation that enveloped the world during Elul.

Indeed, *Chazal* say in *Shabbos* 112b, "If the original generations were like angels, then we are like men; if the original generations were like men, then we are like donkeys. If the difference between the *tenaim*, the compilers of the Mishnah, and *amoraim*, the compilers of the Gemara, was like the difference between angels and men, then where are we?

Today, in our generation, we can say truthfully say, "*Boshnu mikol dor*, we are the lowliest of all generations." There never was a generation like this. We've reached rock bottom. There is nowhere lower to go. Only Hashem knows what the next generation will bring.

We live in a world without Torah, without *chochmah*, without *tzaddikim*, without a teacher. We are without a *kohen* or a *navi* or a leader. We have no one to hold our hands, to strengthen us and guide us.

Today, more than ever, we need the fiery words and lessons of our rabbis and teachers. They have grasped—and actually tasted—the fearful holiness of the High Holy Days, these awesome days that are predisposed for *teshuvah*, regret and correcting our actions. Our teachers have recorded words of reproof and encouragement to arouse *Bnei Yisrael* to repent from their sins, to make peace with their Father in Heaven.

The words of our *chachamim* are like fiery coals. They can enter the heart and pierce the mind. They startle the slumbering soul. Even those who have remained unaware throughout the year can now awaken and rise—to purify, uplift the soul and attain the holy knowledge, fear and true love of the Creator.

Though these words and lessons were spoken many years ago, they are still alive. Our wise teachers speak to us—today. The lessons are still steadfast and truthful, empowered throughout the generations to enjoin the souls of Israel to cleave to their Creator.

★ ★ ★

I thank Hashem with all my heart for all the kindness He has bestowed upon me. I pray that this collection of insights about the High Holy Days should be helpful to every reader in preparing for the upcoming holy days.

This compilation covers *Rosh Chodesh* Elul, *erev* Rosh Hashanah, the two days of Rosh Hashanah, the Ten Days of Repentence, Shabbos *Shuvah, erev* Yom Kippur and Yom Kippur. Whether the reader wishes to extract *mussar*, practical lessons regarding the month of Elul, the proper outlook for Rosh Hashanah or the feeling for the fearful day of Yom Kippur, he will find every detail, every nuance in order and in its proper place. The path of *teshuvah* is clearly marked. Let the reader open his tightly closed heart and purify himself, pour out his soul to Hashem with a pure heart.

I pray to Hashem that this work be an inspiration to the masses to do *teshuvah* and to perfect the service of Hashem. In the merit of the words of the true *tzaddikim* contained within these pages, may Hashem allow me to do complete *teshuvah*. May I merit to spend my entire life in the tent of Torah, going from strength to strength. May I merit to spread Torah and glorify it, with blessing and success, *nachas*, serenity and much Heavenly assistance.

"*Tichleh shanah vekilliloseha veteichal shanah uvirchoseha.* May this year with all its curses finish, and may the new year with all its blessings begin." May Hashem sign and seal His nation in the book for *tzaddikim gemurim*, good life and peace. May the Master of the universe call out to us, "*Salachti*, I have forgiven you!" and sound the great *shofar* announcing the coming of Mashiach and the final redemption, speedily in our days.

Rabbi Dovid D. Meisels
Brooklyn, NY
Elul 5764

Acknowledgements

I wish to express my gratitude to Reb Avraham Yaakov Finkel, the well-known Torah themes, for his highly professional and meticulous translation fro the Yiddish into lucid, conversational English. The original Yiddish text was published under the title Otzer Hamoadim.

I am forever thankful to a dear friend, R' Aryeh Schachter who's help at all times has enabled this book to become a reality. A special thanks for the hard work he put into the pictures.

My special appreciation to Mrs. E. Langer for her superb job of editing the manuscript.

I am indebted to my daughter-in-law, Mrs. S. R. Meisels for her proficiency and talent in arranging the page layout.

I want to express my hakoras hatov to R' Yaakov Moshe Berkowitz, a dedicated friend of my father, Harav Hagaon Rabbi Zalmen Leib Meisels, and a staunch supporter of his kehilla, and benefactor to *kol davar shebikedushah*. It was his suggestion to have this sefer translated into English. His generous support and encouragement enabled to bring this project to fruition, *kedei lezakos es harabbim*.

May Hashem grant much nachas, simchos, and good health to him and his entire mishpachah.

Chapter One

Elul:
Month of Teshuvah

Allusions to Elul

The first letters of each word in the verse, "*Ani ledodi vedodi li,*
I am my Beloved's and my Beloved is mine" *(Shir Hashirim 6:3)*
spell out the word Elul. Who is the "Beloved" in this verse? It is a
reference to Hashem. For by doing *teshuvah* in the month of Elul,
the Jewish people express their desire of coming closer to
Hashem—and Hashem responds by declaring His love for the
Jewish people.

All four words in this verse end with the letter *yud,* with a
numeric value of 10   resulting in a total of 40. This alludes to the
forty days from *Rosh Chodesh* Elul until Yom Kippur, when our
closeness to Hashem reaches its peak.

Another allusion to Elul can be found in the initials of four
words in the verse, "*Umol Hashem Elo-kecha es levavecha ve'es levav
zarecha,* Hashem will remove the barriers from your hearts and
from the hearts of your descendants, so you will love Hashem
your G-d with all your heart and soul." *(Devarim 30:6)* Here is a

clear indication of the power of *teshuvah* to awaken the love of Hashem in our hearts.

> On one *Rosh Chodesh Elul*, Rabbi Mordechai of Lechovitz happened to overhear an old peasant exhorting his colleagues. "Listen, fellows, harvesting time has started. If you'll work hard now, you'll be able to eat all year long. But if you're lazy and goof off, you'll go hungry all year."
>
> Turning to his chassidim, the Rebbe excitedly called out, "Dear brothers! The month of Elul is the source of blessing for serving Hashem for the entire year. Whoever applies himself in this month will experience joy all year long. Serving Hashem will come easily to him. But being lazy in Elul will cause sadness, making it difficult to serve Hashem with heartfelt prayer."

The *B'nei Yissoschor* finds an allusion to the *Yamim Noraim*, the Days of Awe, in the verse, "*Aryeh sha'ag mi lo yira,* A lion has roared; who will not fear?" *(Amos 3:8)* The letters of the word *aryeh—alef, reish, yud, hei—*are the first letters of Elul (*alef*), Rosh Hashanah (*reish*), Yom Kippur (*yud*), and Hoshana Rabbah (*hei*). These are the four times during the year when, overwhelmed with awe and trembling, a Jew is inspired to do *teshuvah*.

Yet another hint at the month of Elul is in the verse "*Ish lere'eihu umatanos la'evyonim,* one to another and gifts to the poor." *(Esther 9:22)* The first letters of each word in this verse again spell Elul. This teaches us that in Elul we should give *tzedakah* freely and generously "and gifts to the poor."

(Ma'amarei Chodesh Elul 41:21)

The Gemara (*Rosh Hashanah 18a*) says that the verse, "Seek Hashem when He may be found, call to him when He is near" (*Yeshayah 55:6*) refers to the ten days between Rosh Hashanah and Yom Kippur. Perhaps it is also an allusion to Elul. The passage urges us not to put off doing *teshuvah* until the last moment, but to repent when He is near. Repent when Rosh Hashanah is near, but not yet here—in other words, at the beginning of Elul. For *Chazal* tell us that in the month of Elul the Heavenly Gates of Compassion are open, affording us the opportunity to make amends for our failings.

(Panim Yafos)

Preparation for Judgement

A person who stands accused of financial wrongdoing or a capital crime is deeply troubled. Fearful of the forthcoming trial, he seeks the advice of the best lawyers for ways to defend himself and gain acquittal.

A person on trial before the Heavenly Court has even more reason to be anxious and alarmed. Hashem, the Judge, knows his innermost thoughts. He needs no witnesses or evidence. Excuses and rationalizations are of no avail. In the Heavenly Court, the only things that can wipe the slate clean are *teshuvah* and good deeds.

It is only logical, then, for a person to examine his past actions and repent for his transgressions before the upcoming Judgment Day on Rosh Hashanah. He should wake up from his year-long slumber and begin to prepare for his day in court at least thirty days before—which is *Rosh Chodesh* Elul. It is then that he should set out on the road to *teshuvah*.

(Menoras Hama'or)

The Mishnah in Avos 4:17 says, "Better one hour of repentance and good deeds in this world than the entire life in the World to Come." Comments the Belzer Rebbe: Do you know what that "one hour of repentance in this world" refers to? It refers to the month of Elul, the month before the coming Days of Awe.

Tipping the Scales

The month of Elul is the time for preparing for the *Yamim Noraim* that lie ahead. It is a time of introspection, when each individual reviews his faults and failings of the past year. Yet we also pray for help from Hashem and deliverance from pain and distress for the entire *Klal Yisrael.*

We should remember that salvation is up to us. The Gemara says: "The world is judged by its majority and each individual, too, is judged by the majority of his deeds—good or bad. If he performs one *mitzvah,* he has reason to be happy, for he has tipped the scale both for himself and for the whole world to the side of merit; if he commits one transgression, woe to him for weighing himself and the whole world on the scale of guilt."

(Kiddushin 40b)

Each of us carries a great responsibility, for the fate of the world may hinge on one single *mitzvah* we perform. Yet when we reflect on it, we realize how flawed we are and how numerous are our shortcomings. We therefore have no alternative but to appeal to Hashem's mercy and kindness—that He answer our prayers, though we have no worthy deeds; treat us with charity and kindness, and save us.

(Kuntres Chiddushei Torah)

Mercy and Favor

The month of Elul has always been a time of reconciliation with Hashem. When Bnei Yisrael committed the sin of the golden calf and the luchos were broken, Moshe pleaded for Divine mercy. It was on Rosh Chodesh Elul when Hashem was appeased and told Moshe to ascend the mountain to receive the second

Tablets. He stayed there for forty days—until the tenth of Tishrei, Yom Kippur. On that day Moshe brought down the second Tablets, which Hashem had given to Bnei Yisrael as a mark of renewed Divine favor.

Ever since then, the forty days from *Rosh Chodesh* Elul until Yom Kippur are fixed for all generations as days of Divine mercy and favor. These forty days also serve as as a token of repentance for the sin of the golden calf, which was built exactly forty days after the giving of the Torah.

(Kaf Hachayim)

Yemei Ratzon

The days of Elul are designated as *"yemei ratzon."* Often translated as "days of favor," the words more precisely mean "days of [Divine] purpose." How is this to be understood?

Hashem created the world for a purpose—so man should obey His will. During the month of Elul, every Jew is inspired to do *teshuvah* and return to doing Hashem's will. It is therefore during Elul that the purpose for which Hashem created the world is being fulfilled. Hence these days are called "days of [Divine] purpose."

(Ohr Hame'ir)

Shofar in Elul

The *Yismach Moshe* explains that in the last psalm *(Tehillim 150)*, "*Hallelu E-l bekodsho,* praise G-d in His Sanctuary," the word *hallelu* occurs twelve times, corresponding to the twelve months of the year. Elul, the sixth month of the year, matches the sixth *hallelu*—"*Hallelu beseika shofar,* praise Him with the blast of the *shofar.*" This alludes to the custom of blowing the *shofar* during the month of Elul.

(Yeitev Panim)

The *shofar* has a special quality—anyone listening to its blasts is jolted and roused to doing *teshuvah*. As it says, "Can a *shofar* ever be sounded in a city and the people not tremble?" (*Amos* 3:6) The Sages instituted that the *shofar* should be sounded the entire month of Elul to remind people to do *teshuvah*.

(Pirkei d'Rabbi Eliezer)

A Month of Shofar

After the sin of the golden calf, which occurred on the seventeenth of Tammuz, Moshe pleaded with Hashem for forty days. At the end of that period—on *Rosh Chodesh* Elul— Moshe was told to ascend the mountain and remain in Heaven for forty days and forty nights to receive the second Tablets.

During each of those forty days, the *shofar* was sounded throughout the camp, and an announcement was made: "Attention please! Let it be known that Moshe went up the mountain. He will not return before forty days and forty nights!" This was done to prevent the people's miscalculation that occurred when Moshe ascended to Heaven the first time, which led to the making of the golden calf. To commemorate the month-long sounding of the *shofar*, we blow the *shofar* during the month of Elul.

(Tur Orach Chaim)

Beis din gives a debtor a thirty-day deferment to pay his bills before his property is confiscated. Similarly, the *shofar* blasts of Elul remind us to pay the debts we have accumulated with our shortcomings. We "pay off the debt" by doing *teshuvah, tefillah* and giving *tzedakah*. We have thirty days to settle our accounts, so we will not be found wanting on Rosh Hashanah.

(Elef Hamagen)

The Unwary Egg

> There once was a poor woman who had no money to feed her children. One day she managed to acquire an egg.
>
> "Dear children," she exclaimed, "let's not eat this egg! If we wait a while, the egg will hatch and we will have a chick. The chick will grow into a chicken that lays eggs every day. They will also hatch, and soon we'll have a flock of chickens. We'll sell the chickens and buy a little calf. The calf will grow into a cow that will give birth to many calves that will grow into cows. Before long we'll have a big ranch with a large herd of cattle. Listen, dear children, this little egg will make us rich!"
>
> In her excitement, the mother held up the egg for her children to see. It slipped from her hand—and cracked wide open on the kitchen floor.

At the start of Elul, everyone makes plans to do *teshuvah*, commits himself to doing more *mitzvos*, and resolves not to transgress again. But no sooner have the Days of Awe passed than he goes back to his old ways, and all his good intentions evaporate. The challenge is to stay on the right path—without dropping the egg!

(Darchei No'am)

No Blessing of the New Moon

We bless every new month of the year, except *Rosh Chodesh* Tishrei. Neither do we mention *Rosh Chodesh* in the prayers of Rosh Hashanah, although Rosh Hashanah is also *Rosh Chodesh* Tishrei.

This is because we want to confuse Satan, the Accuser. By omitting the blessing of *Rosh Chodesh* Tishrei, the Accuser does not know when Rosh Hashanah begins. He will therefore be unable to denounce us before the Heavenly Court.

We find an allusion to this in the verse, "Blow the *shofar* on the new moon, when it is concealed." (*Tehillim* 81:4) This implies that the new moon should be "hidden"—it should not be mentioned.

(Levush 581)

We always bless the new month on the Shabbos preceding *Rosh Chodesh,* because Shabbos is the wellspring of blessing for the entire week. In this way, the Shabbos before *Rosh Chodesh* bestows its blessing on the upcoming month.

Rosh Hashanah is in a different category. It is the anniversary of the beginning of Creation, as we say in *Mussaf,* "Today is the birthday of the world." It is the first moment in time, with nothing preceding it. Before Creation, the concepts of time and Shabbos did not exist. Hashem's glory filled all of existence. Hashem was One, and His name was One. We therefore do not bless *Rosh Chodesh* on the Shabbos before Rosh Hashanah.

(Imrei Emes)

Chapter Two

Selichos

Rising Early for Selichos

In the *Shulchan Aruch*, the chapter "Laws of Rosh Hashanah" (par. 581) begins with the words, "It is the custom to rise early in the morning to recite *Selichos* and supplications." The inclusion of this paragraph is exceptional—as a rule, the *Shulchan Aruch* does not mention customs. Why was this included here?

The *Selichos* service marks the beginning of the *yemei hadin*, the days of judgment. The word *din* in fact has two meanings—both "law" and "judgment."

If a custom is contrary to a law, the rule is that custom overrides the law. Perhaps the author of the *Shulchan Aruch*, Rabbi Yosef Karo, was hinting that our custom of rising early for *Selichos* should override and set aside any harsh *din*—judgments—that may be decreed.

(Rabbi Shalom of Belz)

At the beginning of the Selichos service we say, "Pardon us, our King, for our iniquities are many." The Dubner Maggid points out that this seems to defy logic. We are asking Hashem to forgive us, with the justification that we have so many sins! Surely the fact that we are

13

burdened with transgressions is a strong reason for Hashem to deny us forgiveness. Why, instead of minimizing our offenses, are we stressing our long record of violations?

The Dubner Maggid compares our approach to a debtor who wants to settle with his creditor. The debtor claims that he is penniless and head over heels in debt. Hearing this, the creditor will settle for a minimal amount. We make the same claim. "Pardon us," we plead, "for we have many iniquities." Therefore, we ask Hashem, please come to terms with us and forgive us.

Four Days Before

According to our custom, *Selichos* should be said a minimum of four days before Rosh Hashanah. Therefore, if Rosh Hashanah falls on Monday or Tuesday, we begin saying *Selichos* from the Sunday of the preceding week.

Why is there a required minimum of four days of *Selichos* before Rosh Hashanah?

With regard to the sacrifices that are brought on the *Yamim Tovim*, it says, "*Vehikravtem olah,* You shall offer a fire-offering." (*Bamidbar* 28:19) The exception is Rosh Hashanah, where it says, "*Va'asisem olah,* You shall make a fire-offering." (*Bamidbar* 28:2) This suggests that on Rosh Hashanah, we should *make ourselves* into a sacrifice to Hashem—by submitting ourselves to Hashem's kingship.

The law is that before an animal is offered on the altar, it must be checked for blemishes for four days. Since we consider ourselves as a sacrifice, we, too, must be checked for blemishes—by examining our deeds and doing *teshuvah* for four days before Rosh Hashanah.

(Eliyahu Rabbah)

Beginning on Motzei Shabbos

According to Rabbi Eliezer, the world was completed on the first day of Tishrei. Hashem began the process of Creation six days earlier, on the 25th of Elul. It was on the first day of Tishrei, the sixth day of Creation, that Adam was created. Accordingly, the Jews of Barcelona, Spain had a custom to begin saying *Selichos* on the 25th of Elul.

(Ran on Rosh Hashanah 16a)

Since the 25th of Elul does not always fall on the same day of the week, it is our custom—for the sake of consistency—to always begin saying *Selichos* on *Motzei* Shabbos, the beginning of the first day of the week in which Hashem launched Creation.

(Biur Hagra 581)

We start saying *Selichos* directly after Shabbos, when we are still filled with the joy of the Torah we studied on Shabbos—in addition to the delight of *oneg* Shabbos that still lingers. The Gemara in Shabbos 30b states that the *Shechinah* comes to rest on a person only when he is in a joyous mood that was brought on by a *mitzvah*. It is therefore fitting that we are elated, with hearts brimming over with *simchah*, when we begin to say *Selichos*.

(Leket Yosher)

The Gemara *(Shabbos 119b)* states that by reciting *Vayechulu* on Friday night, one becomes a partner in Hashem's work of Creation. As partners, we have the right to demand access to Hashem and to express our opinions. At the end of Shabbos, we ask Hashem to extend our partnership into *Motzei* Shabbos. Then we can begin *Selichos*, petitioning Hashem to unlock the Heavenly gates and listen to our prayers.

(Rabbi Yissachar Dov, the Belzer Rebbe)

When praying for the rebuilding of the Second Beis Hamikdash, Ezra began by saying, "My G-d, I am embarrassed and ashamed to lift my face to you." (Ezra 9:6) If Ezra felt abashed, shouldn't we feel even more ashamed? How can we dare to approach Hashem?

The Midrash on the verse, "Hashem blessed the seventh day" (Bereishis 2:3) offers a solution. The Midrash says that on Shabbos, Hashem blesses each Jew with a special radiance that lingers on into Motzei Shabbos. On Motzei Shabbos, the continuing glow of Shabbos gives us the courage to approach Hashem with our Selichos prayers.

(Vayageid Yaakov on Selichos)

Feeling humble and inadequate to lead the holy *Selichos* service, the *chazzan* is hesitant to take on the role of spokesman for the community before Hashem. For this reason he is asked to lead the *Maariv* service. He is then entitled to be the *chazzan* for *Selichos*—for one who begins a *mitzvah* should complete it. This way, he will have no misgivings about haughtiness when he leads during *Selichos*.

(Chasam Sofer)

Wearing a Tallis

The *chazzan* wears a *tallis* for *Selichos* because during the *Selichos* service we recite the Thirteen Divine Attributes. (*Shemos* 34:6,7) The Gemara (*Rosh Hashanah* 17b) tells us that when Moshe ascended to Heaven, he beheld Hashem standing like a *chazzan*, wrapped in a *tallis*, reciting the Thirteen Attributes. Hashem told Moshe, "Whenever the Jewish people sin, let them carry out this service before Me, and I will forgive them." Emulating Hashem, the *chazzan* recites the *Selichos* wearing a *tallis*.

(Levush 581)

Chapter Three

Erev Rosh Hashanah

No Tachanun

Tachanun is said in a sitting position, with the head down and resting on the arm—in a posture of despair. But on *erev* Rosh Hashanah we should be in a joyous mood, confident that Hashem will forgive us if we do teshuvah, and that He will grant us a good new year. We therefore do not say *Tachanun* in *Shacharis* on *erev* Rosh Hashanah.

(Avodas Yisrael)

No Blowing Shofar

We do not blow the shofar on *erev* Rosh Hashanah to make a distinction between the sounding of the shofar during Elul, which was instituted by the Rabbis, and the sounding of the shofar on Rosh Hashanah, which is a mitzvah of the Torah.

(Turei Zahav 581)

Not blowing the shofar on *erev* Rosh Hashanah confuses Satan, the Accuser. When he does not hear the shofar blasts on erev Rosh Hashanah, he becomes bewildered. He wonders if Rosh Hashanah has already passed. He believes that he missed the day on which Hashem judges the world, and that he passed up his chance of denouncing the Jewish people. Baffled and perplexed, he is speechless and remains silent.

(Magein Avraham 581)

Annulling Vows

Failure to keep one's vow is a very grave sin—so serious that it can cause the death of one's wife and small children, G-d forbid. We therefore seek to clear ourselves of this sin before we are judged on Rosh Hashanah.

The petitioner declares before a *beis din* of three ordinary people that he regrets having vowed to make a voluntary gift, or for accepting upon himself a custom or various optional good deeds or practices. He now requests the *beis din* to annul all these vows. He then formally declares that he cancels from this time forth all vows that he will make; that he regrets making them; and that they all should be null and void. The judges then state that his vows are annulled.

(Elef Hamagein 581)

Fasting on Erev Rosh Hashanah

A certain city in the king's empire had failed to pay its taxes to the royal treasury. Angry at the long overdue liability, the king came with a mighty army to collect the debt.

When the king was ten miles from the city, the mayor and the city administrators came out to meet him. Since their treasury was empty, they asked, would he be willing to cancel the debt? Feeling sorry for them, the king reduced the amount due by one third.

When the king came closer, the merchants and storekeepers of the city came to greet him and asked him to release them from the remaining debt. Feeling sorry for them, the king cancelled another one third of the liability.

When the king arrived at the city gate, the entire population came out to welcome him. Seeing this massive demonstration of loyalty, the king forgave the entire debt.

On *erev* Rosh Hashanah, the devout and the pious fast. In their merit Hashem forgives one third of Yisrael's transgressions. During the Ten Days of *Teshuvah* even average Jews fast, and in their merit Hashem forgives another third of Yisrael's transgression. Comes Yom Kippur, all Yisrael fast—whereupon Hashem forgives all their transgressions.

(Tur Orach Chayim 581)

Giving Tzedakah

Giving *tzedakah* on *erev* Rosh Hashanah is considered a great mitzvah. In fact, as a result of Jews giving *tzedakah*, the Heavenly Gates of Mercy are opened wide. For in the same measure that we take pity on the poor, Hashem takes pity on us.

(Ohr Hachayim)

A New Knife

Some people have the custom of buying a new knife on *erev* Rosh Hashanah. This is in keeping with the passage (in *Vechol Ma'aminim* in *Mussaf*), "Who cuts a slice of life [*hachoteich chayim*] for all the living." The Ziditchoiver Rebbe said that buying a new knife for Rosh Hashanah and sharpening it is a good omen for sustenance for the entire year.

(Yalkut Mahari)

Buying a new, sharp knife on *erev* Rosh Hashanah awakens the merit of the *mitzvah* of *milah*. For *milah* is the single *mitzvah* that is joyously observed by all Jews—even the most estranged and non-observant Jews.

(Beshem Tzaddikim)

The Value of a Minute

Minchah of *erev* Rosh Hashanah is said in the very last minutes of the year. Yet in the *Shemoneh Esrei* of this final *Minchah* we pray, "Bless on our behalf—O Hashem, our G-d— this year," though all that is left of the year are just a few short minutes!

This teaches us that every minute counts, as our Sages put it, "*Yeshuas Hashem keheref ayin*, Hashem's help comes in the blink of an eye." Even in the last minute of the year, His salvation can come in an instant.

(Rabbi Shalom of Belz, the Sar Shalom)

More Selichos on Erev Rosh Hashanah

Before launching a new project or embarking on a new venture, a person fervently prays that Hashem should bless his undertaking with success. Similarly, on *Motzei* Shabbos we pray at great length for a good and prosperous week.

In the same way, on the day before Rosh Hashanah we get up very early and recite far more *Selichos* than on any other *Selichos* day. Before entering the new year we pray earnestly and intently for a year of blessing, good health and *geulah v'yeshuah,* redemption and salvation.

(Semichas Moshe)

Chapter Four

The Judgement of Rosh Hashanah

Why Judgement on Rosh Hashanah?

Rosh Hashanah was appointed as Judgment Day because it is the day—according to Rabbi Eliezer—on which Hashem created Adam, and judged him for disobeying Him.

In Tishrei the Patriarchs were born, and in Tishrei they died. On Rosh Hashanah, Sarah, Rachel, and Chanah were remembered by Hashem [and they became pregnant]. On Rosh Hashanah Yosef was released from prison, and on Rosh Hashanah our forefathers' bondage ended.

Rabbi Eliezer says: From where do we derive that the world was created in Tishrei? Because it says, "G-d said, 'Let the earth sprout vegetation . . . and trees bearing fruit.'" (*Bereishis* 1:14) In which month is the earth full of grass and trees full of fruit? In Tishrei. That is the season of rain, when the rain comes down and plants sprout, as it says, "A mist rose up from the earth and watered the whole surface of the soil." (*Bereishis* 2:6)

The *Ran* quotes a *Pesikta* which offers a reason why Rosh Hashanah was chosen as Judgment Day. Rosh Hashanah is the day on which Adam was created. Six days earlier - on the 25th of Elul, which was Sunday - Hashem began the work of Creation; on Friday, the sixth day of Creation, Adam was created. That was the first day of Tishrei.

In the first hour of Friday, Hashem conceived the idea of creating Adam. In the second hour, He conferred with the angels whether or not to create him. In the third hour, He gathered the dust from which Adam was to be created. In the fourth hour, He kneaded the dust as one kneads a dough. In the fifth hour He formed man. In the sixth hour, He completed Adam's body, forming flesh, bones, veins, and covering it with skin. In the seventh hour, He blew the soul of life into his nostrils. In the eighth hour He escorted him into *Gan Eden*. In the ninth hour, He commanded Adam not to eat from the Tree of Knowledge. In the tenth hour Adam disobeyed by eating from the Tree. In the eleventh hour, Hashem judged him and condemned him to death. In the twelfth hour, Hashem commuted Adam's death sentence, granting him life, so Adam emerged victorious.

Thereupon Hashem said to Adam, "Let this be a good omen for your children. Just as I judged you today, and I was merciful with you, so will your children be judged by Me every year on this day, and they too will be judged with compassion."

(Ran, first perek of Rosh Hashanah)

Judgment Day in Tishrei

Why has the month of Tishrei been chosen as the month in which Hashem judges the world?

Choosing Tishrei demonstrates Hashem's great compassion. He judges the entire world at a time when He is favorably disposed and full of mercy. For in Tishrei, *Klal Yisrael* is busy doing a great many *mitzvos*: *shofar*, Yom Kippur, *sukkah*, and *lulav*, all of which arouse Hashem's abundant compassion.

(Abudraham)

The Sign of the Scale

The sign of the zodiac for the month of Tishrei is the Scale (Libra), which reminds us to weigh our actions and reflect on our conduct, making sure that we do not transgress Hashem's will. *(Shaar Yissachar)* On Rosh Hashanah, Judgment Day, the good and the bad deeds of every individual are put in the balance to determine which side tips the scale.

What is Being Judged?

When the Gemara says that a person is judged on Rosh Hashanah, it does not mean that a decision is rendered on whether he will go to *Gan Eden* or *Gehinnom*. The verdict reached on Rosh Hashanah pertains only to earthly matters: whether a person will survive or die; whether he will be happy, or suffer agony and distress during the year.

Accordingly, we say in the *Mussaf Shemoneh Esrei* of Rosh Hashanah: "This day is the anniversary of the start of Your handiwork, a remembrance of the first day. For it is a decree for Yisrael, a judgment day for the G-d of Yaakov. Regarding the countries, it is said on this day which is destined for the sword and which for peace, which for hunger and which for abundance, and all creatures are recalled on it to remember them for life or death. Who is not recalled on this day?"

On Rosh Hashanah, a person's deeds determine whether or not he is inscribed for a good year in *this* world. Only at the end of a person's life is he judged whether he merits everlasting life in *Gan Eden*, or—G-d forbid—is condemned to *Gehinnom*.

(Ramban, Shaar Hagemul)

Different Judgements

The Mishnah (*Rosh Hashanah* 1:2) says that the world is judged at four specific times during the year: on Pesach for the grain; on Shavuos for the fruit of the tree; on Rosh Hashanah all mankind pass before Him like young sheep [for the purpose of being tithed]; and on Sukkos they are judged for the water.

The *Ran* asks: Why are the grain, the fruits, and the rain judged at specific times? Aren't these, too, decided when man is judged on Rosh Hashanah? For man is affected by how much rain will fall and how much grain and fruit will grow!

The *Ran* explains that on Pesach, Shavuos, and Sukkos, the world at large is judged, and it is decided how much grain, fruit and rain the entire world will receive. On Rosh Hashanah, however, Hashem decides what share of these gifts each individual will receive.

(Asarah Maamaros, Maamar Chikur Din 2:2)

Decreeing Sustenance

The Gemara (*Beitzah* 16a) says that all of a person's sustenance [for the entire year] is "*ketzuvim*," apportioned for him, [during the ten days] between Rosh Hashanah and Yom Kippur.

Why does the Gemara use the term *ketzuvim*, "rationed," which implies parceling out a measured portion, rather than an ample supply?

According to *halachah*, if a person has made a contract to deliver a specific amount of food or merchandise, he may not go back on his word. Hashem specifies *ketzuvim*, the exact portion of sustenance a person is allotted on Rosh Hashanah. He is then bound by His "contract" and cannot rescind it in the middle of the year.

The Gemara (*Rosh Hashanah* 16b) says, "A person is only judged on the basis of his actions up to that point in time [and not for evil deeds he will commit later in life], as it says, '[An angel told Hagar,] Hashem has heeded the boy's [Yishmael] voice there where he is [in his present state].'" (*Bereishis* 21:17) [Yishmael was saved because at that moment he was still an innocent child.]

On Rosh Hashanah, when *Klal Yisrael* are doing *teshuvah* wholeheartedly, they are *tzaddikim*. Since they are judged only for their present deeds—and they are now free of sin—it is then that Hashem determines the fulfillment of their needs for the entire year. This way, even if they stumble during the year, Hashem will not take away the sustenance He set for the year.

(Rimzei Meir)

Daily or Yearly?

The Gemara (*Rosh Hashanah* 16a) cites a dispute between three *Tanna'im*. Rabbi Yehudah says: All are judged on Rosh Hashanah. Rabbi Yose says: Man is judged every day. Rabbi Nassan says: Man is judged every moment.

How can there be such extreme differences of opinion between the *Tanna'im*?

One day the Baal Shem Tov met Chaikel the water-carrier carrying two heavy pails.

"How are you doing, Chaikel?" the Baal Shem inquired.

"Oy vay, Rebbe," Chaikel moaned. "Things are terrible. I'm shlepping heavy pails up the stairs all day long, and I don't make a living."

The next morning, the Baal Shem again saw Chaikel passing by.

"Well, Chaikel, how are you doing today?" he asked.

Smiling broadly, Chaikel answered, "As you can see, I'm no youngster. But, Baruch Hashem, I still have enough strength to haul heavy pails to the fourth floor. Baruch Hashem, I'm in good health, and I get by."

Turning to his disciples, the Baal Shem Tov said, "Here you have the same Chaikel, the same heavy pails, the same high stairs. Yet yesterday Chaikel bemoaned his lot, and today he is cheerful and content.

"Now you can understand the different opinions of the Tanna'im. True, every individual is judged on Rosh Hashanah. The Heavenly Court decided that Chaikel should be a water-carrier this year. But whether or not Chaikel should be happy with his lot—that is decreed every day."

(Baal Shem Tov)

Accusers and Defenders

Rabbi Akiva says: The Heavenly Court of Justice operates on the same principle as the earthly *Sanhedrin*. Some judges find a defendant guilty, while others move for acquittal. And so it says, "I have seen Hashem sitting on His Throne. with all the hosts of Heaven standing by Him, on His right and on His left." (*1 Melachim* 22:19) How can one speak of G-d's Throne in terms of right and left? The angels on the left are accusing angels, while those on the right are vindicating angels.

(Yalkut Shimoni, Iyov 23)

When Hashem ascends the Throne of Justice to judge the world, the Attribute of Justice positions itself at Hashem's left side and the Attribute of Mercy stands at His right side.

The Attribute of Justice contends that Hashem should judge the world with strict justice, paying the wicked for their evil deeds. The Attribute of Mercy counters that if Hashem remembers all transgressions and punishes man accordingly, no one will be able to bear the dreadful retribution. The Attribute of Justice retorts, "Let the wicked die for their crimes," to which the Attribute of Mercy replies, "Hashem does not desire the death of the evildoer."

(Yalkut Yitzchak)

Rabbi Tanchum says: Only the angels of mercy are standing before Hashem; they are the ones that plead Klal Yisrael's cause. The accusing angels are positioned far away from His Throne.

(Tanchuma, Tazria)

Three Books

Rabbi Kruspedai said: Three books are opened on Rosh Hashanah. One of the totally wicked [people who have more sins than *mitzvos*], one for the totally righteous [people who have more *mitzvos* than sins], and one for those in between [people whose *mitzvos* are evenly balanced with their sins].

The totally righteous are inscribed and sealed immediately in the book of life; the totally wicked are inscribed and sealed immediately in the book of death. The sentence of the in-between people is left pending from Rosh Hashanah until Yom Kippur. If they deserve it, they are inscribed in the book of life; if they don't deserve it, they are inscribed in the book of death.

Rabbi Avin said: What verse supports this? "May they be erased from the book of life, and let them not be inscribed with the righteous." (*Tehillim* 69:29) "May they be erased from the book" refers to the book of the wicked; "of life" refers to the book of the righteous; "and let them not be inscribed with the righteous" refers to the book of the in-between people [who are not inscribed until Yom Kippur].

Rabbi Nachman derives from here: "[Moshe said to Hashem,] If not, erase me now from Your book that You have written." (*Shemos* 32:32) "Erase me now" refers to the book of the wicked; "from Your book" refers to the book of the righteous; "that You have written" refers to the book of the in-between.

(Rosh Hashanah 16b)

Why doesn't the Gemara say "Three books are inscribed" instead of "Three books are opened"?

Perhaps the Gemara is referring to the book mentioned in the Mishnah in Avos 2:1: "All your deeds are recorded in a book." Whatever a person does each and every day is written down in this book. On Rosh Hashanah this book is split up into three sections: righteous deeds, wicked deeds and in-between deeds. According to what is written there, a person is judged: for life, for death, or pending until Yom Kippur.

(Asarah Ma'amaros)

Two or Three?

The *Rif* on *Ein Yaakov* asks: Why is there a need for a book for the *beinonim*, the in-between people? If they do *teshuvah*, they will be inscribed in the Book of the Righteous, and if they don't, they will be inscribed in the Book of the Wicked. What is the purpose of the third book?

The Gemara (*Berachos* 34b) says that in a place where *baalei teshuvah* are standing [in Heaven], even the perfectly righteous cannot stand. A separate book is needed for *baalei teshuvah* because they are on a higher level than *tzaddikim*.

(Likutei Maharil)

Since Hashem really wants the in-between person to be inscribed for life, He enters his name right away in the Book of the *Beinonim*, the in-between. This protects him from accusing angels and makes him immune to new charges. Otherwise, an accusing angel may lodge a complaint against him which will tip the scale to the side of guilt, causing him to be inscribed in the Book of the Wicked.

(Divrei Yoel 7:198)

There is a big difference between a person who does *teshuvah* before Rosh Hashanah and an "in-between" person who does *teshuvah* between Rosh Hashanah and Yom Kippur. The former rightfully deserves to be publicly inscribed for a good year in the

Book of Life, for all to see. He is in no danger from the accusing angels. But the "in-between" person who only does *teshuvah* before Yom Kippur receives his good verdict as a favor. He has to keep it a secret. It must be inscribed covertly in the Book of the *Beinonim,* or the accusing angels may dig up new charges against him—since, they will argue, he doesn't really deserve to receive a favorable verdict.

(D'var Hameluchah 195)

The verdict of the perfectly righteous which is inscribed in the Book of Life is irreversible, even if they sin later on. However, the in-between are inscribed for life provisionally, because their *mitzvos* and sins are evenly balanced. If they sin during the course of the year, the balance is upset, and their judgment is reversed. The verdict of the *beinonim* has to be entered in a separate book, so it can be revoked if they transgress.

(D'var Hameluchah)

Who Is Completely Righteous?

A totally righteous person is one who has more *mitzvos* than sins. A totally wicked person is one who has more sins than *mitzvos*. An in-between person is one whose *mitzvos* are evenly balanced with his sins.

(Rosh Hashanah 16a [see Rashi and Tosafos l.c.])

According to the *Chinuch*, a *tzaddik gamur*, "a totally righteous person," is one who has never sinned. A *rasha gamur*, "a totally wicked person," is one who never in his life fullfilled a *mitzvah*. A *beinoni*, "in-between person," has both *mitzvos* and sins. The amount of *mitzvos* and sins makes no difference. Either way, he is a *beinoni* whose verdict is undecided until Yom Kippur.

(Chinuch 311)

Only One Year

On Rosh Hashanah one is judged only for his actions during the past year. If a *tzaddik* committed one grave transgression during the past year, the Heavenly Court regards him as a *rasha,* and he is sentenced to death. Conversely, if an evildoer fulfilled one major *mitzvah* during the past year, he is judged a *tzaddik* and is inscribed for a good year.

The judgment of the in-between person, who has done neither an outstanding *mitzvah* nor committed a major transgression during the past year, is held in abeyance until Yom Kippur. If he does *teshuvah,* then his repentance is his major *mitzvah* for the year, and he is inscribed for life. If he does not do *teshuvah,* he does not merit life.

That explains why *tzaddikim* sometimes suffer greatly or die, while *reshaim* prosper and flourish. For on Rosh Hashanah, only the deeds of the past year are taken into account. But at the final judgment a person's entire life is reviewed, and the determination of whether or not he enters *Olam Haba* is based on the actions of his entire life.

(Etz Chaim, quoted in Yalkut Yitzchak)

Time of Favor

Why aren't the final decrees of the *tzaddikim* and the *reshaim* also put on hold until Yom Kippur?

If the *beinonim* were judged alongside the *tzaddikim,* in comparison, they would look like *reshaim.* If the *beinonim* were judged together with the *reshaim,* they would be condemned along with the *reshaim* when Hashem's fury is aroused by their sins. So on Rosh Hashanah only the *tzaddikim* and the *reshaim* are judged. The judgment of the *beinonim* is put off until Yom Kippur, which is an "*eis ratzon,* a time of favor," when Hashem forgives our sins. In this way the *beinonim* will be judged favorably.

(Derashos Chasam Sofer)

Inscribed Only

When referring to the sentence of the *beinonim*, the intermediate group, the Gemara says, "If they are deserving, they are inscribed in the Book of Life; if they aren't deserving, they are inscribed in the Book of Death."

Why doesn't the Gemara say that the *beinonim* are "inscribed *and sealed*"?

The *P'nei Yehoshua* explains: The seal of Hashem is *emes*, truth. On Rosh Hashanah He judges with the attribute of *emes*, inscribing and sealing the verdict of true *tzaddikim* and true *reshaim* with the seal of truth. But on Yom Kippur Hashem judges with His attribute of *chesed*, kindness. He forgives transgressions even if the sinner does not deserve to be forgiven. On Yom Kippur Hashem inscribes—but He does not seal, for He does not use His attribute of truth.

(Minchas Chinuch 311)

Tipping the Scales

The *Zohar* says that it happens sometimes that the scales of the world's merits and sins are evenly balanced on Rosh Hashanah. If there is one *tzaddik* whose good deeds tip the scale to the side of merit, the entire world is inscribed for life in the merit of his virtues. If there is one evildoer whose transgressions tip the scale to the side of guilt, the whole world is judged for destruction, G-d forbid.

(Zohar, vol. 2:33)

When the time comes to judge the world, the first to be punished are the people who disdain and humiliate Torah scholars—and especially those who committed the sin of chillul Hashem, desecration of Hashem's name.

(Zohar, vol. 3:231)

Opposing Forces

The forces of Life and the forces of Death confront each other on Rosh Hashanah. The righteous, who come with *teshuvah* and good deeds, are inscribed in the Book of Life. Those who come with their wickedness are inscribed in the Book of Death.

(Zohar 2:33)

There are two pillars of fire blazing in Heaven: one burning with white fire, the other with black fire. Two clerks write down the sentences with black fire on white fire.

(Zohar 3:99)

Merciful Judgement

The Mishnah in *Avos* says, "Do not judge your fellow until you have reached his place." You cannot condemn a person who succumbed to temptation unless you have overcome a similar challenge. Perhaps this is implied by the verse, "Judgment belongs to G-d." *(Devarim 1:17)* Only Hashem Who is all-knowing, and Whose reign extends over the entire world, can understand the extenuating circumstances that caused a person to transgress. And therefore, as the Mishnah *(Avos 1:6)* says, "He will judge everyone favorably."

(Likutei Moharan of Breslov)

The royal butler was caught committing a serious offense. Contrite and ashamed, he stood before the throne, apologizing and begging for leniency.

"You may pronounce your own sentence," the king offered, smiling benignly.

At this, the butler broke into tears.

"Please, your majesty, don't make me pass sentence on myself," he moaned. "I know that I am guilty, and I know the harsh punishment

the law dictates for my crime. But as a commoner, I cannot rule beyond the strict letter of the law; I cannot treat myself with leniency. Only you can do that. Only you can pardon an offender. So please, your majesty, I implore you—you be the one to pass sentence on me!"

We are the servants who transgressed the King's laws. We pray, "Al tavo bemishpat imanu—please, do not make us pass sentence on our own shortcomings. Ki lo yitzdak lefanecha kol chai—For we cannot decide lifnim mishuras hadin, beyond the strict letter of the law.

"We ask You to be our Judge, for You are a King Who pardons and forgives. With great compassion and grace, You will forgive our many sins."

(Kedushas Levi)

Granting Forgiveness

If G-d would not grant forgiveness to transgressors, every sinner would give up hope, reasoning that since the gates of repentance are closed—and he already lost his share in the World to Come—he may as well continue indulging in the forbidden pleasures of this world.

Therefore Hashem, in His mercy, forgives the offenses of one who repents. No matter how gravely a person has sinned, through *teshuvah* he becomes a G-d-fearing person—and can even reach the level of a *tzaddik*.

This is why King David said, "For with You is forgiveness, that You may be feared." *(Tehillim 130:4)* You grant forgiveness to sinners so that, instead of despairing, we will continue to fear You and stay away from wrongdoing.

(Binyan David, Bereishis)

Rabbi Levi Yitzchak of Berditchev once said, "Ribbono shel Olam! If You don't forgive the sins of the Jewish people, I will tell everyone that Your tefillin are not kosher. For the Gemara says: In G-d's tefillin it is written, 'Who is like Your people Yisrael, one nation on earth?' For the Jews crowned Hashem as their G-d, and accepted His Torah. Now, Ribbono shel Olam, if You don't pardon their transgressions, the Jews will be no different than the gentiles. Your tefillin, stating that Yisrael is a unique nation, will contain an untruth—rendering them invalid."

(Yalkut HaGershuni, Tehillim 130)

Who is Judged?

On Rosh Hashanah, an announcement is made in all the Heavens: "Prepare the Throne of Justice for the Holy One, blessed is He, Who is about to sit in judgment of the world!" *(Zohar 3:231)* Hashem judges the whole world and decides what will happen until the next Rosh Hashanah. As it says, "From the beginning of the year to the end of the year." *(Devarim 11:12)* From the beginning of the year, sentence is passed as to what shall transpire until the end of the year.

(Rosh Hashanah 8a)

All people pass before Hashem, one by one, in a single file, as it says, "He Who fashions the hearts of them all, Who comprehends all their deeds." *(Tehillim 33:15)* Although He sees the hearts of all of them and views them with a single glance, He also scrutinizes each one individually, one by one.

(Rosh Hashanah 18a)

The first to be judged are the Jewish people. Afterward the nations of the world are judged. For it is not seemly that the Jewish people, children of Avraham, Yitzchak and Yaakov, should wait outside until the judgment of the other nations is complete. In addition, the Jewish people are tried first, before Hashem's fury is inflamed when He sees the sins of the nations. We are tried when Hashem is filled with compassion, so we will be judged for a good year.

(Rosh Hashanah 16a)

> *The Gemara says (Rosh Hashanah 8b): If a king and a community appear in court together, the king enters first, because it is not proper that the king should stand outside.*
>
> *Explains the Radomsker Rebbe: On Rosh Hashanah we daven two types of tefillos. We say prayers extolling Hashem, Master of the Universe; and we pray for the welfare of the community and our family. "The king enters first" means that we should first daven for the glory of Hashem and share the sorrow of the Shechinah that is with us in galus, "because it is not proper that the King should stand outside," and suffer together with us in exile. Only then should we daven for our personal needs. If we have Hashem's glory in mind when we daven, we will be inscribed for a good year.*
>
> *(Tiferes Shlomo, Rosh Hashanah)*

"He judges the world with righteousness, judges the nations with fairness." (*Tehillim* 9:9) Rabbi Levi expounds: The way Hashem judges the nations is to their advantage. He judges them at night, because when they sleep they do not sin. During the day, however, they violate a great many laws—they steal, they murder, and so on. Hashem judges them at the time that is most beneficial to them.

On the other hand, Hashem judges *Klal Yisrael* during the day rather than at night. When a Jew is asleep he cannot do any good deeds. But as soon as he wakes up in the morning, he begins to do *mitzvos*. He goes to *shul*, davens, hears *krias haTorah*, listens to the rabbi's lecture on *mussar*   so in the daytime, Hashem views the Jews with favor.

(Pesikta Rabbasi)

Mashiach Is Waiting

During his sermon on Rosh Hashanah, the saintly *Yismach Moshe*, ancestor of the Satmar Rebbe, would relate the following:

> *On Rosh Hashanah, the kings and rulers of all nations are standing before the Heavenly Court, anxiously waiting to hear the judgment of their nation. King Mashiach, too, is standing there, hoping that in the coming year the geulah sheleimah, the complete redemption, will come to pass, and the Jewish people will at long last be freed from the galus.*
>
> *When the verdict is read that the Jewish people did not merit to be redeemed, King Mashiach leaves the Court, ashamed and deeply embarrassed, while all the gentile rulers taunt and ridicule him.*

The Satmar Rebbe would repeat these remarks in his inspirational speech before *tekias shofar*. He emphasized that the *Yismach Moshe* knew what transpired in Heaven. His words are not meant in a figurative sense; he stated true facts, and he was qualified to relate them.

(Divrei Yoel, Rosh Hashanah)

Plea for the Defense

Klal Yisrael pleads, "*Ribbono shel Olam!* You are about to judge us. The accusers and the defenders are ready to plead their cases. We beg You, please pay attention only to the defenders who stick up for us. 'May Your eyes see only uprightness.' (*Tehillim* 17:2) Judge us on the basis of our merits."

Hashem answers, "Yes, I will. I will judge you, because I want to clear your name."

When two people are involved in a lawsuit, each one wants to be the first to present his case. But Hashem says to *Klal Yisrael*, "Let's settle our differences in court, and you should present your case first. For if I win, I will actually be the loser; but if you win, I will come out ahead."

Hashem explains, "I triumphed over the generation of the Flood, but I lost out. I lost again when I destroyed the *Beis Hamikdash* and drove My children into exile. But when the Jews erected the golden calf and Moshe defended them and won, I benefited from that. That's why I want you to overcome Me now, too."

Hashem wants to vindicate the Jewish people. Therefore He is called "the true G-d" and "the G-d of Justice." And when the Jews blow the *shofar* on Rosh Hashanah, all accusing angels are silenced and vanish into nothingness.

(Pesikta Rabbasi)

Testimony

Hashem, the Omniscient, knows everything a person has done all year. Nevertheless, when He judges the world, He demands that witnesses testify to each action. Hashem thereby demonstrates that He judges by the rules of the Code of Law, so no one can find fault with the verdict.

If an individual failed to do *teshuvah*, and as a result he stands condemned, Hashem announces in Heaven, "If there is anyone who can put in a good word for him, let him speak up." If someone comes forward and pleads for him, he is saved. If no one comes forward on his behalf, the verdict is handed to the official who will carry it out.

On Rosh Hashanah the testimony given by witnesses about an individual is written down on notepaper. Hashem then waits and defers the sentencing in the hope that the accused will do *teshuvah*. If he does *teshuvah*—even until Shemini Atzeres—all the notes are shredded.

(Zohar 3:99)

Each person's verdict is also recorded on a slip of paper. If one does *teshuvah*, the paper is torn up. If he does not repent, he is handed over to the angels of justice, and they remove his "image of Hashem"— that is, his soul.

(Zohar 1:220)

Who Can Judge?

During the ten days from Rosh Hashanah to Yom Kippur, the saintly *B'nei Yissoschor* wrote the following letter to Hashem:

Ribbono shel Olam! I ask you, how can the angels participate in the proceedings of the Heavenly Court? Do they have any conception of what it means to worry about making a living? How a person suffers from an overpowering evil impulse? The heartache of a father who cannot pay his child's tuition?

The only ones qualified to sit on the Heavenly Court are the souls of the *tzaddikim* who once lived on this world. They can understand the agony and distress of what *Klal Yisrael* is going through. They can judge and decide.

On second thought, the *tzaddikim* who passed away long ago cannot sit in judgment either. They have forgotten how hard it is to surmount temptation; they cannot imagine how difficult life is in our present generation. When a sinner comes before the Heavenly Court, they are very angry with him. They cannot sit on the bench either!

Indeed, the Gemara in *Sanhedrin* 36b says: We do not appoint an old man as a member of the *Sanhedrin*, because he has forgotten the pain that is involved in raising children. For the same reason, *tzaddikim* who died long ago cannot serve on the Heavenly *beis din*.

(Shaarei Yissoschor)

Chapter Five

Toward a Merciful Judgement

Finding the Way

A man was lost in a forest for several days, unable to find his way out. Suddenly, he saw another man at a distance. Joyfully he made his way toward the stranger, thinking, "At last I shall find the way out!"

He asked the man, "My friend, please tell me which is the right way out. I have been wandering about for days."

Said the other fellow, "I don't know the way out either. I too am lost. But one thing I can tell you—don't take the way I've been going, for it will lead you astray. And now let us look for a new way out together."

Said Rabbi Chaim of Sanz, "One thing is certain: we should abandon the way we have been following thus far, for that leads us astray. Now let's look for a new way together."

(Divrei Chaim)

41

The king of a wide-ranging empire decreed that one day each year all his subjects must appear before him and report all their doings during the past year. Failure to appear carried the death penalty.

The people of a distant province were very worried. To get to the royal palace they had to pass a desolate region that abounded with ferocious animals and vicious robbers. To make things worse, they did not know the way.

They chose as their spokesman an inexperienced young man who had never before spoken to the king, and was not sure of the way through the dangerous territory. Afraid that he might not address the king properly, the young man asked to be relieved of his task, but the people would not hear of it. He had to speak on their behalf.

On the way, the young man got lost. The group was in grave danger.

"Please don't depend on me!" he screamed. "I'm lost. Everyone should try to find the trail that leads out of this swamp and gets us to the palace in time. Otherwise we are doomed!"

Hearing this, the people fanned out in all directions, searching for the trail. Fortunately they found it, and they made it to the palace just in time.

Said Rabbi Tzvi Hirsh Meisels of Weitzen: The king is *Hakadosh Baruch Hu.* He decreed that once a year, on Rosh Hashanah, we have to give Him an account of our deeds during the past year. But the road to Rosh Hashanah is fraught with pitfalls and stumbling blocks that prevent us from coming close to Hashem.

The Weitzen Rav concluded: The congregation has chosen me as *chazzan* to lead them in prayer, although I am still quite young, and I am not used to officiating as *chazzan.* But now we are on the way, and I am lost. I don't know which direction to go, and I'm afraid that the accusing angels will block our way.

If you rely on me, we'll *all* be lost! Let everyone search for the right way, the path of *teshuvah.* Let everyone pray that my *tefillos* should be accepted with mercy and favor, and that they should ascend on high to *Hakadosh Baruch Hu*, together with the prayers of *Klal Yisrael.*

(Derashos D'var Tzvi, Rav Meisels of Weitzen)

Wellspring of Tears

The saintly Noda Biyehudah once told the following allegory in his *drasha* on Rosh Hashanah:

A king dearly loved his son, caring for him and buying him the most precious clothes. Spoiled and ungrateful, the son misbehaved and openly insulted his father, the king. The king, deeply hurt, expelled his son from the palace and exiled him to a faraway country. But out of fatherly compassion, he let the boy keep his beautiful royal garments, so wherever he went people would recognize him as the prince and treat him accordingly.

The king told his son, "If you keep your clothes spotless while in exile, one day I will allow you to come back to the palace. If, by accident, your garment gets soiled, make sure to remove the spot immediately. I am sending along your mother to look after you and chastise you when you act up. Be sure to obey her meticulously."

No sooner did the son leave the palace than he sullied his clothes with mud and dirt. His beautiful clothes looked like rags. Although his mother kept warning him to take care of his robe, he ignored her and turned up his nose at her reprimands.

Many months went by, when suddenly it was announced that the king would visit the city. Trumpets were sounded in honor of the king's visit.

"What's the meaning of all this noise, and why are the people so in awe?" the king's son asked.

"Don't you know? The king is coming to town soon! Everyone is afraid that the king might detect some wrongdoing and punish the perpetrator."

Noticing how everyone prepared his finest clothes in honor of the king's visit, the son became worried. "Woe is me," he lamented. "I've dirtied my pure white robe, and I failed to take heed of my mother's admonitions."

He quickly washed and rinsed his royal robe   but to no avail. He then soaked it in clean water for ten days, hoping to eliminate the dirt. When the king arrived, the son had only ordinary workday clothes to greet his father.

"Where is the beautiful royal robe I gave you?" the king sternly asked.

"Dear Father," the son sighed regretfully. "I sullied the clothes you gave me. But I promise that from now on I will keep them spotlessly clean. As proof of my good intentions, here is the water in which I have soaked my dirty clothes. But it takes a long time to remove all the spots."

"Didn't your mother warn you not to stain your robe?" the king reproached.

"It's all my fault," the son admitted. "My mother constantly admonished me, but I paid no attention to her. Please don't be angry with her."

After seeing the water in which the garments had been soaked, and listening to the son protecting his mother, the king took pity on his son and forgave his shortcomings.

The son represents the Jewish people. Our Father brought us to His palace, the *Beis Hamikdash,* where He showed us His great love—especially every year on Yom Kippur, when the *Kohen Gadol* entered the Holy of Holies to atone for our sins.

But we turned our backs on our Father and began to rely on our own power, forgetting that Hashem is our Protector. In the end, we were exiled from Eretz Yisrael and dispersed among the nations of the world.

Even in exile we kept our Jewish garments: the garments of the soul, the Torah and the *mitzvos*. Hashem warned us that in case our souls become stained through our transgressions, we should cleanse it through *teshuvah*. The mother—that is, the holy *Shechinah*—is with us in *galus*, to protect us from our enemies. But we disregarded Her reproof, and stained our holy souls with our sins.

When Rosh Hashanah arrives and we hear the sound of the *shofar*, we come to our senses and tremble in awe of *Hakadosh Baruch Hu*, Who is coming to sit in judgment of us all. Everyone looks with shame at his dirty clothes—the stains on our souls. We attempt to wash them away through *teshuvah* and fasting, soaking them in a wellspring of tears filled with remorse.

On Rosh Hashanah, Hashem asks us, "Where is the pure garment, the holy soul, which I gave you when you came into this world, and which I told you to keep clean?" All we can do is show Hashem the wellspring of the water of our tears of regret, proof of our sincere *teshuvah*.

"*Rabbosai!*" the Noda Biyehudah thundered. "Our Father in Heaven is with us today. Let us offer Him our wellspring of tears of remorse for ignoring the *Shechinah*. Let us do *teshuvah* and beg Hashem to release the *Shechinah* from *galus* and send us the *geulah sheleimah*, the ultimate redemption. Let us ask Hashem to grant us forgiveness for the sake of His Name!"

Precious Tears

It happened in a distant country that the people of one of the provinces rose up against the king. The king's army quelled the uprising. In reprisal, he imposed oppressive fines and taxes on the population and placed heavy restrictions on their commerce and trade.

The wise men of the province held a conference to try to find ways to appease the king and make him rescind the harsh decrees. At the conference, one man spoke up and offered a suggestion.

"For many years I used to be the butler at the royal palace," he explained. "Foolishly, I misbehaved one day, whereupon the king banished me to your province. But I know the king's likes and dislikes, so let me advise you.

"The king is very fond of a certain exquisite beverage. But this beverage is extremely rare and very expensive. If anyone is able to provide this beverage, the king will be extremely grateful and will fulfill that man's every wish.

"Try to procure as much of this drink as you can. Present the drink in sparkling clean glass bottles worthy of the king's good taste. Whoever brings a bottle should write his name on the label, so the king will be able to reward him properly. In fact, I myself will also send a bottle of this beverage to the king.

"When you hand the bottles to the king, express sincere remorse for your wrongdoing, and promise that you will never again revolt against the king. If you do that, I assure you that the king will forgive you, abolish all evil decrees, and treat you favorably and lovingly.

"There's only one thing I ask of you," the former butler continued. "When the king asks who told you about his fondness of this drink, please tell him that his ex-butler revealed it to you. And tell the king that the ex-butler is also sending a small bottle of the precious beverage, since that is all he can afford. If you do that, I'm sure the king will invite me into his chamber and restore me to my former post."

Explained Rav Moshe of Ujhel: The king of the parable is *Hakadosh Baruch Hu*. The beverage He loves so dearly are the tears of remorse the Jewish people shed. Hashem values Jewish tears that come from the heart more than anything in the world. He gathers up and counts those tears, and places them in a treasured vessel, for He is a King Who is appeased through tears.

Let us all pour out our hearts to Hashem, cry out to Him with sincere tears, and He will surely accept our *tefillos* and bless us with a good new year.

(Yismach Moshe)

Meaningful Requests

The saintly Sanzer Rav was wont to use the following parable in his sermon on Rosh Hashanah:

> *A king had a son whom he loved dearly. One day, in a moment of weakness, the son went wrong and offended his father. Deeply hurt, the king expelled his son from the palace and banished him to a distant place where no one knew him.*
>
> *Before long, the boy went hungry and had to sell his beautiful coat to obtain food. When the food ran out, he took a job as an ordinary shepherd. Years went by, and at last, he forgot that he was the crown prince and adopted the crude ways of the shepherds.*
>
> *But there was one thing that troubled him. All the old-time shepherds had cabins with a straw roof to keep them dry in the rain. As a relative newcomer, the king's son did not have a cabin with a straw roof.*
>
> *One day the king passed by in his royal coach. Whoever had a request could write his wish on a slip of paper and throw it into the royal coach, and the king would grant his wish. The prince, too, threw a note into the coach, asking for a straw roof to keep him dry in the rain.*
>
> *Recognizing his son's handwriting, the king was appalled. He realized that his son had forgotten that he was the crown prince. Instead of asking to be readmitted to the palace, he was asking for a straw roof!*

In the long years of our *galus* we have forgotten that we are the children of the King of kings, *Hakadosh Baruch Hu*. Today, on Rosh

Hashanah, our Father is coming very close to us. Now is the time when everyone can express his wish. Remember to pray, "Our Father, our King, bring us back to You." Don't pray for a straw roof or worthless trinkets!

(Divrei Chaim)

Each for Himself

A mother and her child were both gravely ill. Her husband did his utmost to save their lives, bringing in the leading doctors and specialists—but to no avail.

"Your wife and son have an incurable disease," they said. "There is no way we can help them. But since you are Jewish, we advise you to pray to G-d and recite Psalms. Perhaps in His great mercy, He will heal your wife and son."

The husband went to shul and recited Tehillim with deep devotion, imploring Hashem to make his wife and child well again.

When he came home, he told them, "As long as I thought that you could be cured through medical science, I did all I could to restore your health. I got the best doctors, paid for hospitalization, treatments and medications. But now that the doctors have given up hope and said that only prayer and Tehillim can help, I ask that you, yourselves, should beg Hashem to send you a speedy recovery. Don't just rely on my prayers."

Usually, women and children depend on the man of the house to provide their sustenance. But on Rosh Hashanah they cannot rely on his *tefillos*. Each person has to pray for his own well-being, health and prosperity in the coming year.

(Derashos D'var Tzvi, by the author's grandfather,
Rabbi Meisels of Weitzen)

Plea for Mercy

An entire family—husband, wife, and children—were incarcerated. An attorney was retained to defend them in court. When the attorney heard their side of the story, he realized that their case was very weak. It was nearly impossible to win.

"The only thing I can do is this: Since you are a large family, I will appeal for mercy. If you are lucky, the king will have compassion and commute your sentence. But you all have to come along with me to court and weep and moan before the king."

They followed the attorney's advice, and the king released them from prison.

We cannot appeal to Hashem on account of our worthy deeds—for we know that we have no worthy deeds to offer. We ask, instead, that Hashem treat us with charity for His Name's sake. Therefore, everyone—man, woman, and child—should implore G-d to have mercy on the Jewish people. *(Derashos D'var Tzvi, by the author's grandfather, Rabbi Meisels of Weitzen)*

The lion, king of the beasts, was once angry with the other animals. The animals wanted to pacify him, but they did not know how. The clever fox suggested, "I will butter him up by telling him the 300 tales I know."

Happy with the plan, the fox and all the animals set out on the long march to the lion's lair. Midway, the fox cried out, "Woe is me, I have forgotten half of the tales!"

"Well, you still have 150 stories left," the animals said half-heartedly. "That'll be enough to soothe the lion."

At the next stop, the fox moaned, "Oy vay, I've forgotten a hundred more stories."

"Well, let's hope that fifty stories will do," replied the animals.

Arriving at the gate to the lion's lair, the fox exclaimed, "I'm so sorry. I've forgotten all my tales."

Heartbroken and deeply disappointed, the animals cried, "What shall we do?"

Seeing the animals weeping in despair, the fox said, "I have a good idea. Let each of us approach King Lion individually and try to mollify him with our tears and our broken hearts."

The wise fox told the animals that he had 300 stories. If not for that, they would not have set out at all. When the fox saw that they completely relied on him, he told them that he really had no tales and fables, and that each of them individually should appeal to the lion.

Each of us must *daven* to Hashem with broken hearts and humble spirit—and not rely on the prayers of others. Then Hashem will listen to our *tefillos*, as it says, "Hashem is close to the brokenhearted, and those crushed in spirit He saves." (*Tehillim* 34:19)

(Ben Poras Yosef)

Chapter Six

The Date of Rosh Hashanah

Beginning of the Month

When fixing the date for Rosh Hashanah, the Torah says, "In the seventh month, on the first of the month" *(Vayikra 23:24)*, mentioning the month before the day. Conversely, in connection with Yom Kippur and Sukkos it says, "On the tenth day of this month," and "On the fifteenth of this seventh month," listing the day before the month.

A possible reason may be that on Rosh Hashanah, when Jews are being judged, Hashem mercifully includes in His count all the *mitzvos* the Jews are about to fulfill that month. Thus, on Rosh Hashanah He credits them with fasting on Yom Kippur and the numerous *mitzvos* associated with Sukkos and Shemini Atzeres—regarding them as if they had already been fulfilled. This increases the merits of *Klal Yisrael* before the Heavenly Court.

(Vayaged Yaakov by Rabbi Yissachar Dov of Belz)

The Midrash comments that every day of the year Satan denounces Yisrael, but Hashem tells him to come back on Rosh Hashanah, when He sits in judgment. When Rosh Hashanah arrives, Satan shows up with the accumulated charges of the entire year, bringing the sun as a witness.

Says G-d, "The sun is just one witness; I need two witnesses." Satan then wants to bring the moon as his second witness, but the moon is unavailable, for on Rosh Hashanah it is dark and invisible, as it says, "Blow the shofar on the new moon, when [the moon] is covered on our festive day." (Tehillim 81:4) Thus Satan is silenced, unable to bring charges against Klal Yisrael.

(Divrei Yoel, Rosh Hashanah 48)

When Is Rosh Hashanah?

The *Midrash* says that at the end of Elul the angels come to Hashem, asking Him, "Master of the universe, please tell us—when is Rosh Hashanah?"

Hashem replies, "You are asking Me when Rosh Hashanah is? That's not up to Me. Let's you and I go together to the *beis din* down on earth, and find out when they proclaimed Rosh Hashanah." *(Yalkut, Bo 191)*

When the *beis din* in Yerushalayim decides on the date of Rosh Hashanah, Hashem tells the Heavenly angels, "Build a platform, and bring on the angels for the defense to speak up for *Klal Yisrael*, because the earthly court has decided that today is Rosh Hashanah."

But if the witnesses who viewed the new moon were late in coming, so Rosh Hashanah was set for the next day, Hashem tells the angels, "Dismantle the platform, because the earthly *beis din* has designated tomorrow as Rosh Hashanah."

Why does Hashem do this? Because "it is a decree for Yisrael, a judgment day for the G-d of Yaakov." *(Tehillim 81:5)* If the *beis din* declares this day as Rosh Hashanah, Hashem sits in judgment; but if the *beis din* changes the date, Hashem does not judge that day.

(Yerushalmi, Rosh Hashanah)

The Rule of "ADU"

A famous calendar rule is *Lo a'd'u Rosh*. The acronym *a'd'u* means that Rosh Hashanah can never occur on the days designated *a'd'u*: *alef, dalet, vav*. *Alef* - 1, is Sunday; *dalet* - 4, is Wednesday; *vav* - 6, is Friday. Thus, Rosh Hashanah can fall only on Monday, Tuesday, Thursday or Shabbos.

The Midrash says that the angels ask Hashem: "Please tell us—when is Rosh Hashanah?" Hashem answers, "Let us go down together to the *beis din* on earth and find out when they proclaimed Rosh Hashanah."

The date of Rosh Hashanah must be decided by the *beis din* on earth—because there is no day that the Heavenly Court can convene!

How does this work?

Ezra instituted that the *beis din* should convene every Monday and Thursday. The Heavenly Court does not judge whenever the earthly court is in session, so it cannot convene on Monday and Thursday.

Rosh Hashanah cannot begin on Sunday, Wednesday, and Friday (*a'd'u*), so on those days the Heavenly Court cannot meet. Monday and Thursday are also unavailable. This leaves only Tuesday and Shabbos.

But if Rosh Hashanah falls on Tuesday, Yom Kippur—ten days later—comes out on Thursday, a day when the earthly court convenes, so the Heavenly Court will not be able to judge. If Rosh Hashanah falls on Shabbos, Yom Kippur comes out on Monday, again a day on which the earthly court sits, which precludes the Heavenly Court from judging.

Therefore Hashem says, "Let's you and I go down together to the earthly *beis din*. That is where we will be able to judge the Jewish people, for up in Heaven there is not a single day available for judging!"

(Kesones Yosef)

Chapter Seven

The Four Names of Rosh Hashanah

Yom Teruah—Day of Shofar-Sounding

In the Torah, Rosh Hashanah is called *Yom Teruah*, "a day of *teruah*." The *shofar* sound of *tekiah* is a long straight blast; the *teruah* sound is a series of short, broken blasts which resembles sobbing. Rosh Hashanah is called *Yom Teruah*, rather than *Yom Tekiah*, for the sound of the *teruah*—the whimpering sound of remorse and inner turmoil—perfectly symbolizes the spirit of Rosh Hashanah.

The word *teruah* denotes breaking and shattering, which recalls the brokenhearted and contrite mood of a person who repents of his transgression. The word *teruah* is also related to *ur*, "awaken"—a reminder to wake up and do *teshuvah*.

(Menoras Hama'or 293)

Yom Hazikaron—Day of Remembrance

Rosh Hashanah is called the Day of Remembrance, because on that day Hashem remembers the deeds we did throughout the year. When judging us, Hashem remembers the merit of our Fathers, Avraham, Yitzchak, and Yaakov, and the merit of *Akeidas Yitzchak.*

Why did our Sages give Rosh Hashanah the name Yom Hazikaron, "Day of Remembrance," when the Torah describes Rosh Hashanah as Yom Teruah, "Day of Shofar-Sounding" (Bamidbar 25:1)?

The Gemara (Rosh Hashanah 16a) states: Hashem says to the Jewish people, "Recite for Me on Rosh Hashanah [verses that mention] kingship, remembrance and the shofar — kingship, so that you may proclaim Me king over you; remembrance, so that your remembrance may rise favorably before Me; and through what? Through the shofar."

Hashem tells us what we should do to be remembered favorably before Him on Rosh Hashanah: let the shofar blasts prompt us to accept Him as our King! Yom Teruah, "Day of Shofar-Sounding," is therefore a name that honors the Jewish people, whose merits will be remembered by Hashem through the sounding of the shofar.

On the other hand, the Sages attach the name Yom Hazikaron to Rosh Hashanah in honor of Hashem. On that day Klal Yisrael crown Hashem as their King and as King of the entire world, and submit themselves to His judgement.

(Toras Emes)

Yom Hadin—Judgment Day

On Rosh Hashanah, Hashem judges the entire world. Hashem does us a great favor by judging us once every year—for that way our transgressions do not accumulate to the point where they are beyond atonement.

If not for the annual *Yom Hadin*, the world's sins would continue to accumulate, until it would reach the stage where it would have to be destroyed. This is why Rosh Hashanah is a *Yom Tov*, a day of celebration.

(Sefer Hachinuch)

Rosh Hashanah—Head of the Year

Chazal call the *Yom Tov* by the name Rosh Hashanah, although this name is not mentioned anywhere in the Torah. The Torah denotes the day as *tekufas hashanah*, "the repetition of the year" (*Shemos* 34:22), implying that the new year is a replay of the past year. Only in *Yechezkel* 40:1 is there mention of the name Rosh Hashanah.

Perhaps this is because in the days before the destruction of the *Beis Hamikdash*, all Jews were righteous people, faithful servants of Hashem. On Rosh Hashanah, they could look back on a year filled with *mitzvos* and good deeds. They wished that the new year would be a duplicate of the previous year, rather than the beginning of a new year with temptations and stumbling blocks. This is why the Torah speaks in terms of "repetition of the year."

Living after the destruction of the *Beis Hamikdash*, Yechezkel *Hanavi* saw a generation of Jews burdened with sins and transgressions. On Rosh Hashanah they sought forgiveness for their failures of the past year, committing to do better in the coming year. They did not look back at the evils of the past year; rather, they looked forward to improvement in the new year. Therefore *Chazal*, who lived after the destruction of the *Beis Hamikdash*, designated the day as Rosh Hashanah, "Beginning of the Year."

(Chasam Sofer)

Why didn't Chazal call the *Yom Tov Techilas Hashanah*, "beginning of the year," instead of "head of the year"?

In man, the head is the primary organ of the body. Similarly, Rosh Hashanah is the most important day of the year. For on Rosh Hashanah we are judged, and decisions are rendered that will affect our destiny for the entire year.

(Likutei Torah)

The Gemara in *Eruvin* 41a says, "The body follows the head." This may be taken as an allusion to Rosh Hashanah, which is the head of the year. Whatever will happen during the coming year is determined on Rosh Hashanah. It is our prayer that on Rosh Hashanah, we will merit that the entire coming year will bring happiness and good tidings.

(P'ri Tzaddik, Rosh Hashanah)

We should spend the day of Rosh Hashanah immersed in praying and learning Torah. This may be compared to a builder who is about to put up a new house. Before he starts, he draws a blueprint of the planned construction. Rosh Hashanah, the first day of the new year, is the blueprint of the year that lies ahead. Whatever a person does on Rosh Hashanah becomes the pattern of his conduct throughout the year. The praying and studying he does on Rosh Hashanah will set the standard for the coming year.

(Rabbi Pinchas of Koret)

Chapter Eight

Customs of Rosh Hashanah

No Hallel on Rosh Hashanah

It is not appropriate to recite *Hallel*, a collection of joyful hymns, on the solemn and fateful day of Rosh Hashanah—the *Yom Hadin*, Judgment Day.

The Gemara relates that the angels asked Hashem, "Why don't the Jewish people sing songs of praise to You on Rosh Hashanah and Yom Kippur?" Hashem replied, "Is it possible that the King should be sitting on the Throne of Justice with the books of life and death open before Him, and Yisrael should sing hymns of praise?"

(Rosh Hashanah 32b)

We have a tradition that on Rosh Hashanah and Yom Kippur the souls of our deceased parents come down to pray together with us. This is implied by the phrase, "The books of the living and the dead are open before Him." We know that the dead cannot sing hymns to Hashem, as it says, "The dead cannot praise

G-d." *(Tehillim* 115:17) Since the souls of the dead are praying with us, we do not sing *Hallel* so as not to embarrass them.

(Chasam Sofer)

Not In Our Merit

At the Parting of the Sea, the Jews sang *shirah* because G-d saved them when He saw that "they had faith in Hashem and in Moshe, His servant." *(Shemos* 14:31) Since they were saved in their own merit, it was fitting for them to sing Hashem's praises. However, on Rosh Hashanah we hope to be judged favorably in the merit of our ancestors, not in our own merit. It therefore is not appropriate to recite the joyous *Hallel*.

(Chasam Sofer, Sermons for Elul)

Since we are confident that Hashem will inscribe us for a good year, why shouldn't we recite *Hallel* on Rosh Hashanah? It is likely that we are judged favorably because of the death of a *tzaddik* who passed away that year, for the death of the righteous atones for the Jewish people. *(Moed Katan* 28a) But the Sages tell us that the death of the righteous is a greater loss to G-d than the breaking of the *Luchos* (Tablets). *(Yerushalmi Yoma* 1:1) In the face of such a momentous tragedy, how can we recite *Hallel*?

(K'sav Sofer, Rosh Hashanah)

Every year on the first night of Rosh Hashanah, the saintly Rebbe Reb Elimelech of Lizhensk saw Eliyahu Hanavi in a dream, who revealed to him what was being said in Heaven. In 1773, Eliyahu Hanavi related to him that the world endures because of the prayers of three tzaddikim: The Rebbe Reb Elimelech himself; his brother, the Rebbe Reb Zishe of Hanipol; and the Rebbe Reb Shmelke of Nikolsburg. Reb Elimelech wondered why Eliyahu Hanavi had not mentioned the prayers of his rebbi, the Rebbe Reb Ber, the great Maggid of Mezritch. Later that year, on the 19th of Kislev, the Rebbe Reb Ber passed away. It was then that Reb Elimelech understood why Eliyahu Hanavi had not mentioned the Rebbe Reb Ber.

(Mekor Chaim)

L'David Mizmor on Rosh Hashanah

The *Rema* explains that one of the reasons for saying *Tashlich* near the banks of a river or the edge of the ocean is because by looking at the ocean, one recognizes that G-d created the world. Two-thirds of the earth is covered by the sea, and it is only by the grace of G-d that the entire globe is not covered by water. Standing at the water's edge, we watch the waves buffeting the shore, eager to inundate it; but Hashem helps the sand resist the unrelenting surge of the waves, allowing mankind to live on dry land.

One of the passages in *L'David Mizmor* reads, "For He founded [the earth] upon seas." *(Tehillim 24:2)* The fact that the land defies the relentless pounding of the waves is proof that "the earth is Hashem's and all that it holds." *(Tehillim 24:1)* This realization arouses a person to *teshuvah*, and it is therefore recited on the night of Rosh Hashanah.

(Divrei Yoel, Rosh Hashanah)

When Shlomo built the Beis Hamikdash, he wanted to bring the Ark into the Holy of Holies. But the gates clung to each other, preventing him from entering. Shlomo uttered twenty-four prayers, yet he was not answered.

Shlomo proclaimed, "O gates, lift up your heads! Up high, you everlasting doors, so the King of glory may come in." (Tehillim 24:7) Thinking that by "the King of glory" he meant himself, the gates rushed upon him to swallow him. They cried, "Who is the King of glory?" (24:8) Replied Shlomo, "Hashem, mighty and valiant, Hashem valiant in battle!"

Still, the doors did not open. The same dialogue was repeated, and when the doors asked again, "Who is the King of glory?" Shlomo replied, "Hashem, Master of Legions, He is the King of glory!"

Even so, the doors did not open. But as soon as Shlomo prayed, "O Hashem, do not reject Your anointed one; remember the loyalty of Your servant David" (2 Divrei Hayamim 6:42), he was answered immediately, and the door opened.

At that moment the faces of all of David's enemies turned black like the bottom of a pot, and all Yisrael knew that G-d had forgiven David the sin [of Batsheva]. (Shabbos 30a)

The Gemara in Avodah Zarah 4b says: It was not like David to behave the way he did [in connection with Batsheva]. So why did he commit this act? G-d ordained it, in order to teach that if a person has sinned [and doubts that his teshuvah will be accepted] you can tell him, "Look at David [who sinned, and whose teshuvah was accepted]. You, too, will be forgiven!"

We recite the psalm where this episode is related, "LaShem haaretz umlo'ah" (Tehillim 24), on the night of Rosh Hashanah, because it demonstrates that Hashem accepts the teshuvah of every Jew.

(Divrei Yoel, Rosh Hashanah)

Saying the psalm *L'David Mizmor* brings the blessing of prosperity, because it promises Hashem's blessing to one who serves Him with sincerity.

(Chida)

Leshanah Tovah

The *Shulchan Aruch* says: Although throughout the year one should say the *Shemoneh Esrei* in a low voice, on Rosh Hashanah and Yom Kippur one is allowed to raise his voice slightly when reciting the *Shemoneh Esrei*. The *Rema* comments that on the first night of Rosh Hashanah it is customary to wish each other, "*Leshanah tovah tikaseivu,* May you be inscribed for a good year."

How does the *Rema's* comment relate to the *Shulchan Aruch's* statement about raising one's voice in the *Shemoneh Esrei*?

A beggar collecting alms for himself mumbles in a low voice because he is embarrassed. But someone collecting tzedakah for a worthy cause speaks up loud and clear. Since he is asking for money to help others, he is not embarrassed.

The *Rema* wonders, how we can ask Hashem for favors in a raised voice, when we "knock on G-d's doors like beggars and paupers," and the kindness that Hashem bestows on us is considered to be *tzedakah*? The *Rema's* comment explains that since we wish each other "*Leshanah tovah tikaseivu,*" we are praying for the welfare of others, not just for ourselves. There is no need for us to be embarrassed, and we may therefore raise our voices when *davening* the *Shemoneh Esrei* on the *Yamim Noraim*.

(Sifsei Shimon, Michtavim)

Inscribed and Sealed

On the night of Rosh Hashanah, after *Maariv,* we wish one another "*Leshanah tovah tikaseiv veseichaseim,* may you be inscribed and sealed for a good year." Why do we say both inscribed and sealed? Isn't the verdict for in-between people—as we are advised to consider ourselves—only sealed on Yom Kippur?

Our wish *veseichaseim,* "may you be sealed," is a special prayer. We wish that when Hashem graciously inscribes us in the book of life, our lives should be guided by the Torah and filled with *mitzvos* and good deeds. This wish is sealed for everyone on Rosh Hashanah— even for the in-between people.

(Amaros Tehoros)

Two Angels

On the night of Rosh Hashanah, two angels accompany a Jew and listen as he wishes his friends, *"Leshanah tovah tikaseiv veseichaseim,* May you be inscribed and sealed for a good year.*"* Inspired by the warmhearted friendship and unity among *Klal Yisrael,* they ascend to Heaven and plead for a good and sweet year for *Klal Yisrael.*

(Tzemach Tzedek)

Significant Omens

Abbaye said: Since symbols are meaningful, everyone should eat foods that symbolize blessings for the new year: pumpkin, fenugreek, leek, beet and dates, since these are regarded as symbols of fertility and quick growth.

(Kerisos 6a)

On Rosh Hashanah we pray primarily for the spread of Hashem's glory throughout the world: "And so may Your Name be sanctified instill Your awe upon all Your works   And so too, grant honor to Your people   that You, Hashem, alone will reign over all Your works."

Our prayers are not for worldly requests. We only hint at material prosperity by eating foods that are omens for a good new year.

(Imrei No'am, Rosh Hashanah)

Why do we delight in eating the symbolic foods on Rosh Hashanah? Isn't that contrary to the solemn spirit of Rosh Hashanah? The symbolic foods are not expressions of joy. Instead, they demonstrate our confidence in the favorable judgment that will be rendered on Rosh Hashanah.

(Chasam Sofer, Rosh Hashanah Sermons)

The Maharshal—Rabbi Shlomo Luriah, the great Talmudist and author of

Yam shel Shlomo—did not eat fish on Rosh Hashanah. Although he was fond of fish, on Rosh Hashanah he abstained from his favorite delicacy. Why was this? After all, the Gemara says that fish is one of the symbolic foods we should eat on Rosh Hashanah.

This statement holds true, however, only if we eat the symbolic foods with the purest of intentions, solely for the sake of the mitzvah. But if we eat these delicacies because we enjoy them, we are merely satisfying our physical desires, and the symbolic value of the food is lost.

Since the Maharshal loved to eat fish, he was afraid that he might not eat them for the sake of the mitzvah. Rather than indulge in mundane pleasure, he did not touch the fish.

(Ma'or Vashemesh, Rosh Hashanah)

Round Challahs

Round challahs are shaped like a crown, an allusion to the Rosh Hashanah prayer, "*Uvechein lecha hakol yachtiru,* And so, all shall ascribe the crown to You." In addition, a circle has neither a beginning nor an end, making it a fitting symbol for long life.

(Toras Moshe)

Challah Dipped in Honey

The Sages tell us that when one does *teshuvah* arising out of the love of G-d, all of his intentional sins are converted into *mitzvos*. Honey, too, has the quality of turning bad things to the good. As the *Rema* rules *(Shulchan Aruch, Yoreh Dei'ah 84):* Non-kosher meat that falls into a pot of honey disintegrates. Since it is absorbed in the honey, it loses its identity and may be eaten. Honey is thus the only substance that has the power to turn forbidden food into kosher food.

By dipping the challah into honey we suggest that, just as honey turns bad into good, so should our *teshuvah me'ahavah* turn our transgressions into *mitzvos*.

(Keren LeDavid, Rosh Hashanah)

Another reason for dipping the challah in honey is based on *Tehillim* 81. This is the special psalm for Rosh Hashanah, for it says, "Blow the *shofar* at the moon's renewal, at the time appointed for our festive day." *(Tehillim 81:4)* The verse refers to Rosh Hashanah, which occurs on the first day of Tishrei, when the *shofar* is blown. The last verse of the chapter reads, "He would feed him with the finest wheat, and with honey from a rock sate you." (81:17) This indicates that we should dip the challah, which is made of wheat, in honey.

(Imrei No'am)

Apple Dipped in Honey

The *Shechinah* is likened to an apple tree in the verse, "Like a fruitful, fragrant apple tree among the barren trees of the forest, so is my Beloved (Hashem) among the fruitless idols of the nations." *(Shir Hashirim 2:3)* By dipping the apple—the symbol of the *Shechinah*—in honey, which is a sticky substance, we express our attachment to Hashem, as it says, "You who cling to Hashem, your G-d, you are all alive today." *(Devarim 4:4)*

(Likutei Torah by the Maggid of Tchernobel)

The Gemara *(Shabbos 88a)* asks, why are the Jewish people compared to an apple tree? Just as an apple tree produces fruit before its leaves sprout, so did *Klal Yisrael* say, "We will do" before "We will hear." They were ready to accept the Torah before they knew what its laws entailed.

By eating an apple, we ask Hashem to deal with us measure for measure, fulfilling our requests before we even utter them.

(Divrei Yoel, Rosh Hashanah 28)

A bee has two opposite qualities: its sting is painful, but its honey is sweet. By dipping the apple in bee honey, we pray to be released from the painful sting of Middas Hadin, the Divine Attribute of harsh Justice, and to be judged by the sweetness of Middas Harachamim, G-d's Attribute of Mercy.

(Midrash Pinchas)

Honey symbolizes material values, as it says, "How sweet to my palate is your word, more than honey to my mouth." (*Tehillim* 119:103) By dipping an apple in honey we hint that the apple—that is, the Torah—is our first concern, and the honey is only secondary. We say a *brachah* over the apple, but not over the honey, to demonstrate that in our view, the Torah take precedence over worldly values.

But we cannot disregard material concerns altogether. As the Sages have stated, "Without 'flour' the Torah cannot survive." Therefore we ask "that You renew for us a good and a sweet year." "Good" represents the Torah, and "sweet" represents material needs.

(Vayaged Yaakov 13)

Good and Sweet

We wish each other "a good and sweet year," because "a good year" alone is not enough. For we say "*Gam zu letovah*, it's all for the best," no matter what occurs. What we pray for is a "good year" that is also a "sweet year," a year that is visibly and unmistakably good.

(Rabbi Shlomo of Lentchitz)

Pomegranate: Fruit and Seeds

The pomegranate, with its abundance of seeds, represents the Jewish people. Even the unworthiest among the Jewish people are as full of *mitzvos* as a pomegranate is full of seeds.

(Amaros Tzaddikim)

Elisha ben Abuyah, Rabbi Meir's rebbi, abandoned Judaism. Because of his shameful deed, he was given the derogatory name Acher, "the other one." In spite of Acher's apostasy, Rabbi Meir continued to learn Torah from him.

The Gemara asks, how could Rabbi Meir learn Torah from the apostate Acher? Answers the Gemara: Rabbi Meir found a pomegranate; he ate the fruit inside, and the peel he threw away. He only learned the good things from Acher, and discarded the worthless teachings.

By eating a pomegranate we symbolically ask Hashem to emulate Rabbi Meir, to consider only our good deeds and disregard our shortcomings.

Fish

It is a universal custom to eat fish on Rosh Hashanah, because fish multiply at a prolific rate. Since they live in water, they are invisible to the human eye and are not harmed by an *ayin hara*, "evil eye." Thus, eating fish is a good omen that we may greatly multiply and not be hurt by an *ayin hara*.

Since fish do not have eyelids, their eyes are always open. By eating fish on Rosh Hashanah we call upon Hashem to look down from Heaven and protect us from all evil, as it says, "He neither slumbers nor sleeps, the Guardian of Israel." (*Tehillim* 121:4)

(Elef Hamagein 583)

The Head and Not the Tail

We pray to be "as the head and not as the tail." We want to start doing Hashem's will "as the head," when we are young, in the prime of life. We do not want to start doing *teshuvah* "as a tail," at the tail end of life, when our youthful vigor has waned.

(Sifsei Shimon, Michtavim)

We say "as a head," but not, "that we may be a head." We are not praying to be the one and only leader, for that position is reserved for *Mashiach*, may he come soon and announce the final redemption.

(Toras Shimon Hashaleim)

May Our Merits Increase

Carrots are an omen for increase, since the Yiddish word for carrots is *mehren*, a word which can also mean "to increase."

When eating carrots on the night of Rosh Hashanah we say, "May our merits increase." Does it make sense to ask to increase our merits? If a person has merits, he need not pray that they should increase. If he has no merits, how does it help to pray for an increase in merits that do not exist?

The *Zohar* says: If Hashem wants to favor a person, He counts that person's future *mitzvos* as if they had already been done. "May our merits increase" asks that all the *mitzvos* and customs we will perform in the upcoming month of Tishrei should be regarded as if they had already been done.

(Mikra Kodesh)

"May our merits increase" means that we should do *teshuvah* out of love of Hashem, rather than out of fear of punishment. The Sages teach that when a person does *teshuvah* out of love of Hashem, all his sins are converted into *mitzvos,* and his merits increase greatly.

(Toras Chaim)

Why do we speak in the plural form—"May *our* merits increase"—rather than, "May *my* merits increase"? When the masses repent, their *teshuvah* is considered as *teshuvah me'ahavah*, "*teshuvah* motivated by love of G-d," in which case all their sins are counted as merits. We use the plural form and say, "our merits," because we want to be included in the *teshuvah* of the masses, so our transgressions are judged as merits.

(Divrei Yoel)

No Nuts on Rosh Hashanah

It is customary not to eat nuts and almonds on Rosh Hashanah, because the numeric value of the Hebrew word *egoz* (nut) is 17, the same as that of the Hebrew word *cheit* (sin), not counting the *alef* of *cheit*. In addition, nuts increase saliva and cause coughing, which interferes with praying.

(Rema 583)

No Sleep During the Day

We don't sleep during the day on Rosh Hashanah, for we have a tradition that says: "He who sleeps on Rosh Hashanah, his *mazal* also becomes listless and drowsy." (*Yerushalmi Rosh Hashanah*)

Sleeping is a sign of laziness and lethargy. On the *Yom Hadin*, Judgment Day, one must be alert and lively. Do more and more *mitzvos, daven* more, learn more and say *Tehillim*!

(Kaf Hachayim)

The Gemara says that during the first three hours of the day, Hashem judges the world. By sleeping during those hours a person shows that he is not concerned about the judgment he will receive. To show our anxiety about the forthcoming decree, we get up earlier than usual on Rosh Hashanah.

(Elef Hamagein 584)

Learning Mishnayos

It is a custom to learn the four chapters of *Meseches Rosh Hashanah* at the four meals of Rosh Hashanah, one chapter at each meal. This is a good omen to be inscribed for a good year.

(Elef Hamagein)

Chapter Nine

The Rosh Hashanah Prayers: Shacharis

Adon Olam

Rabbi Yehudah *Hechasid* said: When a person recites *Adon Olam*, concentrating on the meaning of the words, I assure him that his prayers will be accepted in Heaven, and that Satan will not disrupt his *tefillos*.

(Matteh Moshe)

On Rosh Hashanah it is customary for the *chazzan* to chant *Adon Olam* with a solemn melody. This is the day that Hashem completed His work by creating *Adam Harishon*. He thereby became the *Adon Olam*, the Master of the Universe. It is therefore fitting to chant *Adon Olam* with a slow, reflective melody.

(Ohel Shlomo)

Pesukei D'zimra

On Rosh Hashanah everyone *davens* with extraordinary devotion, concentrating on the special *tefillos* that are the hallmark of the day.

73

Regrettably, people tend to rush through the important portions of the Rosh Hashanah service we say every day, such as *Pesukei D'zimra* and *Shema*.

This is a mistake. For when we say these *tefillos* on Rosh Hashanah with proper intent and concentration, we elevate all the prayers we said routinely and without *kavanah* all year.

(Yosher Divrei Emes)

Hamelech — O King

The *chazzan* raises his voice and loudly proclaims "*Hamelech*, O King!" to demonstrate to the whole world that we accept G-d's kingship and acknowledge His absolute sovereignty.

(Elef Hamagein 584)

With Bowed Heads

Some people make it a practice to say the *Shemoneh Esrei* on Rosh Hashanah and Yom Kippur with a bowed head. This is done as an expression of awe of Hashem and His judgment.

(Tur 582)

Hamelech Hakadosh, the Holy King

In the *Shemoneh Esrei* of the Ten Days of Repentance, we say "*Hamelech hakadosh,* the holy King," instead of, "the holy G-d," the phrase used the rest of the year. The term "holy King" implies absolute power and strict judgment. Before pleading for mercy, we acknowledge Hashem's mastery and the fact that He now sits in judgment.

(Levush 582)

Le'eylah Ule'eyla

During the Ten Days of Repentance we say in the Kaddish, *"Le'eyla ule'eyla,* Exceedingly beyond any blessing," rather than just *"Le'eyla,* Beyond any blessing," the phrase used throughout the year. For during this period of judgment, G-d's majesty is even more pronounced than it is during the rest of the year.

(Levush 582)

The Torah Reading

The Torah reading of the first day of Rosh Hashanah is from *parshas Vayeira,* the chapter beginning with the words, "Hashem remembered Sarah." (*Bereishis* 21) We read there that Hashem allowed Sarah to conceive, and the Gemara says that this happened on Rosh Hashanah. The text then continues relating the birth of Yitzchak.

(Beis Yosef 584)

The *Oheiv Yisrael,* the Apter Rav, comments that the reading of this chapter serves as a remedy to help barren women conceive.

On Rosh Hashanah, when Rav Levi Yitzchak of Berditchev read the parshah of "Hashem remembered (pakad) Sarah," 180 barren women conceived—the numeric value of pakad.

(Rabbi Shalom of Belz)

The Haftorah tells the story of Chanah. Heartbroken at being childless, Chanah ardently implored Hashem to grant her offspring. On Rosh Hashanah her prayer was answered; she conceived and later gave birth to Shmuel *Hanavi.*

Chapter Ten

Avinu Malkeinu

Reciting Avinu Malkeinu

The Gemara (*Taanis* 25b) tells us how this prayer originated. One year a severe drought ravaged Eretz Yisrael. Despite fasting and fervent prayers, not a drop of rain fell. The great sage, Rabbi Eliezer, led the multitude in prayer, but still no rain fell.

Then Rabbi Akiva stepped forward and began a five-sentence prayer, each of whose verses began with *Avinu Malkeinu*. The first one was, "Our Father, our King, we have sinned before You." Immediately, it began to rain.

When the Sages saw that this prayer formula, beginning with *Avinu Malkeinu,* was answered, they added other requests as the need arose, and they ordained that these verses be recited on fasts and during the Ten Days of Repentance.

(Shulchan Aruch 584)

Opening the Doors of the Ark

The doors of the *Aron Hakodesh* are kept open while *Avinu Malkeinu* is recited. When a petitioner appeals to a mortal king, he wants to offer his plea in the king's private chamber, where no outsiders will interfere. So, too, when we implore "*Avinu Malkeinu,* our Father, our King," we open the doors of the Holy Ark, the seat of His holy Torah, where Satan and his accusing angels have no access.

(Tiferes Uziel)

Why Mention Sin?

The *Beis Yosef* says that verses that mention sin should be omitted on Rosh Hashanah, and the first verse "We have sinned" should therefore be left out on Rosh Hashanah.

According to *Machzor Vitry*, all the verses of *Avinu Malkeinu* should be recited, because the mentions of sin refer to the transgressions of previous generations, of which we, too, must repent.

Perhaps *Machzor Vitry* may be understood together with a statement by the *Magen Avraham*. When reciting *Tehillim* on Rosh Hashanah, one may say the passage, "We have sinned like our forefathers, we have gone astray and done evil" (*Tehillim* 106:6), even though it mentions sin. Since it is said as a prayer and not as a confession of sins, it is not considered a self-indictment.

In saying, "We have sinned before You," we refer to the sins of our forefathers who worshiped idols. But we are not like that. For we say in the next verse, "We have no King but You."

(Toras Moshe)

One Rosh Hashanah, the holy Berditchever offered the following defense on behalf of Klal Yisrael: "Ribbono shel Olam! Even if a Jews stumbles and sins, in the end he will do a mitzvah, for he will give tzedakah and do favors for others to atone for his sin."

This is why we say, "Our Father, our King, we have sinned for You!" True, we have sinned—but our sin will turn out to be "for You." For the sin will result in a mitzvah.

(Kedushas Levi)

Perfect Teshuvah

In *Avinu Malkeinu* we pray that we may return in perfect *teshuvah*, which means *teshuvah* out of love of Hashem. For if a person does *teshuvah* out of love rather than fear of Hashem, all his transgression are counted as *mitzvos*.

(Darash Av 167)

A Complete Recovery

Sometimes a person's recovery requires the surgical removal of an organ or a limb. He recovers, but it is not "a complete recovery."

We pray that Hashem may send a *refuah sheleimah*, "a complete recovery"—the patient should be completely healed, with all his organs and limbs intact.

(Darash Av 167)

Inscribe Us in the Book of Good Life

In a department store, some items move faster than others do. If an article does not sell, the manager reduces the price to attract customers. But there is one item that is needed by everyone all the time, and that is bread. The baker never has to reduce the price of bread!

On Rosh Hashanah, people pray for different things: one person *davens* for healing, another for *parnassah*, for *shidduchim*, for riches. But there is one thing everyone *davens* for: their lives! When G-d sees that life is in such great demand, He raises the price. In return for the gift of life, He demands that we *daven* with *kavanah*. That's why we fervently *daven*, "Inscribe us in the book of good life!"

The Book of Redemption and Salvation

Why the double expression *"Geulah vishuah,* redemption and salvation"?

> *Sometimes after serving his term, a convict is released from prison—but he is immediately indicted for another crime. His release from prison is "redemption," but not "salvation." We pray that Hashem should "redeem" us from our distress, and that our "redemption" should be the ultimate "salvation" from all our troubles.*
>
> *(Darash Av, 167)*

The repetitive *"Geulah vishuah,* redemption and salvation," tells us that we should not believe in a *geulah* before the coming of Mashiach. We pray for a *geulah vishuah,* the redemption that is the final salvation.

(Divrei Yoel)

The Book of Sustenance and Support

We pray that we should merit both aspects of this verse: "The book"—that we should be able to learn Torah; and "sustenance and support," that we should be able to learn Torah without worrying about *parnassah.*

(Tiferes Shlomo)

> *A person cries at three points in his life—when he is born, when he is weaned and when he gets married. When he is born he cries because*

after being nourished in his mother's womb, he is afraid that he might not be fed in the outside world. He cries for the same reason when he is weaned. When he gets married, he cries because he is afraid to take on the responsibility of providing for his wife and family.

All three incidents indicate a lack of faith in Hashem. A person should know that Hashem, Who sustained him before he was born, will support him all his life. So we pray with complete trust that Hashem will inscribe us in the "book of sustenance and support."

(Maharsham, Vayechi)

The Book of Merits

"Inscribe us in the book of merits" is followed by, "Inscribe us in the book of forgiveness and pardon." This sequence is patterned after the system of buying and selling. Buying merchandise on credit costs more than paying for it in advance. Hashem sends *tzaddikim* abundant *parnassah* without trouble on their part, because they prepaid for it by the *mitzvos* they performed. But a person who asks Hashem for sustenance before he performed *mitzvos* will have to struggle to earn his livelihood, because he wants it on credit.

We are asking first that Hashem should inscribe us in the Book of Merits, that all the *mitzvos* we perform daily should be considered as pre-payment. Having paid with our *mitzvos*, we ask for "forgiveness and pardon" at the cash price, because we established our credit-worthiness with the *mitzvos* and good deeds we have performed.

(Tiferes Uziel)

The Pride of Yisrael Your People

The Gemara *(Pesachim 87a)* says: Hashem sent the Jewish people into exile among the nations so converts should join them. Unfortunately, it did not work out that way. While only a few converts have joined us, there are many Jews who have abandoned Judaism.

"The plan did not work out," we say to Hashem. "Do not wait for *Klal Yisrael* to increase by the addition of converts. Start by sparing the remnant of Yisrael from more losses, so we will remain faithful Jews who serve You with devotion."

(Avodas Yisrael)

Open the Gates of Heaven

How does a person know that the gates of Heaven have opened to allow his prayers to enter? When he feels his heart opening up and a fountain of faith surging up from below, it is a sign that the gates of Heaven have also opened up.

(Toras Avos)

Those Who Went into Fire and Water

Why the strange wording, "who went into fire"? Why don't we simply say, "for the sake of those who were burned"?

During the persecutions of the Spanish Inquisition, the Jews were forced to convert to Christianity. Those who refused to bow to the cross were burned at the stake. In those tragic times, there were Jews who asked, "Where's the auto-da-fe? We are eager to give up our lives *al kiddush Hashem!*" They took their children along, and with joy in their hearts they marched to the roaring pyre to die a martyr's death. They willingly went into the fire to sanctify Hashem's name.

(Devar Hameluchah)

Act for Your Sake and Help Us

The prior verse says, "Act for Your sake, if not for ours." What additional request is in the words, "Act for Your sake, and help us"?

The saintly Yismach Moshe of Ujhel once exclaimed in his sermon on Rosh Hashanah: "Ribbono shel Olam! You know that my sins stand in the way of the geulah sheleimah. If my death would atone for the sins of Klal Yisrael, and the geulah sheleimah would come, I am prepared to surrender my body and soul, even if I will not be resurrected at techiyas hameisim. I am willing to die, as long as Your great Name will be sanctified."

Our initial prayer is, "Help us, if not for our sake." If we do not merit seeing the salvation of *Klal Yisrael*, we ask You to "act for Your sake," even if we lose our share in the World to Come—as long as You help *Klal Yisrael*.

Next we pray, "Act for Your sake and help us." Bringing the *geulah sheleimah* confers honor on Your Name—particularly when no one is missing at the final redemption. Therefore it is fitting for You to help us.

(Devar Hameluchah)

We Have No Worthy Deeds

The last verse of *Avinu Malkeinu* is said in a subdued tone of voice. This can be explained with a parable:

The owner of a retail store came to a wholesale house with a long list of items he wanted to order. In a loud voice, he called out, "Bring me 100 yards of silk, 200 yards of lining material, 50 yards of cotton, 100 yards of wool, 20 boxes of buttons "

When the order was neatly packed and placed on the counter, the secretary presented the invoice. Seeing the amount he owed, the merchant turned pale and asked to see the boss.

He whispered to the owner, "I am out of cash, my bank account is overdrawn. Could you please let me have the merchandise on credit? I'll pay you in monthly installments."

On Rosh Hashanah we approach Hashem with a long list of requests. In a loud voice we announce, "Give us good life, sustenance, help and redemption, healing for the sick   "

When the list is ended, we very quietly whisper to Hashem, "Be gracious with us and answer us, though we have no worthy deeds. Treat us with charity and kindness, and save us."

(Maggid of Dubno)

Chapter Eleven

Blowing
the Shofar

Three Verses

The blowing of the *shofar* is mentioned in three verses:

- "Speak to *Bnei Yisrael* and say: The first day of the seventh month shall be a day of rest for you. It is a sacred holiday for remembrance [and] sounding [of the ram's horn]." (*Vayikra* 23:24)

- "The first day of the seventh month shall be a sacred holiday to you when you may not do any mundane work. It shall be a day of sounding [the ram's] horn." (*Bamidbar* 29:1)

- "Blow the *shofar* at the moon's renewal, at the appointed time for our festive day." (*Tehillim* 81:4)

A Wake-Up Call

The Rambam says: Although the sounding of the *shofar* on Rosh Hashanah is a Torah decree, [to be observed whether or not one understands it,] it contains an allusion, as if the *shofar* is saying: "Awake, sleepers, from your sleep! Arise, slumberers, from your slumber! Scrutinize your deeds! Repent with contrition! Remember your Creator!"

To those who forget the truth in the vanities of time, and throughout the entire year devote their energies to vanity and emptiness—peer into your souls! Improve your ways and your deeds, and let everyone abandon his evil path and thoughts.

(Rambam, Hilchos Teshuvah 3:4)

A Call to Arms

Since man is made of the dust of the earth, he is by nature slow and inert. He has to be goaded into action. In war, the troops are roused by martial music and the sounding of trumpets to fight the enemy. On Rosh Hashanah, the *Yom Hadin,* the *shofar* is the ideal instrument to spur a person to do *teshuvah.* The broken sound of *teruah* suggests a person's brokenhearted remorse. It also reminds us to break our lusts and overcome our temptations.

(Sefer Hachinuch 805)

Ten Allusions to the Mitzvah of Shofar

Rabbeinu Saadiah Gaon lists ten symbolic allusions for the blowing of the shofar on Rosh Hashanah:

1. Rosh Hashanah marks the anniversary of the day Hashem became Sovereign of the universe. We blow the *shofar,* since it is customary to sound the trumpets at the coronation of a new king.

2. Just as a king may proclaim a period of amnesty before he punishes wrongdoers, the *shofar* blasts proclaim, "Whoever wishes to repent—let him do so now; if not, let him not complain later."

3. At Mount Sinai, when the Jews accepted the Torah, "the sound of the *shofar* continually increased and was very great." (*Shemos* 19:19) On Rosh Hashanah the *shofar* reminds us to renew that commitment.

4. The *shofar* reminds us of the admonitions of the prophets and their calls to repentance, as it says, "When I bring a sword upon a land [the sentry] blows the *shofar* and warns the people." (*Yechezkel* 33:2-3)

5. The *shofar* reminds us to pray for the rebuilding of the destroyed *Beis Hamikdash,* of which the *navi* lamented, "I shall not be silent, for the sound of the *shofar* have you heard, O my soul, the shout of war. Destruction upon destruction has been proclaimed " (*Yirmeyah* 4:19-20)

6. The *shofar,* a ram's horn, reminds us of *Akeidas* Yitzchak, the Binding of Yitzchak, when Avraham sacrificed a ram as a substitute for Yitzchak. (*Bereishis* 22) Thus may our remembrances ascend before Him for the good.

7. The sound of the *shofar* inspires fear and trembling in the hearts of all who hear it, as the *navi* asks, "Can a *shofar* be blown in a city, and the people not tremble?" (*Amos* 3:6)

8. The *shofar* reminds us of the great and awesome Judgment Day of the future, which the *navi* describes as, "a day of *shofar* blowing and shouting." (*Tzefaniah* 1:16)

9. The *shofar* makes us yearn for the ingathering of the exiles, of which it is said, "It will be on that day that a great *shofar* will be blown and then they will prostrate themselves to Hashem on the holy mountain in Yerushalayim." (*Yeshayah* 27:13)

10. The *shofar* recalls the resurrection of the dead, which will be accompanied by the sounding of a *shofar,* as it says, "All the inhabitants of the world and dwellers of the earth you shall hear when a *shofar* is sounded." (*Yeshayah* 8:3)

(Rabbeinu Saadiah Gaon)

Purpose of Creation

On Rosh Hashanah Man was created, and Hashem blew into his nostrils the soul of life. The blowing of the *shofar* reminds a person that he was created for the sole purpose of doing Hashem's will. This spurs him to do *teshuvah* and rectify his shortcomings.

(Tzvi Latzaddik)

Trumpets and Shofar

"With trumpets and *shofar* sounds, call out before the King, Hashem." *(Tehillim 98:6)* The saintly Berditchever would relate the following parable to shed light on this verse:

> *While on a hunting expedition, a king got lost deep in a dark forest. Searching for a way out, he ran into some coarse, uncultured peasants. Much to his chagrin, his ardent requests for directions were met with stony silence.*
>
> *At last, exhausted and near collapse, he spotted a refined hunter emerging from the shrubbery. "I am lost," the king said faintly. "Would you please show me the way out of this forest?"*
>
> *Realizing that it was the king, the kindhearted hunter guided him all the way back to the palace. The grateful king rewarded the hunter, giving him a large sum of money and a splendid uniform of the royal honor guard. The man's hunting outfit was displayed in the royal treasure house, in honor of the great favor he had done for the king.*
>
> *After a time, this man was arrested and charged with a serious violation of the law, punishable by a long prison term and a heavy fine. Deeply despondent, the man asked the manager of the treasure house to let him wear his special hunting outfit—the one that was kept on display—to his trial before the king. His request was granted.*

At the trial, the king saw the accused wearing the hunting outfit. He was reminded of the day the hunter had rescued him, thereby saving both his life and the monarchy.

"Case dismissed!" the king's voice rang out. "The accused is granted a pardon."

Hashem, the King of kings, approached all the nations, but none of them were willing to accept the Torah. *Klal Yisrael* was the only nation to embrace the Torah, crowning Hashem as their Sovereign and Master.

On Rosh Hashanah, when we are judged for our failings, we put on the garments we wore on the day we received the Torah and crowned Hashem as our King. What is this garment? The Torah describes it as, "The sound of the *shofar* growing continually much stronger." *(Shemos* 19:19) By blowing the *shofar*, we awaken G-d's love for *Klal Yisrael* which blossomed at *mattan* Torah. May Hashem forgive our transgressions and inscribe us for a good and blessed year.

(Kedushas Levi)

Recalling the Shofar

A noble king enjoyed listening to the lyrical musical compositions his children sang and played for him. Whenever he was depressed, the sound of his children's choir, accompanied by harp and violins, would always cheer him up.

In the course of time, the princes became disloyal and rebelled against their father. Infuriated with their folly and arrogance, the king expelled them from his palace, sending them into exile.

The princes suffered greatly in their remote exile. They finally came to realize how badly they had hurt their kind father. Remorseful over their disobedient behavior, the children sent groups of singers to their father to perform the musical compositions they used to sing for him as youngsters, hoping that the sound of the old tunes would reawaken the king's love for them.

The devout Jews of former generations knew how to blow the *shofar* with the proper intentions and mystical thoughts. G-d was pleased when hearing their *shofar* blasts, and as a result, the gates of Heaven were opened.

We are now in exile, banished from the King's palace, the *Beis Hamikdash*. Although our *shofar* blasts are not blown with the proper profound intentions, nevertheless, the *shofar* blasts are the same that were sounded by the Jews of old, blown according to the instructions of the Sages. Our *tefillah* is that Hashem may accept our *tekias shofar*, answer our prayers, redeem us from *galus*, and rebuild His palace, the *Beis Hamikdash*.

(Divrei Yoel, Rosh Hashanah)

Hashem's Command

The *mitzvah* of *shofar* has profound kabbalistic significance, which the saintly Sages had in mind during the *shofar* blowing. But in Heaven, the simple intention of blowing the *shofar* because Hashem commanded it is cherished greatly.

(Ma'or Vashemesh, Rimzei Rosh Hashanah)

The Gemara (Rosh Hashanah 16a) says: Rabbi Yitzchak asked, "Why do we blow the shofar on Rosh Hashanah?" [Surprised at the question, the Gemara exclaims:] You ask, "Why do we blow?" Hashem told us to blow! [How can you ask such a question?]

Perhaps when Rabbi Yitzchak asked this question, his intention was to ask, "What are the mystical reasons for blowing shofar?" To this the Gemara answers: The paramount reason is to perform the mitzvah because "Hashem told us to blow," and to fulfill Hashem will. This stands much higher than all mystical intentions.

(Ma'or Vashemesh)

Sign of Submissiveness

A mighty king appointed his only son as governor of one of the provinces of his vast empire, on condition that all taxes he collected be transferred to the royal treasury. After a few years, the son decided to keep the tax money, refusing to hand the funds over to the royal treasury. The king adamantly demanded the money, but the son turned a deaf ear to all requests for payment.

When the king's repeated warnings were ignored, he decided to launch an invasion of the province. Seeing the massive imperial forces coming down on his defenseless territory, the son decided to surrender. But how was he to communicate with his father over the din of roaring guns and clattering chariots? The only way to reach his father was by alerting him with trumpets and announcing his unconditional surrender through a loudspeaker.

Klal Yisrael is the only son of Hashem *Yisbarach.* The spiritual taxes we pay are the *mitzvos* we dutifully perform. A person who has been lax in performing the *mitzvos* and wants to mend his ways has great difficulty getting through to his Father in Heaven, to ask forgiveness for his past failings. But on Rosh Hashanah, the *shofar* serves as a "loudspeaker," transcending all obstacles and opening the Gates of Heaven, where our *teshuvah* is readily accepted.

(Emes L'Yaakov)

Confusing the Satan

On Rosh Hashanah, Satan looks around, focusing on the people who were inscribed for death and noting their names. But when the Jews blow the *shofar*, he becomes confused and does not recognize the people who were inscribed for death. If a person fails to do *teshuvah*, however, Satan is able to identify him and eagerly carries out the verdict.

(Zohar, vol. 2:237)

The common excuse people give for neglecting to serve Hashem properly is that they were too busy earning a livelihood. Preoccupied, they were unable to concentrate on davening and doing mitzvos. The Satan contends that this is not a valid excuse. A Jew has to focus on doing mitzvos, no matter what!

But when we blow the shofar and the Satan becomes confused—to the point that he is unable to accuse Klal Yisrael—he himself proves that when you are preoccupied, you cannot concentrate. Thus Satan's charge is discredited.

(Rabbi Simchah Bunim of P'shischa)

Rabbi Yitzchak said: If the *shofar* is not blown at the start of the year, [and Satan is not confused by the *shofar* blasts,] bad things will happen in the end. Comments *Tosafos*: This does not refer to a year when Rosh Hashanah falls on Shabbos, in which case it is forbidden to blow the *shofar*.

Tosafos explains why Satan becomes confused. When he hears the first series of *shofar* blasts, he is slightly baffled. But when he hears the second set of blasts, he is sure that this heralds the end of the world, the day about which it says, "He will eliminate death forever" (*Yeshayah* 25:8), and Satan, the Angel of Death, will be slaughtered. Terrified, he goes into hiding, and is too confused to accuse the Jewish people.

(Rosh Hashanah 16b)

The Satmar Rebbe suggests another reason for Satan's bewilderment. Every year when we blow the shofar, the shofar blasts of all the tzaddikim of previous generations are added to our present shofar sounds, and a great and holy crescendo rises up to Heaven. Every Rosh Hashanah, as new shofar blasts are joined to the ones of the previous years, the noise in Heaven grows stronger.

Satan remembers the sound of last year's shofar blasts. He is now confronted with a much louder noise. Afraid that enough shofar blasts have accumulated in Heaven to bring about the final redemption, he is panic-stricken, thinking that what he hears is the "shofar of Mashiach," trumpeting his demise.

The Satmar Rebbe concluded: The Satan's fears are not unfounded. Mashiach can come today when our modest tekios are added to those of the tzaddikim of past generations. Let's not miss the opportunity. Entreat Hashem wholeheartedly and accept His absolute sovereignty, for with sincere prayer it is possible to bring the final redemption.

It is not enough to just recite the phrase, "Repentance, Prayer and Charity remove the evil of the decree." We must do it!

(Divrei Yoel)

From Justice to Mercy

One of the verses of Shofaros reads, "G-d has ascended with a *teruah* blast, Hashem, with the sound of the *shofar*." (*Tehillim* 47:6) The verse mentions both the name *Elo-kim*, denoting the attribute of Justice, and the name *Hashem*, which signifies the attribute of Mercy.

When Hashem ascends to take His seat on the Throne of strict Justice, He is accompanied by Heavenly *shofar* blasts. When *Klal Yisrael* raise their *shofars* to blow for Hashem, He is overcome with Mercy—and He rises from the Throne of harsh Justice and moves to the Throne of Mercy. Instead of judging with strict Justice, He decides with Mercy.

(Midrash Rabbah, Emor)

If the shofar blowing causes Hashem to move to His Throne of Mercy, every year should be a good and bountiful year. So why is it that there is so much misery and suffering?

The sound of the shofar is effective only if it prompts people to do teshuvah. The word shofar is related to the phrase, "shapperu ma'aseichem, improve your deeds."

(Yismach Moshe, Rosh Hashanah)

Shofar After Torah Reading

Unlike all other *mitzvos*, which we do as early in the day as possible, the mitzvah of shofar blowing is delayed until after the Torah reading. Why?

In the days of the Roman rule in Eretz Yisrael, the authorities outlawed *shofar* blowing. To enforce their decree, they placed guards in all *shuls* to make sure that the *shofar* was not sounded.

Expecting the Jews to blow the *shofar* early in the morning, the guards waited till noon. When no *shofar* blowing took place, they left. It was then that the *shofar* was sounded. This practice, rooted in distress, became an established custom, so we likewise postpone the *shofar* blowing until after the Torah reading.

(Beis Yosef 585)

The Shofar's Curve

The *shofar* is bent to remind us to be subservient to Hashem and bow to His will.

(Tur)

How to Blow

The *toke'a* blows the *shofar* from the right side of his mouth. He does so in keeping with the verse, "The Satan was standing at his right to accuse him." (*Zechariah* 1:3)

(Matteh Moshe)

During the blowing, the *toke'a* should point the *shofar* upward, conforming to the verse, "G-d has ascended with the blast, Hashem with the sound of *shofar*." (*Tehillim* 47:6)

(Rema 585)

The *shofar* blowing serves as a reminder of *Akeidas* Yitzchak, the Binding of Yitzchak; it is meant to arouse Hashem's compassion for the Jewish people. Thus, by blowing the *shofar* the *toke'a* acts as a defense lawyer for the Jewish people, and in that capacity he must stand when he addresses the court.

(Matteh Moshe)

The *shofar* is covered while the *brachos* are recited. This is similarly related to *Akeidas* Yitzchak. The *Midrash* says that before building the altar on which to sacrifice his son Yitzchak, Avraham kept Yitzchak hidden, for fear that Satan would injure Yitzchak and render him unfit to be offered.

(Elef Hamagein)

Lamenatzei'ach Livnei Korach

The *shofar* is covered while the *brachos* are recited. This is similarly related to *Akeidas* Yitzchak. The *Midrash* says that before building the altar on which to sacrifice his son Yitzchak, Avraham kept Yitzchak hidden, for fear that Satan would injure Yitzchak and render him unfit to be offered.

(Elef Hamagein)

This psalm praises Hashem with the words "For Hashem, most High is awesome." (*Tehillim* 47:3) Before the *shofar* blowing, Satan gets ready to present his charges and accusations against *Klal Yisrael*. Reluctant to meet Satan, Hashem retreats to a very lofty and awesome region in Heaven where Satan and his minions have no access. But we want our *tefillos* to reach Hashem in His lofty abode. What does Hashem do? He opens a doorway beneath His Throne of Glory, allowing the *tefillos* of *Klal Yisrael* to rise up to Him.

(Aron Eidus)

Min Hameitzar

Before the *shofar* blowing we recite seven verses aloud, beginning with "*Min hameitzar*," which is an expression of prayerful hope. The acronym of the following six verses form the words "*Kra Satan*, tear up Satan," implying that through the *mitzvah* of blowing the *shofar*, Hashem should do away with Satan's accusations.

(Ma'or Vashemesh)

The Sounds of the Shofar

The Torah describes Rosh Hashanah as *Yom Teruah*, a day of sounding the [ram's] horn. Thus the *teruah* sound is the primary sound, and a *teruah* must always be preceded and followed by a *tekiah*, a long, clear blast. The *mitzvah* requires that three sets of *tekiah-teruah-tekiah* be sounded.

An uncertainty arose whether the *teruah* sound is a moaning sound, consisting of three short, broken blasts, called *shevarim;* a sobbing sound, consisting of nine very short staccato blasts, which we call *teruah;* or a combination of the two: *shevarim-teruah*.

In order to satisfy all three alternatives, we blow three series of *tekiah-shevarim-teruah-tekiah*, three series of *tekiah-shevarim-tekiah*, and three series of *tekiah-teru'ah-tekiah*—a total of thirty blasts which are blown after the Torah reading.

(Rosh Hashanah 34a)

Rabbi Aharon of Karlin offered the following poignant interpretation of the various shofar sounds:

Hashem created man upright and flawless. Through his sins, man became warped and twisted. By turning to the shofar in teshuvah, he is straightened out again.

This thought is reflected in the sounds of the shofar: tekiah-shevarim-teruah-tekiah. The first tekiah, a straight, clear sound, represents man's original rectitude and virtue. The broken shevarim sound is indicative of the spiritual breakdown that comes as a result of sinning. This is followed by the sobbing teruah sound, which mirrors the sinners's brokenheartedness, inner turmoil and deep remorse, the forerunners of teshuvah. The culmination is reached in the steady tone of the final tekiah, which signifies the inner tranquility of the baal teshuvah whose missteps have been forgiven.

The clear, straight sound of the *tekiah* suggests "love," a person's straightforward feeling of adoration. The *shevarim-teruah* sound represents "awe and fear"—a person who is afraid shakes and trembles. The sounds of the *shofar* tell us to resolve anew to love Hashem and be in awe of Him, keeping His Torah and fulfilling His *mitzvos*.

(Hayashar Vehatov)

Tekiah Gedolah

The final sound at the end of *Mussaf* is a *tekiah gedolah*, a long, drawn-out *tekiah*, which is reminiscent of the long blast of the *shofar* that signaled the end of Hashem's revelation at Sinai and the withdrawal of the *Shechinah*, as it says, "When the ram's horn sounds a long blast, they will be allowed to go up the mountain." *(Shemos 19:13)*

(Maharil, K'tzei Hamatteh)

The long blast of the *tekiah gedolah* awakens Hashem's mercy. The Torah tells us that at the Giving of the Torah, "there was a sound of a *shofar*, increasing in volume to a great degree." *(Shemos* 19:19) The Sages comment that the longer the sound went on, the stronger it became. This was unlike the sound produced by man: the longer he blows, the weaker the sound becomes.

We blow a long *tekiah* with diminishing strength. What message are we sending with the diminishing sound of the *shofar*? After 210 years of Egyptian bondage, *Bnei Yisrael* did not listen to Moshe, "because of shortness of breath and hard work." *(Shemos* 6:9) All the more so is it hard for us, after two thousand years of *galus* and oppression, to obey Hashem. The steadily weakening sound of the *tekiah gedolah* conveys this plea for Hashem's compassion.

(D'var Hameluchah)

The Gemara (Berachos 34b) says: In a place where baalei teshuvah are standing [in Heaven] the perfectly righteous cannot stand.

The Shelah says that the straight sound of the first tekiah symbolizes the tzaddik, who has not sinned. The broken shevarim sound stands for the sins that cause an inner breakup in a person's soul, which leads to the weeping sound of the teruah. When he does teshuvah, he is straightened out again like the second tekiah sound.

The final tekiah gedolah, extended tekiah, indicates that a baal teshuvah is on a higher level than a tzaddik who has never sinned.

(Vayageid Yaakov, Rosh Hashanah 24)

The Berditchever's Plea

Before the *shofar* blowing, the holy Berditchever offered the following plea to Hashem on behalf of *Klal Yisrael*:

Ribbono shel Olam! You wrote in Your Torah, *"Yom teruah yihyeh lachem,* It shall be a day of the sounding of the [ram's] horn." The Sages said the word *teruah* is mentioned three times, so the *teruah* sound is blown three times. Before and after every *teruah* a *tekiah* sound must be blown, which gives us nine blasts. Then there is the doubt whether *teruah* is a staccato sound or *shevarim,* a moaning sound, or a combination of the two. By blowing all possible variations we obtain thirty sounds.

These thirty sounds are blown before *Mussaf.* In *Mussaf* we blow another thirty sounds, and in the repetition of *Mussaf* thirty more sounds, and in the last *Kaddish* ten additional sounds, for a total of one hundred blasts.

We blow one hundred blasts for the one blast You mention in the Torah! And tomorrow on the second day of Rosh Hashanah we blow yet another one hundred blasts. We blow in every *shul* across the world two hundred blasts for You, and this has been done ever since You gave us the Torah — an innumerable number of *shofar* blasts!

Therefore we beg You, *Ribbono shel Olam*—sound the great *shofar* for our freedom! *Klal Yisrael* has been reciting this prayer three times a day, for more than 1800 years since the destruction of the *Beis Hamikdash.* Why don't You answer their prayers?

(Shaar Yissachar)

Blowing Twice

The Gemara asks: Why do we blow the *shofar* before *Mussaf,* and again during *Mussaf?* The double sounding shows how greatly we cherish the *mitzvah.* This confuses the Satan so much that he is unable to bring charges against *Klal Yisrael* before the Heavenly Tribunal.

(Rosh Hashanah 16b [Rashi])

The Satan knows that at the coming of *Mashiach,* Satan and the evil impulse will be put to death. He assumes that the first *shofar* blast signifies the *teshuvah* of *Klal Yisrael.* This causes him anxiety. When he hears the second series of blasts, he assumes it is the *"Great Shofar"* which signals the final redemption, and that his own demise is near. This upsets him so much that he is speechless, unable to accuse the Jewish people.

(Rosh Hashanah 16b [Tosafos])

The second series of *shofar* blasts is meant to tell us that after we leave *shul*, we should not forget the awe-inspiring *davening* we just completed. The impression should carry over into our homes, where we should conduct ourselves in a way befitting the holy day.

(Seder Hayom)

Broken Hearts

When we blow the sobbing sound of *teruah*, Hashem is reminded of the broken hearts of *Klal Yisrael*. His attribute of Mercy is awakened, and He bestows on us His bountiful flow of kindness.

(Midbar Kadesh, Rosh Hashanah)

G-d Ascended With a Teruah

The *shofar* blowing on Rosh Hashanah prods us to do *teshuvah* during the Ten Days of Repentance. The sound of the *shofar* is a semblance of the voice of Hashem, as it says, *"Elo-kim* ascended with a blast, Hashem with the sound of the shofar." (*Tehillim* 47:6) It is as if Hashem is inherent in the sound of the *shofar*, inspiring us to do *teshuvah*.

(Tiferes Shlomo, Rosh Hashanah)

The Skill of Blowing Shofar

The Gemara (*Rosh Hashanah* 29b) says: Blowing the *shofar* and taking bread from the oven [after it is baked] are skills, not work.

What is the connection between blowing the *shofar* and bread?

The Sanzer Rav explained: The *shofar* blowing awakes Heavenly compassion and draws down Divine favor, ample sustenance and all good things to this world to benefit *Klal Yisrael*. In this way, blowing the *shofar* brings about an abundant flow of "bread," sustenance and all good things.

(Beis Pinchas)

Rabbi Shlomoh Kluger once said to the toke'a (the person who blows the shofar): The Sages are quite right when they say: Blowing the shofar is a skill (chochmah), and not work. But regarding chochmah it says, "The beginning of chochmah (wisdom) is fear of Hashem." (Tehillim 111:10) Fear of Hashem is the first requirement for being a toke'a.

(Avodas Yisrael)

Rachel Is Weeping

"A voice is heard on high." (*Yirmeyah* 31:14) In a figurative sense, this applies to the "voice" of the *shofar*. If in Heaven the sound of the *shofar* is heard, inspiring people to do *teshuvah*, then "Rachel weeps for her children." Hashem answers her plea and promises, "Your children will return to their borders."

(Mar'eh Yechezkel)

Shofar Blowing in Auschwitz

Rabbi Zvi Hirsch Meisels, *zt"l*, the Veitzener Rav, arrived in Chicago after the Second World War and became one of the community's most prominent and beloved *rabbanim*. Rabbi Meisels was a renowned *rav* before and during the war in Veitzen, Hungary, and highly regarded as a *halachic* authority.

Since Hungarian deportations did not begin until 1944, Rabbi Meisels was still carrying on extensive correspondence with his colleagues in Hungary as late as 1943, concerning a volume of responsa he had issued before the war. After coming to Chicago, Rabbi Meisels compiled the correspondence he had managed to save and published it, in 1955, in *"Mekadshei Hashem,"* which included letters from *Rabbanim* who had been killed *al kiddush Hashem* by the Nazis.

The volume is preceded by a section that details several horrific episodes that occurred in Auschwitz. Among them is an extraordinary series of events that culminated on Rosh Hashanah 5705, 1944. May the translated excerpt presented here serve as a source of strength and inspiration when we come before the Heavenly Tribunal.

★ ★ ★

From time to time, transports of hundreds or thousands were sent from Auschwitz to other camps or places of work. One Rosh Hashanah the lot fell on a transport of approximately one thousand men to be sent to some other place.

Through miracles and the mercy of Hashem, I was able to smuggle a *shofar* into the camp. On Rosh Hashanah I went from block to block with the *shofar* in my hand, although this was fraught with great danger from the wicked Nazis and *kapos*. But I had the merit, through His great mercy, to blow the full hundred blasts of the *shofar* approximately twenty times that day. This greatly restored the broken spirits of the inmates and somewhat eased their consciences to know that even in Auschwitz, they had the merit of fulfilling the *mitzvah* of *tekias shofar.*

Due to the confusion and preparations being made for their journey, the transport of one thousand men had not heard the *shofar*. They were standing at the gate ready to leave. When I approached them and informed them that I had a *shofar*, they begged me to once again sound the *shofar* so they, too, could fulfill the *mitzvah* before they left to their unknown destination.

The voices and cries that broke out from the men upon hearing the *shofar* still ring in my ears—especially the quavering voice of the *makri*, who was my dear friend Reb Yehoshua Fleischman of Deberecin, *hy"d*. He cried out in a wailing tone, "*Tekiah, teruah, tekiah.*"

Indeed, I could not focus my attention on blowing the *shofar* according to the prescribed *halachah*. I experienced the *Sheloh HaKadosh's* interpretation of the *shofar* sounds. *Tekiah*—what was originally so straight and orderly had become *shevarim*—so many of our holy communities had become broken. And the final *tekiah*—our hopes and prayers to Hashem that we should merit to return to a speedy redemption.

Fourteen hundred boys had been locked up in one of the blocks, condemned to the crematorium. They found out that I had a *shofar*. Tearfully they pleaded that I enter their block and blow the one hundred blasts so they, too, could have the merit of this precious *mitzvah* in their last moments before they were burned *al kiddush Hashem*.

I did not know what to do. It was extremely dangerous, for the Nazis could come at any time. If I were found among them there was no doubt that I, too, would be taken to the crematorium, for it was well known that the wicked *kapos* would not allow me to escape. I stood there contemplating what to do, with great doubt in my mind whether I was permitted to endanger my life to sound the *shofar* for the boys. But the boys cried bitterly, with cries that could crush any heart. "*Rebbe, Rebbe*, come for Hashem's sake; have pity on us and grant us the merit of hearing the *shofar* in our last moments."

My son Zalman Leib, who was with me, begged me not to put my life in danger. Had I not already done so twenty times that day? Was that not sufficient?

I looked at my entreating son and realized that he was right. On the other hand, the cries of the boys gave my soul no rest. A great pity welled up in my heart for them, and I thought that perhaps this great *mitzvah* would protect them in their time of danger. Others who heard the cries of the boys pleaded with me on their behalf, and assured me that the merit of the great *mitzvah* would allow me to escape unharmed.

I decided that I would not turn the boys down. I immediately began to bargain with the wicked *kapos*, who stubbornly refused to allow me into the block. After many entreaties, and for a substantial sum that was raised on the spot, they acquiesced to our demands. They warned me, however, that if I heard the sound of the gate bell—the signal that the SS were coming—then my fate would be sealed together with that of the boys, for under no circumstances would they allow me to leave the block.

I stationed my son Zalman Leib outside to observe the street and warn me if he saw SS men approaching the gate—even if I was in the middle of the *shofar* blasts. Then I entered the block.

The truth must be written that my decision did not conform to *halachah*, for I knew full well that it is forbidden to endanger one's life for the *mitzvah* of *shofar*. But my decision at that moment was based mainly on the fact that my life had little value anyway. For who in Auschwitz knew how many days he had left to live? Daily we saw thousands of our brethren killed and burned or falling dead in the fields from hard labor, like sheaves after the harvest. Our lives had no value. This was my main reason, even though I knew it had no basis in *halachah*.

Where is the pen and who the writer who can transcribe the emotions of my heart as I entered the block? I met the sea of eyes of the youngsters who pressed forward to kiss my hand and my clothes. They cried with bitter tears and wailing voices to the heart of Heaven.

When I began to recite the verse *Min Hameitzar,* they stopped me and begged me to say a few words before the *shofar* service. In my emotional state, I could not speak; my tongue cleaved to its palate and I could not open my mouth or my lips. I was also fearful of the delay, for the Nazis could come at any moment.

But the boys would not let me continue, and I finally acceded to their entreaties. I spoke words of *drash* focusing on the verse, "*Bakeseh l'yom chageinu,*" explaining that truly Hashem's design and purpose for this Holocaust was, at this moment on Rosh Hashanah, hidden and concealed from us. But we were not to despair, for even if a sharp sword is placed on one's throat he should not desist from seeking mercy ...

I cannot hold back the words. I must speak so future generations will know of the great *mesiras nefesh* and the holy words that my ears heard from these young boys a short while before they were martyred.

After the *shofar* blowing, as I was about to leave, one boy stood up and cried out: "Dear friends, the Rabbi has strengthened us by telling us that even when a sharp sword is on our throats we should not despair of mercy. I say to you, however, that while we can hope for the best, we must be prepared for the worst. For the sake of Hashem, my brothers, let us not forget in our last moments to cry out *Shema Yisrael* with fervent devotion."

With heart-rending voices and with great enthusiasm, they all cried out *Shema Yisrael*.

Afterward, another boy stood up and said to me, "We are not going to give the *Rebbe* a *yasher koach* for his great *mesiras nefesh* in providing us with our last *mitzvah*, that of *tekias shofar*. But all of us together bless you that in this merit, Hashem *Yisbarach* should help that the *Rebbe* will leave here alive and well." All of the boys answered, "*Amen.*"

As I was leaving, a few of the boys approached me and tearfully asked if I could provide them with a morsel of bread, so they could fulfill the *mitzvah* of *seudas* Rosh Hashanah, the Rosh Hashanah feast, in their last moments. For a full twenty-four hours, from the time they had been locked up, not a drop of food or water had passed through their lips, and they believed that according to *halachah*, one was forbidden to fast on Rosh Hashanah. To my great sorrow, there was no way that I could fulfill their request and re-enter their block.

That bitter day was a fast day for them. Still fasting, they were taken to the crematorium. May the Almighty speedily avenge their blood.

(Responsa Mekadshei Hashem, vol. 1, pp. 10-13)

Chapter Twelve

The Rosh Hashanah Prayers: *Mussaf*

Impoverished of Deeds

The moving prayer the *chazzan* chants before *Mussaf* opens with the words, "*Hineni he'ani mima'as,* Here I am, impoverished of deeds." A parable will explain its significance:

> Once a month, the wealthy owner of a small-town department store would go on a buying trip to the big city. A gracious fellow, he also bought merchandise for his friends, who would give him lists of the items they needed and the money to pay for them. If the money did not cover the cost of the goods they ordered, he would advance the shortage and be repaid when he returned.
>
> When the kind merchant passed away, the local store owners appointed an agent, who was an impoverished fellow, to do the buying for them. Knowing that the needy agent could not lay out any money, they were careful to send along enough funds to pay for all their purchases.

The *chazzan*, who is the agent of the community, declares, "I am poor in good deeds and short in merits that would stand you in good stead before the Heavenly Court. So don't rely on me. Prepare enough *mitzvos* and good deeds so you will be inscribed for a good new year on your own merits."

(Rabbi Hillel of Kolomey)

In Distress I Call on G-d

A mighty king had two sons. The older one he appointed ruler of one of his provinces. The younger one—a delicate and sensitive boy, whom the king loved dearly—remained with his father.

The king wanted his younger son to succeed him as monarch of the realm. When the prince grew up, the king sent him to his older brother's royal palace to be trained and prepared for his responsibilities.

Wishing to stay in touch with his beloved young son, the king told him to write a letter at the end of each day, reporting the events of the day. The king also ordered him to come home once a year on the anniversary of his coronation.

The older brother realized that the young prince was the father's favorite, and understood that his brother would succeed his father as king of the realm. In jealous retaliation, he abused and tormented his younger brother, forcing him to perform menial jobs and humiliating him in public. Aware of the daily messages his brother was writing to his father, he ordered the post office to confiscate and destroy all the letters.

At long last, on Coronation Day, the young prince returned home. Seeing his son, haggard, battered, and wearing disheveled clothes, the king was aghast and furious.

"My dear son!" he exclaimed. "Look at you! What has happened to you?"

"Father, do not trouble yourself," the prince replied soothingly. "Simply rejoice over the fact that I came home alive. And please, make sure that from now on, I will live in peace and tranquility."

The king is Hashem, the King of kings, *Hakadosh Baruch Hu*. The two sons are Eisav and the Jewish people. G-d designated Eisav to rule the world, while the Jewish people consider this world to be the lobby to the World to Come. The daily letters are our *tefillos* to Hashem and our Torah study, but the *yetzer hara* captures and tries to destroy these letters. Once a year, we appear before G-d on His Coronation Day—Rosh Hashanah.

As we approach Hashem on Rosh Hashanah, we cry out, *"Min hameitzar karasi Kah—*In distress I call on G-d. *Anani bamerchav Kah—*answer us, and bring us relief!" *(Tehillim 118:5)* Please release us from the darkness of *galus* and bring us the light of redemption. Remove us from distress to relief, from subjugation to freedom. *(Emes LeYaakov)*

Grant Honor to Your People

In the *Shemoneh Esrei* of the *Yamim Noraim* we pray, "And so, O Hashem, grant honor to Your people." Why do we pray for honor, when our Sages praise a person who shuns honor and recognition?

The more honor that is bestowed on the Jewish people, the greater is Hashem's glory manifest in the world. One may pray on Rosh Hashanah for all his material needs, for if the Jews live happy and contented lives, G-d's name will be exalted and praised by the people of the world.

(S'fas Emes, the Gerer Rebbe)

A World of Mercy

The Sages tell us that Hashem originally intended to create the world with *middas hadin*, the Divine attribute of strict Justice. But when He realized that that the world could not endure with strict Justice, He employed *middas harachamim*, His attribute of Mercy, to bring the world into being.

Every year in the month of Tishrei-on the anniversary of Creation-Hashem's original plan of creating the world with the attribute of Justice is revived. Therefore we pray, "Make Your word come true and endure forever"-referring to the word by which G-d actually created the world: with *middas harachamim*, the attribute of Mercy.

(Divrei Yoel)

Concealment and Faith

"His concealment is uprightness; His advice is faith; His accomplishment is truth." Even when the logic of G-d's ways is hidden from us, we should have faith—believing that His actions are fair and upright.

(Ohel Torah)

Hunger or Abundance

We say in *Mussaf*, "Regarding countries, it is said on this day which is destined for hunger and which for abundance."

This presents a difficulty, for the Mishnah says that the world is judged on Pesach for the grain that will grow that year. If the fate of the harvest is decreed on Pesach, why do we say that on Rosh Hashanah the decision regarding hunger or abundance is made?

Eretz Yisrael is different from all other countries, in that the main events in Jewish life revolve around the month of Nisan, the month of the Exodus. When the Mishnah says that the harvest is judged on Pesach, it is referring to the harvest of Eretz Yisrael. The determination of the size of the harvest of the rest of the world is made on Rosh Hashanah.

(Yaaros D'vash)

Exalted Baalei Teshuvah

At the close of the *Shemoneh Esrei* of *Mussaf*, the chazzan chants, "For You hear (*shome'a*) the sound of the *shofar*, and You give ear (*ma'azin*) to the *teruah*, and none is comparable to You."

Why do we praise G-d for hearing the *shofar*? After all, we too hear the *shofar*! What sort of praise is this?

> *A king had two servants. One was a long-time faithful attendant who never caused him any grief. The other, while also loyal, did cause trouble for the king one time. The servant instantly regretted his mistake. The king accepted his apology, and he loyally served the king ever after. But while the king appreciated the repentant servant, his true affection was reserved for the servant who had never offended him.*

The above parable illustrates the mindset of a human king. But *Hakadosh Baruch Hu* deals with us in a different manner. He loves a *baal teshuvah* even more than one who has never sinned, as the Sages say: The level of *baalei teshuvah* is so exalted that not even perfect *tzaddikim* can stand in their division in *Gan Eden*.

(Sanhedrin 99a)

The *Shelah* explains that a perfect *tzaddik* may be compared to a *shofar*. Like the straight sound of the *tekiah*, he is upright and without failings. A heartbroken *baal teshuvah* is likened to the broken *teruah* sound.

The verb *shome'a*, hear, denotes hearing from a distance, while *ma'azin*, give ear, implies listening from close by. "For You hear the sound of the *shofar*" alludes to the *tzaddik* who never sins—Hashem hears him from afar. But "You give ear to the *teruah*" refers to the *baal teshuvah*. Hashem listens to him from close by, for a regretful *baal teshuvah* is closer to Hashem. "And none is comparable to You"—for Hashem is a compassionate and merciful King.

(Leshon Chassidim)

Interrupting with a Niggun

The moving prayer *Unesaneh Tokef* contains the words, "*Ki lo yizku be'einecha badin*, For they cannot be vindicated in Your eyes in judgment." After reciting the words "*Ki lo*, for they cannot," the saintly Sanzer Rav would pause while intoning a lively *niggun*. Only after that would he resume, reciting the words "*yizku be'einecha badin*, they *will* be vindicated in judgment." Singing the *niggun* separated the negative "*ki lo*, they cannot," from the rest of the verse. Rather, we *will* be vindicated in judgment.

(Chiddushei Binyan Tzvi)

Count and Calculate

In the *Unesaneh Tokef* we say, "You count and calculate . . . the soul of all living things." What is the significance of this repetitious phrase?

These words contain a strong justification for *Klal Yisrael*. Tragically, in the wake of countless massacres and persecutions by our enemies, the number of Jews in the world has declined sharply. At the same time, the world population has increased profusely. We ask that G-d should *count*—compare the number of Jews of the past to the present dwindling tally, remembering those who perished *al kiddush Hashem*, and then *calculate* their merits. That will lead Him to inscribe us, the meager remnant, for a good and fruitful year.

(D'var Hameluchah)

Teshuvah, Tefillah, and Tzedakah

We recite these words aloud and with deep feeling at the end of the *Unesaneh Tokef*. But why is *tzedakah* mentioned after *teshuvah* and *tefillah*?

For a possible answer, let's turn to the Gemara in *Bava Basra* 9b. It says there that Yirmeyah cursed the people of Anasos who wanted to kill him, stating, "May they be caused to stumble before You." (*Yirmeyah*

18:25) Explains the Gemara: Even when they try to give *tzedakah*, may Hashem make them stumble by causing them to give to people who are unworthy of receiving *tzedakah*, so their gift does not count as *tzedakah*.

If one wants to earn the merit of giving true *tzedakah*, he must first do *teshuvah* and *tefillah*. Otherwise, he will end up giving charity to unworthy people or institutions. And so *teshuvah* and *tefillah* are mentioned before *tzedakah*.

(Divrei Yoel, Rosh Hashanah)

From Dust to Dust

In *Mussaf*, the congregation tearfully recites, "Man's origin is from dust, and his destiny is back to dust." If man originates from dust, why is it tragic that he returns to dust?

Although man was created from dust, he is able to rise to lofty spiritual heights. How tragic it is if he ends his life without having risen higher than the dust!

(Chiddushei HaRim)

Man is also likened to a broken shard. *Halachah* rules that a shard of an earthenware vessel that has been contaminated with a forbidden substance cannot be made kosher, for the substance it has absorbed cannot be expelled. The vessel must be broken. In a figurative sense, it may be said that a person who has sinned cannot make amends, unless he returns to G-d with a broken heart, as it says, "A heart broken and humbled, O G-d, You will not despise." *(Tehillim 51:19)*

(Sefer Baal Shem Tov)

In the Absence of an Advocate

In the *Shemoneh Esrei* of *Mussaf* we say, "Since we have no lawyer to defend us against [Satan] who reports transgressions, may You testify for the sake of Yaakov's [offspring] regarding the observance of Your decrees [*chok*] and ordinances."

How does Hashem defend us? When Satan brings charges against *Klal Yisrael*, Hashem really wants to help us, even though we do not have enough merits to outweigh our shortcomings.

Complains Satan, "Why do You favor the Jews when they are short on good deeds?"

Hashem replies, "*Klal Yisrael* observe many *chukim—mitzvos* that have no known reason—solely because they want to fulfill My will. It is only fair that I fulfill their wish and help them, although I have no valid reason for doing so."

(B'nei Yissoschor)

The numeric value of Yaakov is 182 (yud, ayin, kuf, beis—10+70+100+2=182), and the name Satan adds up to 359 (sin, tes, nun—300+9+50=359). After wrestling with Satan and subduing him, Yaakov's name was changed to Yisrael, with a value of 541 (yud, sin, reish, alef, lamed—10+300+200+1+30=541). The name Yaakov (182) was increased by the value of Satan (359), for 182+359=541. Since Yaakov defeated Satan and seized his name, we are called Bnei Yisrael, "the offspring of the one who overcame Satan."

(Agra DeTzvi)

Chapter Thirteen

Tashlich

Tashlich by Water

Tashlich is recited on Rosh Hashanah after *Minchah*. The *Rema* explains why the *Tashlich* prayer is said near a body of water.

As you gaze at the expanse of the ocean, you realize that at Creation, the entire planet was originally covered with water. Then Hashem commanded the water to gather in seas and rivers so the dry land may be seen, enabling man to live and flourish there. You see the waves lapping at the beach, trying to flood the earth, but the sand forms a formidable barrier that defies the mighty waves, proof of Hashem's awesome might.

This is also why we recite the psalm *L'David Mizmor* on Rosh Hashanah. For it says there, "He founded [the earth] upon the seas." The sea, as much as it tries, cannot drown the earth. This is proof that "Hashem's is the earth and its fullness, the inhabited land and those that dwell in it." (*Tehillim* 24:1)

These thoughts inspire a person to do *teshuvah*.

(Divrei Yoel, Rosh Hashanah)

Cast Away

The word *Tashlich* means "cast away," for on Rosh Hashanah we cast away our sins. The ceremony is called *Tashlich* because it says, "You will cast [*vesashlich*] all their sins into the depths of the sea." *(Michah 7:19)*

The *Arizal* says that when saying the passage, "Hurl into the depths of the sea all their sins" *(Michah 7:19)*, one should intend that all his sins should be cast away. One should also have in mind that the Satan, who is ready to lodge his accusations, should be hurled into the depths of the Heavenly sea.

(Rannenu Tzaddikim)

Akeidas Yitzchak

We say *Tashlich* on the banks of a stream to recall the merit of the *Akeidah,* the binding of Yitzchak. The Midrash *(Tanchuma Vayeira)* says that when Avraham was on his way to offer Yitzchak as a sacrifice, the Satan tried to deter them by turning himself into a raging river to block their path. But Avraham our Father resolutely walked into the river. When the water reached his neck, he exclaimed, "Save me, Hashem, for the waters have reached until the soul!" *(Tehillim 69:2)*

"I am drowning!" he cried. "You chose me and You promised me, saying, 'I am One, and you are one, and through you My Name will become known throughout the world.' You told me to offer my son Yitzchak as a sacrifice, and I did not hesitate for a moment. Now that I am on my way to the *Akeidah,* I find myself stuck in the middle of this stream. If I or my son Yitzchak will drown, who will fulfill Your command? Through whom will Your Name be sanctified all over the world?"

Hashem immediately accepted his plea and pledged, "Through you My Name will be sanctified all over the world."

Hashem took Satan to task, and the river dried up immediately. Avraham's merit rose to even greater heights, for he had shown how ready he was to fulfill Hashem's will.

We say *Tashlich* near a river or a lake in the hope that the *zechus* of Avraham *Avinu's* willingness to enter the raging river will stand us in good stead in the judgment of the *Yom Hadin.*

(*Derashos Maharil, Rosh Hashanah*)

A King's Coronation

In ancient times kings were crowned on a riverbank *(Horayos* 12a) to signify that their kingdom should flow smoothly and continuously like a river. On Rosh Hashanah, when we proclaim the Holy One, Blessed be He, as King, we acknowledge our dependency on His mercy at the water's edge.

(*Otzar Hatefilos*)

Washing Off Transgressions

The water of a stream never stands still. It flows continuously, moving forward from place to place. On Rosh Hashanah, we should let go of our bad habits and transgressions, wash them off and let them flow away. Let us do *teshuvah*   and may our sins sink to the bottom of the sea!

(*Toras Ha'olah*)

Wouldn't it be preferable to burn or bury our sins, so they are completely annihilated? Why do we cast them into the sea, where they continue to exist?

The Gemara (Avodah Zarah 39a) says, "Any animal on land has a counterpart in the sea. The unclean animal on land has a counterpart in the sea that is clean, and vice versa."

Evidently, the sea has the power to cleanse the unclean and purify it. We cast our sins into the sea, where they are transformed into merits and mitzvos. We therefore say in the Tashlich prayer, "Hurl into the depths of the sea all their sins" (Michah 7:19), so our sins will be transformed into merits when we do teshuvah out of love of Hashem.

(Divrei Yoel 29)

A stream or lake is reminiscent of the way water has the power to cleanse a person of his impurities the moment he immerses in it. A person can similarly instantly rid himself of his transgressions by doing *teshuvah.*

(Levushei Mordechai Hechadash)

The purpose of *teshuvah* is to "walk in all His ways and holding fast to Him." *(Devarim* 11:12*)* This can only be attained near a body of water, for water symbolizes *taharah,* "purity."

(Divrei Yoel, Mo'adim)

Through the Year

The Gemara (*Horayos* 12a) says: One should learn Torah on the bank of a river. Just as the waters of the river keep moving forward, so may one's knowledge continue to advance. By saying *Tashlich* by a riverbank we express our wish that our fervent prayers of Rosh Hashanah should carry forward through the entire year.

(Maharshak, Sefer Hachayim)

Living Fish

We say *Tashlich* at a body of water that contains living fish so the *ayin hara,* evil eye, should not harm us. Fish, which live calmly, unseen by man, are not affected by the evil eye.

(Darkei Moshe 583:2)

Living fish are abruptly caught in the fisherman's net. They remind us that we are in danger of being caught in the net of the *malach hamaves,* the angel of death. The thought of our mortality prompts us to do *teshuvah*.

(Levush 596)

The eyes of fish are always open. We pray that Hashem may guard and protect the Jewish people with open eyes and with mercy all year long.

(Shelah, Rosh Hashanah)

This thought is alluded to in the *mizmor* of *Rannenu Tzaddikim*, "Sing forth, O you righteous" (*Tehillim* 33:1), which we recite at *Tashlich*. It says there, "Truly the eye of Hashem is on those who fear Him." (*Tehillim* 33:18)

(P'nei Hamayim)

Shaking Out Pockets

It is customary to shake out one's pockets at *Tashlich* when reciting the words, "Hurl into the depths of the sea all their sins." *(Michah 7:19)* We symbolically rid ourselves of our sins and resolve not to transgress again.

(Matteh Efraim 595:4)

The custom is to shake the pockets three times. According to the *Arizal,* the custom is to specifically shake a corner of the *tzitzis.*

(Ta'amei Haminhagim beshem HaArizal)

Chapter Fourteen

The Second Day of Rosh Hashanah

Yoma Arichta—One Long Day

The two days of Rosh Hashanah are considered to be one long day; both days are treated with equal sanctity. This is in contrast to the second day of the other *Yamim Tovim*, which are celebrated because of doubt as to the correct day of *Rosh Chodesh*.

Why is this? The Ten Days of *Teshuvah* between Rosh Hashanah and Yom Kippur parallel the Ten Commandments. The first two commandments were uttered by Hashem Himself, while the other eight commandments were pronounced by Moshe. Accordingly, the two days of Rosh Hashanah, corresponding to G-d's utterance, are considered as one long day.

(Attributed to Rabbi Yonasan Eibschutz)

When the Beis Hamikdash was standing, the new month was sanctified on the basis of testimony by witnesses who saw the new moon. On Rosh Hashanah, which is on the first day of the month of Tishrei, the beis din could not declare the new month until the witnesses arrived. Still, everyone kept the first day as a Yom Tov, since there was the possibility that witnesses would arrive and beis din would declare the new month. If the witnesses were late in coming—arriving after the afternoon tamid offering had already been brought—the beis din ruled that that day would be considered Yom Tov, even if there was no time to interrogate the witnesses, since everyone had already been keeping the laws of Yom Tov; and the next day, too, would be Yom Tov, since that was really the first of the month. It was then decided to always celebrate Rosh Hashanah for two days, even in Eretz Yisrael.

(Rosh Hashanah 30b)

The Gemara says that when Satan hears the sound of the *shofar*, he becomes confused and is unable to complain about the failings of *Klal Yisrael*. But what about when the first day of Rosh Hashanah falls on Shabbos? Since we do not blow the *shofar*, Satan will not be baffled. Will he be able to present his charges against *Klal Yisroel*?

The solution is *yoma arichta*. Since the two days of Rosh Hashanah are considered one long day, the final judgment will be rendered only on the second day—when we do blow the *shofar*. Hearing the *shofar* blasts, Satan will be confounded and incapable of lodging complaints against *Klal Yisrael*. In the absence of Satan's charges, *Klal Yisrael* will be judged favorably and inscribed for a good year.

(Taamei Haminhagim, quoting Divrei Shmuel)

Forty-Eight Hours

The *Baal Hatanya* says: In the verse, "*Cham libi bekirbi*, My heart grew hot within me" (*Tehillim* 39:4), the numeric value of the word *cham*, "hot" is 48 (*ches*=8; *mem*=40). This alludes to the 48 hours of the two days of Rosh Hashanah. It tells us to use the holy hours of Rosh Hashanah for fervent *davening* and learning.

(Sefer Hatanya)

Shehecheyanu on the Second Night

When we recite *Kiddush* or light the candles on the second night of Rosh Hashanah, we say the *brachah Shehecheyanu*—just as we do on the first night. But since both days are like one continuous day, we really do not need to say *Shehecheyanu* again on the second day. It is customary, therefore, to place a new fruit on the table, or to put on a new garment, so the *Shehecheyanu* said in the *Kiddush* may apply to the new fruit or garment.

The Benefit of Two Days

The *Zohar* says that Hashem is doing us a great favor by letting us celebrate Rosh Hashanah for two days. On the first day, the Divine attribute of strict Justice holds sway, and those who are judged on the first day are in great jeopardy. On the second day, the Divine attribute of Mercy prevails—assuring everyone who is judged on that day of a favorable judgment.

This is hinted at in the verse, "After two days He will make us whole." (*Hoshea* 6:2) Hashem heals us and grants us life, by letting us celebrate Rosh Hashanah for two days. This may also be alluded to in the passage, "Proclaim His salvation day after day." (*1 Divrei Hayamim* 6:23) Our salvation lies in the fact that our judgment is pushed off from the first day to the second day of Rosh Hashanah.

(Arvei Nachal)

Chapter Fifteen

Rosh Hashanah on Shabbos

No Avinu Malkeinu on Shabbos

Avinu Malkeinu was composed by Rabbi Akiva to be recited in times of distress. On Shabbos every Jew feels as though all his worldly work is done, and nothing is lacking. For this reason we do not pray for our personal concerns. Therefore, we do not say *Avinu Malkeinu* when Rosh Hashanah comes out on Shabbos.

(Ran, Rosh Hashanah)

Why, then, do we continue to insert the verse, "Zochreinu lechayim, Remember us for life, O King who desires life" into Shemoneh Esrei on Shabbos? Isn't this also a personal request?

Perhaps we recite "Zochreinu lechayim" for the sake of evildoers who are inscribed immediately for death. They are in mortal danger every moment of the day. We pray that Hashem should have pity on them, granting them time to do teshuvah, rather than seal them for death on this day.

(Sifsei Tzaddik)

The *Avinu Malkeinu* prayer corresponds to the middle *brachos* of the weekday *Shemoneh Esrei*, which contain personal requests. These *tefillos* are not said on Shabbos and *Yom Tov*.

For example:

"*Avinu Malkeinu, chonneinu*, Be gracious with us," matches the *brachah*, "*Chonein hadaas*, Gracious Giver of knowledge."

"*Avinu Malkeinu, hachazireinu biseshuvah sheleimah*, Return us to You with perfect repentance," parallels, "*Harotzeh biseshuvah*, Who desires repentance."

"*Avinu Malkeinu, shelach refuah*," conforms with "*Refa'einu*, Heal us."

"*Chaddeish aleinu*" corresponds with "*Bareich aleinu*."

"*Hareim keren*" matches "*T'ka beshofar gadol*."

When Rosh Hashanah falls on a weekday, on a day when the middle *brachos* of the *Shemoneh Esrei* would ordinarily be said, we recite the *Avinu Malkeinu*. But these *brachos* are never said on Shabbos—and therefore we do not recite *Avinu Malkeinu* on Shabbos.

(Levush 584:1)

No Shofar on Shabbos

The Sages decreed that the *shofar* should not be sounded on Shabbos. They reasoned as follows:

Everyone is required to blow the *shofar*, but not all are skilled at blowing the *shofar*. It is possible that a student may take the *shofar* on Shabbos and go to an expert to learn how to blow, and he would thereby carry it four cubits in the public domain. Carrying an object on Shabbos in a public domain is one of the 39 Biblically forbidden labors. To prevent this possible desecration of Shabbos, our Sages forbade blowing the *shofar* on Shabbos.

(Rosh Hashanah 29b)

The Torah exempts one who is unavoidably prevented from performing a mitzvah. (Bava Kamma 28b) Perhaps the Gemara means to tell us that since this person cannot fulfill the mitzvah, the Torah fulfills it for him. When Rosh Hashanah falls on Shabbos, and we are prevented from doing the mitzvah of blowing the shofar—Hashem Himself blows the shofar for us! He does it in the most accomplished manner, with all the mystical intentions, so Klal Yisrael should be granted a good year.

(Reb Bunim of Pshis'cha)

As we say in the daily Shemoneh Esrei, "Teka beshofar gadol lecheiruseinu, Sound the great shofar for our freedom." For when Hashem is the toke'a, we will surely witness the geulah sheleimah.

(Razin De'Oraisa)

The Power of Shabbos

The Gemara (*Shabbos* 12a) says if one visits a sick person on Shabbos, he should say to the patient, "May the Shabbos have compassion." This indicates that the *kedushah* of Shabbos has the power to bring recovery. When Rosh Hashanah falls on Shabbos, there is no need to blow the *shofar*—for the Shabbos itself arouses Heavenly compassion.

(Divrei Chaim, the Sanzer Rav)

The sound of the shofar fills the listener with awe and trepidation, inspiring him to do teshuvah. Shabbos also creates this sense of respect in people—in fact, according to the Gemara, on Shabbos even an unlearned person is afraid to tell a lie. When Rosh Hashanah falls on Shabbos, there is no need to blow the shofar, because Shabbos has the same effect as the shofar does—imbuing a person with awe and inspiring him to do teshuvah.

(P'ri Tzaddik)

We Didn't Mean It

Read backwards, the initials of the phrase, *"Tik'u bachodesh shofar,* Blow the *shofar* at the moon's renewal" (*Tehillim* 81:4) form the word Shabbos. This acronym suggests a praise of *Klal Yisrael.*

At the sounding of the *shofar,* G-d moves from His Throne of Justice to the Throne of Mercy. Despite this benefit, we do not blow the *shofar* on Shabbos out of fear that someone might forget that it is Shabbos and end up carrying his *shofar.* This proves that we are absentminded and negligent by nature. We therefore ask Hashem to forgive our transgressions, for when we sinned throughout the year it was certainly out of forgetfulness.

(Derashos D'var Tzvi)

Shabbos and Yom Tov

The Mishnah dealing with the subject of blowing the *shofar* when Rosh Hashanah falls on Shabbos begins with the words, "When the *Yom Tov* of Rosh Hashanah falls on Shabbos." Metaphorically, this may be interpreted as follows: When Rosh Hashanah falls on Shabbos, it is a *Yom Tov,* a happy day, for *Klal Yisrael.* Why is this so?

On Shabbos it is forbidden to write. Inscribing in the Book of Life, however, is saving a life, and saving a life overrides the Shabbos. So when Rosh Hashanah falls on Shabbos, it is permissible to only inscribe for life—inscribing for death, which does not override the Shabbos, is strictly forbidden. Therefore, it is truly a *Yom Tov.*

(Beis Avraham, quoting Kedushas Levi)

According to the Kabbalistic writing of the holy Ari, Rabbi Yitzchak Luria, the soul has three stages, in ascending order: nefesh, ruach, and neshamah. On Rosh Chodesh a person receives an additional nefesh; on Yom Tov he receives an additional ruach; and on Shabbos he receives an additonal neshamah, the neshamah yeseirah.

When Rosh Hashanah falls on Shabbos he receives all three extra souls at once: those of Shabbos, Yom Tov, and Rosh Chodesh. Therefore the Mishnah says, "When the Yom Tov of Rosh Hashanah falls on Shabbos." It is a Yom Tov, a source of happiness, when Rosh Hashanah falls on Shabbos, for then the three souls coincide.

(Rabbi Elimelech of Lizhensk)

The Power of Kugel

Someone once asked the Belzer Rebbe, "What is the significance of eating kugel on Shabbos?"

Explained the Rebbe, "You should know that kugel has the power of turning *middas hadin*, the Divine attribute of strict Justice, into *middas harachamim*, the attribute of Mercy."

Retorted the questioner, "If so, why do we have to blow the *shofar* on Rosh Hashanah to turn the *middas hadin* into *middas harachamim*, when the same result can be achieved by eating kugel?"

Replied the Rebbe with a twinkle in his eye, "That's why we don't blow the *shofar* when Rosh Hashanah falls on Shabbos. The kugel we eat on Shabbos has the same effect in Heaven as blowing the *shofar*: it turns *middas hadin* into *middas harachamim*."

(Divrei Baruch, Rosh Hashanah)

Chapter Sixteen

The Fast of Gedaliah

Historical Background

In *Yirmeyah* 40 and 41 we read that after the destruction of the first *Beis Hamikdash* by Nebuchadnezzar, King of Babylonia, the Jewish population was taken into exile to Babylonia. A small remnant remained in the abandoned towns of Eretz Yisrael. Nebuchadnezzar appointed Gedaliah ben Achikam as governor of the remaining Jews in Eretz Yisrael.

Gedaliah encouraged the despondent people to return to their farms. "Do not be afraid to serve the Chaldeans. Stay in the land and serve the king of Babylonia, and it will go well with you. I am going to stay in Mitzpah, but you may gather wine and figs and oil, and settle in the town you have occupied." (*Yirmeyah* 40:9-10)

Many Jews who had fled to Ammon, Moab, and Edom, upon hearing "that the king of Babylonia had let a remnant stay in Yehudah, and that he had put Gedaliah ben Achikam in charge of them, returned from all the places to which they had scattered. They came to the land of Yehudah, to Gedaliah at Mitzpah, and they gathered large quantities of wine and dried fruit." (*Yirmeyah* 40:11-12)

Yochanan and all the army officers came to Mitzpah and warned Gedaliah that King Baalis of Ammon had sent Yishmael ben Nesaniah to assassinate him. But Gedaliah would not believe them.

Yochanan said to Gedaliah, "Let me go and strike down Yishmael before anyone finds out. Otherwise he will kill you, and the remnant of Yehudah will perish."

But Gedaliah told Yochanan, "Do not do such a thing. What you are saying about Yishmael is not true."

> "*It happened in the seventh month, the month of Tishrei, that Yishmael, who was [a Jew] of royal descent and one of the king's commanders, came with ten men to Gedaliah ben Achikam at Mitzpah; and they ate together there at Mitzpah. Then Yishmael and the ten men who were with him struck down Gedaliah with the sword and killed him, because the King of Babylonia had put him in charge of the land. Yishmael killed also all the Jews who were there and the Chaldean soldiers who were stationed there.*" (*Yirmeyah* 40)

Afraid of the wrath of the king of Babylonia, the small remnant of Jews fled to Egypt and dispersed there, while Eretz Yisrael remained desolate and uninhabited.

To commemorate this day, the Sages instituted *Tzom Gedaliah*, the Fast of Gedaliah, on the third of Tishrei. The Gemara notes that the establishment of a fast to commemorate this day, just as a fast was instituted to commemorate the destruction of the *Beis Hamikdash*, indicates that the death of the righteous is equivalent to the burning of the House of G-d.

(Rosh Hashanah 18b)

Why We Commemorate the Death of Gedaliah

The Gemara in *Rosh Hashanah* asks: Who killed Gedaliah ben Achikam? The Gemara answers, Yishmael ben Nesaniah killed him.

Why does the Gemara ask this question? The *navi* (*Yirmeyah* 41:2) says explicitly who the murderer was!

Maharsha explains that the Gemara lists *Tzom Gedaliah* as one of the four public fasts, three of which memorialize tragic national events. *Tzom Gedaliah* is different—it commemorates the tragic death of a *tzaddik*.

The Gemara's question implies another question. If we fast for the death of Gedaliah, why don't we fast for the deaths of other *tzaddikim*? But in that case, we would have to fast every day of the year, because there is not a day in the year which is not the *yahrzeit* of a *tzaddik*.

The Gemara answers that Gedaliah's death is different, for he was killed by Yishmael ben Nesaniah. As a result, all the Jews in Eretz Yisrael fled to Egypt, which was a national tragedy.

Maharsha suggests an alternative answer. Since this assassination took place during the Ten Days of *Teshuvah*, Yishmael ben Nesaniah should have had an impulse to do *teshuvah*. Instead, he killed Gedaliah, thereby bringing untold trouble on the Jewish people. This is alluded to in the verse, "In two days He will make us whole again, on the third day He will raise us up, and we will be whole by His favor." (*Hoshea* 6:2) On Rosh Hashanah, the first two days of the Ten Days of *Teshuvah*, we all pray for life; but on the third day—the day Gedaliah was killed, which caused a downfall for *Klal Yisrael*—we need to pray for a double dose of Heavenly mercy. We ask that we be uplifted from the downfall of Gedaliah's murder, and inscribed for a year of life.

(Maharsha, Rosh Hashanah 18b)

The *P'nei Yehoshua* offers yet another answer to this question. Usually, the death of a righteous man brings atonement for the generation. The tragedy of the *tzaddik's* death is tempered somewhat, so a fast is not needed. But since Gedaliah was killed by Yishmael ben Nesaniah, a Jew of royal lineage, we cannot say that his death provided atonement. On the contrary—it led to a great calamity for *Klal Yisrael.* Therefore the Sages decreed a fast on the day of Gedaliah's *yahrzeit.*

(P'nei Yehoshua, Rosh Hashanah 18, s.v. Umi)

Secluding the Kohen Gadol

The first Mishnah in *Maseches Yoma* states that on the third day of Tishrei [which for us is *Tzom Gedaliah*] the *Kohen Gadol* was sequestered in the officials' chamber. Another *kohen* was prepared as his substitute. If the *Kohen Gadol* was disqualified by becoming *tamei,* the other *kohen* could take over.

(Yoma 2a)

Yom Tov on the Third of Tishrei

The Gemara *(Rosh Hashanah 18b)* says that the third of Tishrei [which for us is *Tzom Gedaliah*] was established as a *Yom Tov,* because on that day the mention of Hashem's name on legal documents was abolished.

The Greek rulers of Eretz Yisrael had forbidden the Jews to mention G-d's name. When the *Chashmonaim* gained the upper hand and defeated the Greek forces in the days of Chanukah, they ordained that people should mention the name of Hashem on all bills and notes. For example, they would write, "In the year so-and-so of Yochanan, *Kohen Gadol* to G-d the Most High."

When the Sages heard about it, they said, "Tomorrow this borrower will pay his debt, and the note with the name of Hashem on it will be thrown into a pile of trash." So the Sages put an end to the practice. That day, the third of Tishrei, was declared a *Yom Tov.*

Chapter Seventeen

The Ten Days of Teshuvah

Bein Kesseh Le'Asor

The *aseres yemei teshuvah*—Ten Days of Repentance that fall between Rosh Hashanah and Yom Kippur—are called *bein kesseh le'asor*, between *kesseh* and *asor*. *Kesseh* is derived from the verse, "Blow the *shofar* at the moon's renewal, when the moon is covered—*bakesseh*—on our festive day." *(Tehillim 81:4)* Which festive day? Rosh Hashanah, which falls out on the first of the lunar month. *Asor* is the tenth, referring to Yom Kippur, the tenth of Tishrei.

Hashem Seeks Our Teshuvah

Out of His abundant love for *Klal Yisrael*, Hashem *Yisbarach* does not desire the death of the wicked; instead, He hopes that the wicked will return from their evil deeds. Hashem would much rather repay a person for the good he does than extract punishment for his misdeeds. So Hashem, with love and grace, sets aside specific times to

135

be close to us, ready and eager to accept our *teshuvah*. The Gemara says that Hashem is most accessible between Rosh Hashanah and Yom Kippur.

(Rosh Hashanah 18a)

"Seek out Hashem when He is accessible, call upon Him when He is near." *(Yeshayah 55:6)* Yeshayah also says, "May the wicked one forsake his path and the deceitful man his thoughts, and let him return to Hashem Who will show him mercy, and to our G-d, for He is abundantly forgiving." *(Yeshayah 55:7)* With the goal of *teshuvah* in mind during the *aseres yemei teshuvah*, we pray more intently, we say *Selichos* early in the morning, and we are more meticulous than ever in observing the *mitzvos*.

(Matteh Moshe)

Praiseworthy is the person who does not let a moment pass during these days without engaging in the service of Hashem or reflecting on *teshuvah*. According to the holy Arizal, during these ten days one should conduct himself as on *Chol Hamo'ed* (the intermediate days of *Yom Tov*), limiting himself to only the most essential work, and spending the rest of the day meditating on *teshuvah*. Happy is the person who focuses his thoughts on G-d's kindness and arouses people who are spiritually asleep, urging them to do *teshuvah*.

(Yaaros D'vash by Rabbi Yonasan Eibes 136)

Why Ten Days?

The Arizal says that on each day of the *aseres yemei teshuvah*, one can repair all the errors and misdeeds he made on that day of the week throughout his life. On Sunday of *aseres yemei teshuvah*, for example, he can repent and atone for every mistake he ever made on a Sunday.

In that case, seven days of repentance should be enough—one for each day of the week. Why are there ten?

The first two days of the *aseres yemei teshuvah* are Rosh Hashanah, when Jews everywhere gather in shul to crown G-d as Ruler of the world. People are not thinking of their individual sins and failings. Once G-d has been placed as the exalted King, there are seven additional days to reflect on individual wrongdoings, cleansing ourselves from sins for the final and tenth day of *aseres yemei teshuvah*—Yom Kippur.

(Divrei Yechezkel)

Rabbi Nehora'i said: The ten days between Rosh Hashanah and Yom Kippur correspond to the ten trials that Avraham *Avinu* passed with flying colors. Ten is also the number of commandments *Klal Yisrael* received at Sinai.

Midrash Harninu cites the ten sacrifices offered on Yom Kippur: one bull, one ram, seven sheep, and one goat. There are ten admonitions in the verse, "Wash yourselves, purify yourselves, remove the evil of your deeds from before My eyes; cease doing evil. Learn to do good, seek justice, vindicate the victim, render justice to the orphan, take up the grievance of the widow   Come now, let us reason together, says Hashem. If your sins are like scarlet they will become white as snow; if they have become red as crimson, they will become white as wool." *(Yeshayah 1:16-18)*

The word "*vayomer*, and he said" recurs ten times in the story of Creation, indicating that Hashem created the world with ten utterances. *(Bereishis 1, 2:18)* The word "*yom*, day" also is found ten times, referring to the ten days of *teshuvah*.

(Matteh Moshe)

A Community's Repentance

Although *teshuvah* and crying out to Hashem are always welcome from individuals, between Rosh Hashanah and Yom Kippur they are even more desirable and will be accepted immediately. The proof— "Seek Hashem when He can be found." *(Yeshayah 55:6)*

But this is only true of an individual's repentance. When an entire community repents, crying out from the depths of their hearts, they are always answered immediately, no matter what time of year. Note the plural tense in the verse in *Devarim*: "What nation is so great that they have G-d close to it, as Hashem our G-d is whenever we call Him?" *(Devarim 4:7)*

(Rambam, Hilchos Teshuvah 2:6)

480 Hours

The primary time for doing *teshuvah* is from Rosh Hashanah through Hoshana Rabbah. From Rosh Hashanah until Yom Kippur there are ten days, 240 hours. Yom Kippur through Hoshana Rabbah is also ten days, adding up to a total of 480 hours. This is hinted at in the verse, "Praise Him with drums—*tof*—and dance—*machol.*" *(*Tehillim 150:4) The numeric value of *tof* is 480 (*tav*=400; *pei*=80), and the word *machol* also means "forgiveness." We praise Hashem for giving us 480 (*tof*) hours in which to attain pardon and forgiveness (*machol*).

(Kesef Nivchar, Vayakhel)

After Rosh Hashanah

Why do the Days of Repentance immediately follow Rosh Hashanah? On Rosh Hashanah everyone does *teshuvah* mentally, regretting his failings and resolving to turn over a new leaf. But this is not enough. *Teshuvah* must also be done in a practical manner, through good and charitable deeds. Many of these cannot be carried out on *Yom Tov*. We can set things right during the weekdays of the Ten Days of *Teshuvah*.

(Avnei Nezer, Sochatchover Rebbe)

Yemei Ratzon, Days of Favor

The Ten Days of *Teshuvah* is a period of Divine judgment, yet these days are designated specifically as *yemei ratzon*, "days of favor." How are we to understand this seeming inconsistency?

The Gemara (*Avodah Zarah* 4b) says that during the first three hours of the day, the Holy One, blessed be He, judges with unmitigated strictness. During the second three hours, He occupies Himself with the Torah, which is termed "truth." This means that Hashem judges with *emes*, and will not overstep the strict letter of the law—yet will be stern and uncompromising. So it is that every day, after the fist six hours, the judgment is completed and irreversible, and praying is useless.

During the Ten Days of *Teshuvah*, however, the judgment does not end after six hours. It continues throughout the day. Throughout this time, while the judgment is in progress and the final decree is not set, a person can pray for mercy.

When a trial is in session, the judge may not intimidate the litigants by displaying anger. Only after the verdict was rendered may the judge show his displeasure at the wrongful party. In the same way, G-d does not display anger during these ten days. Although these days are *yemei din*, "Days of Judgment," they are also *yemei ratzon*, "Days of Divine Favor."

(Yaaros D'vash)

Akeidas Yitzchak

Why do we recall *Akeidas* Yitzchak during *Selichos* each day of the Ten Days of *Teshuvah*? When Avraham tied Yitzchak to the wood of the altar, he asked Hashem to give his descendants Ten Days of *Teshuvah*. Why did he make this request at the moment of the *Akeidah*?

Hashem told Avraham that He considered his willingness to go through with the *Akeidah* as if he had actually performed the *Akeidah*.

Avraham understood that whenever a person is sincerely ready to give up his life for the sake of G-d, it counts as though he had actually sacrificed himself—and he becomes a different person.

There are sins that cannot be wiped out through *teshuvah* alone. Only the sinner's death, together with his *teshuvah,* brings about atonement. But since Hashem reckons a person's willingness to offer his life as if he had actually sacrificed himself, *teshuvah* alone is enough to grant forgiveness, since he is now reborn as a different person— even for sins that can be erased only by death.

Avraham therefore prayed at the *Akeidah* that during the Ten Days of *Teshuvah,* Hashem should accept the willingness of *Klal Yisrael* to sacrifice themselves for His honor as an actual sacrifice, and accept their *teshuvah* alone, even for sins that are not cancelled by *teshuvah.*

During *Selichos,* we pray that Hashem should pardon even the gravest sins through *teshuvah,* because of our readiness to sacrifice for the sake of Hashem and the Torah.

(B'nei Yissoschor, Tishrei)

May Hashem Shine His Face Upon Us

The Gemara (*Rosh Hashanah* 18b) interprets the verse "Seek Hashem when He can be found" as referring to the Ten Days of *Teshuvah,* for it is then that the *Shechinah* is present in the synagogues and halls of study.

The Sages forbid gazing at the face of a wicked man. Since Hashem observes all the ordinances of the Torah, He surely complies with the prohibition against gazing at the face of an evildoer. We must therefore do *teshuvah* so Hashem will be able to look at us and "shine His face upon us." (*Bamidbar* 6:25)

(Yismach Moshe of Ujhel)

Attaining a Pure Heart

The verse says in *Tehillim* (51:12), "Create a pure heart for me, O Hashem." Can we expect to receive the gift of a pure heart without any action on our part? We have to prepare ourselves, by fasting and turning away from mundane pleasures.

During the Ten Days of *Teshuvah* it is a *mitzvah* to fast, but only until noon—for the main purpose of fasting is to tame our bodily desires. Those who do not fast should be careful not to overeat, for when one is overly satiated it is impossible to rise to the spiritual level of "a pure heart." One should eat in moderation, just enough to still his hunger, but not more.

(Likutei Torah, Ki Savo)

The Power of Tzedakah

The *navi* exhorts *Klal Yisrael*, "Establish yourself through *tzedakah*." (*Yeshayah* 54:14) *Klal Yisrael* responds by giving *tzedakah* openhandedly, especially during the Ten Days of *Teshuvah*.

The *tzedakah* one gives during those days is like planting a seed. Before planting, one must plow the earth, for a seed thrown on solid ground will not take root and sprout. The same holds true for the *tzedakah* one gives throughout the year: it does not yield fruit in Heaven unless it is given in the spirit of the Ten Days of *Teshuvah*, when a Jew is as meek and lowly as earth that has been softened by plowing.

When a person gives *tzedakah* he must crush his haughtiness, concentrating only on the plight of the needy. He should say to himself, "The poor man to whom I give my donation is a fellow Jew, and I am no better than he is. Why should I be satiated while he goes hungry? Both of us have the same Father in Heaven. In the Ten Days of *Teshuvah*, we are both equally awestruck as we stand before the Heavenly Court. All Jews, rich and poor alike, are being judged."

The *tzedakah* one gives during the Ten Days of *Teshuvah* makes a tremendous impact in Heaven, and its merit weighs heavily in the donor's favor.

(Likutei Torah, Derushim LeSukkos)

Chapter Eighteen

Shabbos Shuvah

Shabbos of Return

The Shabbos before Yom Kippur is called Shabbos *Shuvah*, which, literally translated, means "Shabbos of Return." This alludes to the final redemption, which will usher in the World to Come—an era that will be completely and exclusively Shabbos. By calling the Shabbos before Yom Kippur by this name, we express our hope that the final redemption will arrive. In this way, Shabbos will immediately return to the world—and this time, it will last forever.

(Degel Machaneh Efraim)

The Sages tell us that observing Shabbos is equivalent to keeping all the *mitzvos* of the Torah, because Shabbos has the power to drive away evil influences and spiritual pollution. The name Shabbos *Shuvah* reminds us that by observing Shabbos, one is guaranteed that his *teshuvah* is accepted.

(Lechem Min Hashamayim)

The Sermon

It is customary for the rabbi to give a lengthy sermon on Shabbos *Shuvah*. The Midrash says that when the rabbi gives a speech on Shabbos *Shuvah*, Hashem forgives the transgressions of the listeners. Even when a harsh decree has been sealed, when Hashem hears the congregation answer *"Amein yehei shemei rabba"* in the *Kaddish* after the rabbi's speech, He will forgive them and reverse the fateful verdict.

(Birkas Shmuel)

It is customary for the rabbi to begin his *derashah* on Shabbos *Shuvah* with a lengthy *halachic* exposition. This is followed by words of inspiration, admonition, and exhortation to do *teshuvah*.

The Kabbalists suggest the following reason: Before saying *krias Shema* in *Shacharis* we recite *Pesukei DeZimra*, "Verses of Praise." But *zimra* also means "to cut off." (*Shabbos* 73b) Thus *Pesukei DeZimra* can be translated as "verses that cut off." Why is this so?

Our prayers, and especially the *Shema* and the *Shemoneh Esrei*, are greatly prized in Heaven. Knowing this, the destructive angels want to interfere with our *tefillos*, preventing our prayers from rising to Heaven. Before saying the *Shema* we recite *Pesukei DeZimra*, verses that "cut off," to drive away the destructive angels. In this way we can say *Shema* and the *Shemoneh Esrei* undisturbed, and our *tefillos* are accepted in Heaven.

The same is true of the rabbi's *derashah* of *mussar*, urging the congregation to mend their ways and *daven* with greater *kavanah*. Since his *derashah* spurs people to doing *teshuvah*, it is valued very highly in Heaven. Aware of this, the destructive angels try to disrupt the *mussar* speech. To counteract these angels, the rabbi begins by giving a *halachic* discourse, which has the power to chase away the destructive angels.

(Beis Shmuel Acharon, Parshas Emor)

Wearing a Tallis

It is customary for the rabbi to wear a *tallis* when giving the *derashah* for Shabbos *Shuvah*. He does so in honor of the congregation.

Another reason is to protect himself from an *ayin hara* that may be cast on him during his *derashah*. In fact, the *Zohar* expressly says that *tzitzis* form a protective shield against the *ayin hara*.

(She'eilos Uteshuvos Lev Chaim 3:9)

"Zishe! Zishe!"

At the Third Meal on Shabbos *Shuvah*, the saintly Rebbe Reb Zishe, engaging in a dialogue with himself, used to cry out, "Zishe! Zishe! When are you finally going to do *teshuvah*?"

Replying to his own question, he said resolutely, "Today I'll start doing *teshuvah!*"

"But you said the same yesterday, and you didn't do it!" he retorted.

"But now I'll really do it, I promise!" Reb Zishe assured himself.

The Sanzer Rav was wont to repeat Reb Zishe's exchange with himself every year at *shalosh seudos* on Shabbos *Shuvah*, which never failed to make a profound impact on the assembled *chassidim*.

(Darchei HaChaim)

Thirteen Attributes of Mercy

The eighth day of the Ten Days of *Teshuvah* is called *Shelosh Esrei Middos*, "The Thirteen Attributes of Mercy," because in the *Selichos* prayers of that day we recite the hymn beginning with the phrase "*Shelosh esrei middos.*"

It was on this day that the first *Beis Hamikdash* was inaugurated. The construction was completed in the month of Kislev, but Hashem ordered the inauguration to be postponed until the following Tishrei, the month of Avraham's birth, in order to invoke the merit of Avraham *Avinu*.

It was on this day that Shlomo said his timeless prayer, in which he pleaded, "If Your people are defeated by an enemy because they sinned against You, and they return to You and praise Your Name and pray and supplicate to You in this Temple, may You hear from Heaven and forgive the sin of Your people Israel, and return them to the land that You gave to their forefathers."

(1 Melachim 8:33-34)

Ever since, that day has been set aside as a day for *teshuvah* and prayer for Hashem's favorable acceptance of the *tefillos* of *Klal Yisrael.*

(B'nei Yissoschor)

Chapter Nineteen

Erev
Yom Kippur

Eating on Erev Yom Kippur

The day before Yom Kippur is considered a semi-*Yom Tov*, and it is a *mitzvah* to eat two festive meals on this day. Indeed, Rabbi Chiya said, "One who eats on *erev* Yom Kippur is considered by the Torah as meritorious as if he fasted on both the ninth and the tenth of Tishrei." (*Berachos* 5b)

Passing the market on his way to school, a child of a wealthy home regularly would snatch an apple from one of the stands. After a while, the needy fruit seller complained about it to the boy's father. Ashamed and upset at his son's behavior, the father chided and lectured the boy. When his admonishments did not help, the father thought of a different strategy to teach his son the error of his ways. He arranged to have his son brought to school each day accompanied by an entourage of servants and a marching band. In the face of this display of pomp and esteem, the boy did not dream of mischief or filching apples.

147

The yetzer hara encourages a person to pursue all the worldly pleasures he can attain. Had the Torah merely decreed that one must eat and drink on erev Yom Kippur, people would overindulge and gorge themselves, becoming intoxicated to the point where there would hardly be a minyan for the Kol Nidrei service.

To preclude such excesses, the Torah enhanced the mitzvah with the ornament of fasting, stating that eating on erev Yom Kippur is considered as fasting for two days. With this is mind, a person will feel subdued at his erev Yom Kippur meal and control his mundane desires, eating and drinking only for the sake of the mitzvah so he can fast on Yom Kippur.

(Meshalei Yaakov)

The Remorseful Pharmacist

In Hanipol, the town of the Rebbe Reb Zishe, there lived a pharmacist who led a very sinful life. One day he came to see the evil of his ways. He called on Reb Zishe, seeking his advice on how to do *teshuvah*.

Reb Zishe prescribed a rigorous regimen of fasting and mortification.

"But Rebbe," the pharmacist moaned, "if I fast that much, I'm going to die for sure!"

"Well, I have no other remedy," Reb Zishe replied. "But I have a brother, the Rebbe Reb Elimelech. He is a kindhearted soul. Go and call on him; he might be able to help you."

So the penitent pharmacist traveled to Lizhensk and poured out his heart to Reb Elimelech.

"You don't have to fast," the Rebbe told him. "Go ahead and eat fresh rolls and fish every day, and don't forget to drink whiskey. Then have soup, a juicy steak, and dessert. There's just one thing. Before you start your meal, you must come in to see me."

Relieved at hearing this and looking forward to having a sumptuous meal, the pharmacist entered the Rebbe's study the next day. The Rebbe gazed at him intently, and with his spiritual power of looking into a person's soul, the Rebbe began to enumerate and outline each and every sin the pharmacist had committed on a given day in his past.

Shocked and ashamed, the pharmacist broke into tears and blacked out. When he came to, the Rebbe Elimelech told him, "Now you can have your meal!"

Naturally, the man had lost his appetite. He refused to take a bite. But the Rebbe Elimelech insisted that he eat. He even appointed a guard, who made sure that the man ate his meal.

Day after day, the pharmacist had to be forced to take food. In the process, he became a true *baal teshuvah*.

Commented the Baranover Rav: This is how one should feel when eating the *seudah* of *erev* Yom Kippur. Recalling one's missteps and realizing that tomorrow is Yom Kippur, a person loses his appetite—and he must force himself to eat for the sake of the *mitzvah*.

(Divrei Emunah, Shuvah Yisrael)

> *Rabbi Elimelech of Lizhensk wondered, "Why are the meals of erev Yom Kippur considered a form of fasting, as if you had afflicted yourself?" The answer becomes clear once you begin to ponder the holiness of the upcoming Yom Kippur day. One quickly becomes overwhelmed with awe. In that frame of mind, how can you possibly indulge in eating? Can there be a greater ordeal than to sit down to a meal at a time like this?*

(Beis Rebbi)

The Expensive Fish

One *erev* Yom Kippur, a wealthy Polish squire sent his servant to the market to buy fish. There was a shortage of fish, and the only fish available cost two golden ducats, an exorbitant amount. Eager to buy the fish for the meal of *erev* Yom Kippur, a poor Jewish tailor outbid the servant and offered three ducats. When the servant offered four, the tailor raised the bid to five golden ducats and bought the fish.

Arriving home empty-handed, the servant told his master about the poor Jewish tailor who had outbid him.

Angry at the audacity of the Jew, the squire summoned the tailor to the palace.

"What do you do for a living?" the *poritz* asked.

"I'm a simple tailor," the Jew replied timidly.

"How did you have the nerve to buy such an expensive fish?" the *poritz* growled.

"Sir, today is a special day for us Jews," replied the tailor. "G-d told us to eat and drink today to show that we are confident that our Creator in Heaven will forgive our sins. If necessary, I would have paid twice as much for that fish."

Moved by the sincere faith of the simple Jew, the *poritz* said, "You did the right thing, Moshke. More power to you." Wishing him a happy holiday, he sent him home to enjoy the fish.

(Tur, Hilchos Yom Kippur 604)

Atoning for Improper Meals

According to the great *tzaddikim*, eating on *erev* Yom Kippur atones for all the meals you ate without the proper intention all year. Since the purpose of eating on *erev* Yom Kippur is to give you strength to fast on Yom Kippur, the meals of *erev* Yom Kippur have the power to restore and instill *kedushah* into the meals of the entire year.

(S'fas Emes)

The Feast of Yom Kippur

The Gemara in *Taanis* 26b says, "There never was a greater *Yom Tov* than Yom Kippur," for that was the day on which Moshe brought the second *Luchos* (Tablets) down from Heaven. Since we cannot make a festive meal on Yom Kippur, we have the *Yom Tov seudah* on *erev* Yom Kippur instead.

(S'fas Emes)

The Affliction of Eating

The Torah says, "You must afflict yourselves on the ninth of the month." (*Vayikra* 23:32) Why does the Torah speak of affliction when it is a *mitzvah* to savor food and drink on the ninth day of the month, which is *erev* Yom Kippur?

The Arizal explains that eating on *erev* Yom Kippur is a source of pain. The *yetzer hara* either tries to convince a person not to eat at all, or he persuades him to overeat and gorge himself, instead of just eating for the sake of the *mitzvah*. The agony of having to overcome both these blandishments of the *yetzer hara* is truly an affliction.

(Imrei Yehoshua)

Meals that Heal

As a reward for eating on *erev* Yom Kippur (with the intention to be able to fast on Yom Kippur), Hashem will save us from sickness, pain, and suffering.

A fascinating *gematria* supports this idea. The verse says (*Shemos* 23:25), "You will then serve Hashem your G-d, and He will bless your bread and your water. I will banish sickness from among you—*mikirbecha*."

The numerical value of *mikirbecha*-362 (*mem, kuf, reish, beis, chaf*-40 + 100 + 200 + 2 + 20 = 362) is the same as the *gematria* of the word Yom Kippur (*yud, vav, mem, chaf, pei, vav, reish*-10 + 6 + 40 + 100 + 80 + 6 + 200 = 362). Hashem will repay us for eating on *erev* Yom Kippur by "banishing sickness from among us."

(Ateres Yeshua)

The Berditchever's Defense

The saintly Berditchever, the great defender of *Klal Yisrael*, sheds a new light on the verse in *Hashkiveinu*, "Remove the Satan from before us and behind us."

Twice a year, Satan denounces *Klal Yisrael* before the Heavenly Tribunal. On *erev* Yom Kippur, when Jews are fulfilling the *mitzvah* of eating lavishly, he accuses them of eating more than the gentiles. Again on Purim, he lodges the same complaint, charging that Jews eat more than the gentiles.

Immediately the angels jump to the defense, proving that by eating an opulent meal on Purim, *Klal Yisrael* want to fulfill Hashem's *mitzvah*. They remove the Satan *milefaneinu*, "from before us," pointing out that on the day *before* Purim, the Jews fast—on Taanis Esther. Then the angels remove the Satan *me'acharainu*, "from behind us," indicating that Jews eat a big meal on *erev* Yom Kippur so they can fast on Yom Kippur, the day "behind" *erev* Yom Kippur.

Satan's indictments of Jews eating excessively on Purim and *erev* Yom Kippur are removed by the *taanis* that is held *milefaneinu*, "before us"—which is Taanis Esther— and the fast *me'achareinu*, "behind us," which is Yom Kippur.

(Kedushas Levi)

Chapter Twenty

Yom Kippur - Holiest Day of the Year

Masechta Yoma

Why is the tractate dealing with Yom Kippur called *Yoma,* "the Day," unlike those of the other *Yomim Tovim,* which are appropriately named 153153*mesechtos Pesachim, Sukkah* and *Rosh Hashanah*?

Because Yom Kippur is "the Day"—the holiest day of the year. Accordingly, the first Mishnah of *Yoma* begin with the words *"shivas Yomim,* seven days." The number seven signifies *kedushah,* holiness, and the *kedushah* of Yom Kippur is on the same level as that of Shabbos, the seventh day.

This is why the Torah speaks of Yom Kippur in terms of *Shabbas Shabboson,* "a Sabbath of Sabbaths." (*Vayikra* 23:32) There are six other *Yomim Tovim:* one day of Rosh Hashanah, two days of Sukkos, two days of Pesach, and one day of Shavuos. On these six days of *Yom Tov* all labor associated with the preparation of food is permitted. But the seventh day of *Yom Tov*—Yom Kippur—has the same *kedushah* as Shabbos: no labor at all may be performed. Thus, Yom Kippur is the Shabbos of the other six "Shabbosos"—the other *Yomim Tovim.*

153

Shabbos is called "a semblance of the World to Come." Yom Kippur has an even greater semblance of the World to Come, because on Yom Kippur we do not eat or drink, just as there is neither eating nor drinking in the World to Come.

Yom Kippur resembles the World to Come in yet another aspect. It is the only day of the year on which Satan is unable to lodge accusations against *Klal Yisrael*. The *gematria* of the word *haSatan* is 364 (*hei*=5, *sin*=300, *tes*=9, *nun* = 50; 5+300+9+50=364), for Satan denounces Yisrael 364 days of the year. But on the 365th day—Yom Kippur—Satan is powerless, just as he will be in the World to Come.

(Maharsha, Yoma 2a)

Yom HaKippurim in Plural

The day is called *Yom HaKippurim,* literally, "Day of Atonements" in the plural, because a twofold atonement is provided: for the living and for those who have died.

(Ba'eir Heteiv, Orach Chaim 621:8)

Why do the dead need atonement? If their children or grandchildren do not live according to the Torah, they are held partially responsible for failing to give them the proper education and guidance. They therefore require Hashem's forgiveness even after their passing.

(Chasam Sofer)

Fasting on Yom Kippur

Fasting on Yom Kippur is a positive commandment of the Torah, as it says, "You shall afflict yourselves." (*Vayikra* 23:27) Whoever does not fast on Yom Kippur violates a negative commandment, for it says, "If anyone does not afflict himself on this day, he shall be cut off [spiritually] from his people." (*Vayikra* 23:29) By fasting one fulfills both a positive and a negative commandment.

The *mitzvah* of fasting on Yom Kippur is greater than putting on *tefillin* or wearing *tzitzis*, because fasting entails physical distress. A person should rejoice over the discomfort he feels from fasting—for by suffering hunger, he is fulfilling a *mitzvah*. Those who complain about the discomfort and long for the fast to end surely do not receive one thousandth of the reward that is bestowed on people who rejoice over the *mitzvah* of fasting.

In fact, the *simchah* takes away the discomfort of fasting, whereas griping about fasting only sharpens the hunger pangs!

(Elef Hamagein, 611)

No Brachah Over Fasting

Fasting—abstaining from eating—is a passive action, and a *brachah* is not recited over *not* doing something.

(Avnei Nezer)

Just One Day

Outside of Eretz Yisrael we observe the *Yomim Tovim* for two days, because of doubt as to the correct date. The Sages did not ordain Yom Kippur to be observed for two days, however, because fasting for two days would be harmful to one's health.

(Rema 624:5)

In addition, if one observed Yom Kippur for two days because of doubt, then if the second day is actually Yom Kippur, the first day would be *erev* Yom Kippur—a day when it is forbidden to fast!

(Magein Avraham 624)

A *mitzvah* based on a doubt is not accepted by Hashem as fully as a *mitzvah* that is certain. Yom Kippur, the *Yom Tov* that atones for our sins, must be observed on a date that is certain—for how can a doubtful day bring atonement for sins that are definite? The Sages did not decree two days of Yom Kippur so the atonement of *Klal Yisrael* should be granted on a day that is not clouded by doubt.

(Derashos Chasam Sofer)

No Shoes

The *teshuvah* of *Klal Yisrael* brings an atmosphere of *kedushah* to the entire world. The earth on which we walk becomes spiritually hallowed and uplifted. We must not step on such *admas kodesh*, holy ground, while wearing shoes—just as Hashem told Moshe, "Remove your shoes from your feet, for the place upon which you stand is holy ground." (*Shemos* 3:5)

(Menachem Tzion)

In the wake of Adam's sin the earth was cursed. We wear shoes so our feet will not touch the doomed earth. But on the holy day of Yom Kippur the curse is lifted, and the earth becomes sanctified. We do not have to avoid stepping on it, and therefore there is no need to wear shoes.

(Agra DePirka)

The late Satmar Rav ruled that on Yom Kippur one should not wear sneakers or any footgear with solid soles, even rubber soles. Since people wear such casual shoes every day during the summer months, it is not considered an affliction.

(Machzor Divrei Yoel)

The Kittel

One reason for wearing a *kittel*, a white robe, on Yom Kippur is that we want to look like angels. Since on Yom Kippur we are free of the *yetzer hara*, we resemble the angels who do not have a *yetzer hara*.

The dead are buried shrouded in a *kittel*. We wear a *kittel* on Yom Kippur to remind ourselves that man does not live forever. There comes a time when a person will have to render an accounting of his deeds. Thoughts such as these lead a person to do *teshuvah*. (*Rema, Orach Chaim* 610:4) This also indicates our readiness to give up our lives for the sake of sanctifying Hashem's name.

The white *kittel* symbolizes the idea that by forgiving us, Hashem washes away and whitens our sins, as it says, "Be your sins like scarlet, they will become white as snow." (*Yeshayah* 1:18)

(Maharshal)

The white *kittel* causes us to resemble the *Kohen Gadol*, who performed the Yom Kippur service wearing white garments.

(Yismach Moshe)

Shedding Tears

It is commendable for a person to cry to Hashem, shedding tears on the holy day of Yom Kippur. A parable will help explain it:

A king ordered a magnificent castle to be built. To discourage invaders, he fortified the castle with two defenses: an impenetrable high wall, and a deep, water-filled moat surrounding it.

In times gone by, *Klal Yisrael* was protected by a mighty wall, the *Beis Hamikdash*, to deter Satan and the *yetzer hara*. Unfortunately, we have lost this stronghold. We now depend on our second line of defense, the water-filled moat of our tears, to ward off the onslaught of the *yetzer hara*. May our tears arouse Hashem's compassion, so He will protect us from our enemies who are trying to ruin us.

(Tiferes Uziel)

No Time to Relax

A shipping magnate ordered a large freighter to be built to sail the oceans, carrying cargo to distant lands. As the ship was being built, the builders ran into many difficulties. They worked hard to make sure the ship was seaworthy.

At last, the vessel was launched into the harbor. But the sailors discovered yet more problems with the new ship. They spend countless hours working on the safety of the ship before allowing it to head for the ocean on its maiden voyage.

At last, sailing out in the open sea, the sailors began to relax. "All right, mates," they said to each other. "After all the trouble we've had, now we can finally relax and go to sleep."

But one bright sailor spoke up. "Don't you see, we're in greater danger now than ever before! If we ran into snags earlier, at least we were on dry land. But if something goes wrong now, out here in the middle of the stormy ocean, our lives are at risk. So how can you relax and go to sleep?"

During the month of Elul we begin working hard at improving our conduct. This is followed by the *Selichos* days and Rosh Hashanah, when our ship is launched from the dry dock into the harbor. We work even harder doing *teshuvah* and good deeds before our ship finally moves into the open ocean—which is Yom Kippur.

Don't think you can relax now! We are in a perilous situation. Now is the time for crying out to Hashem. On Rosh Hashanah we were inscribed, but today our fates will be sealed. We are in the middle of a turbulent sea. Everyone should tremble with awe of the holy day of Yom Kippur.

So let us *daven* to Hashem and do *teshuvah* with all our heart, so Hashem will grant us a year of *geulah* and *yeshuah*.

(Mishlei Yaakov)

Day of Reconciliation

The Gemara in *Yoma* 87a relates that Rav once had a complaint against a certain butcher. By *erev* Yom Kippur the butcher had not come to him to appease him. Rav said, "I will go to placate him."

Rav Huna met him along the way and asked, "Where are you going?"

Rav replied, "To placate So-and-so." As he said this, Rav thought: I am afraid that I will cause his death. [He knew that the butcher was a difficult person and would not take advantage of his offer at reconciliation.]

Rav went there and remained standing in front of the butcher, who was busy chopping an animal's head. The butcher glanced up. Upon seeing Rav, he said, "Go away! I will have nothing to do with you!"

While he was chopping the head, a bone flew off, striking his throat and killing him.

This teaches us that spurning an offer at reconciliation has very grave consequences. On the holy day of Yom Kippur, Hashem comes to reconcile with us, offering to forgive all our sins. Turning Him down, refusing to do *teshuvah*, is a grave sin. We should engage in introspection, examine our past deeds, be remorseful over our shortcomings and resolve not to sin again. In the merit of our *teshuvah* we will be inscribed for a year of *geulah* and *yeshuah*, with the coming of *Mashiach*

Chapter Twenty One

Kol Nidrei

Coming Closer to Hashem

The solemn *Kol Nidrei* service moves even simple Jews to do *teshuvah*. For Hashem infused the night of Yom Kippur with the power to suspend all worldly desires. In his mind's eye, a person reviews his past actions and realizes how far he has strayed from the right path.

But *teshuvah* is more than resolving not to transgress again. *Teshuvah* means deciding to learn more Torah, do more *mitzvos*, and *daven* with more concentration and true devotion.

This is the underlying thought of the verse, "For on this day atonement shall be made for you to cleanse you of all your sins; you shall be clean before Hashem." (*Vayikra* 16:30) Hashem has given the power to this day to cleanse you of all your sinful desires, but "you shall be clean before Hashem"—you must respond by arousing yourselves to do *teshuvah*.

(*Divrei Chaim, the Sanzer Rav*)

The Open Aron Hakodesh

The *Aron Hakodesh* is left open while the *sifrei Torah* are carried around the synagogue before *Kol Nidrei* to indicate that the Gates of *Teshuvah* are always open.

(Imrei Noam)

Inviting the Transgressors

Before *Kol Nidrei* is recited, a formal declaration, *Al Daas Hamakom*, is made by the elders of the congregation, inviting the participation of even *avaryanim*, "transgressors."

This declaration dates back to the time of the *anusim*, also known as Marranos, the Spanish Jews who were forced to convert to Christianity. While outwardly living as gentiles, they secretly retained their Jewishness. On Yom Kippur they risked their lives, gathering in hidden cellars for the *Kol Nidrei* service, asking Hashem's forgiveness for behaving like non-Jewish *avaryanim*, "transgressors," throughout the year.

This ancient declaration was incorporated into the standard *Kol Nidrei* liturgy, for today, as in the period of the *anusim*, there are transgressors who are drawn to the synagogue on Yom Kippur. With this declaration we invite these people to pray with us, so their prayers will rise to Heaven together with those of all of *Klal Yisrael.*

Permission to Transgressors

The Sages teach that a public fast in which Jewish sinners do not take part is not considered a fast. This is derived from the fact that *chelbenah*, galbanum, which has a foul aroma, was included among the spices of the *ketores*, the Temple incense.

Rabbeinu Bachya explains that this shows us that we should not ignore the sinners of Yisrael by excluding them from our fasts and prayers. For whenever transgressors repent, atone for their sins, and join with the righteous, the Name of G-d is sanctified. If not for that, the righteous would be held accountable for the sinners—because all Jews are responsible for one another.

(Kereisos 6b)

Baruch Shem Kevod Malchuso- Blessed Is The Name

All year this verse is recited silently. Only on Yom Kippur is it said aloud.

At Yaakov's deathbed his children affirmed their loyalty to G-d, proclaiming the verse *Shema* [the word "Yisrael" in that context refers to Yaakov]. Yaakov replied with the words: "Blessed is the Name   " The Sages taught: Should we say these words because Yaakov said them? Yes. But on the other hand, Moshe did not transmit them to us, for they are not found in the Torah. Therefore, let us say them in low voice.

(Pesachim 56a)

Moshe heard this beautiful prayer from the angels and taught it to *Klal Yisrael.* We dare not say it aloud, because we are sinful and unworthy of praising Hashem with a phrase used by the angels. On Yom Kippur, however, when *Klal Yisrael* rises to the level of angels, we, too, may proclaim it aloud.

(Levush 619:2)

"I Have Forgiven According to Your Words"

Hashem said these words to Moshe in response to his prayer after the sin of the spies maligning Eretz Yisrael. (*Bamidbar* 14:20)

Perhaps the phrase "*Kidvarecha,* According to your words," may be applied to Yom Kippur. It is as if Hashem is saying, "I will forgive you according to the sincerity of your remorse and the depth of your *teshuvah*. If you repent with all your heart and do *teshuvah* out of love, I will totally wipe away your transgressions and turn them into merits."

(Tiferes Shlomo)

Forgiveness

One *Kol Nidrei* night, before reciting the verse, "I have forgiven according to your words," the Kozhnitzer Maggid said the following:

Ribbono shel Olam! No human being can fathom Your infinite power; but neither can anyone comprehend how utterly weak I am. Only You know that. You know that, unlike every year, this year I am too frail to lead the *davening* for *Kol Nidrei*. You also know that in spite of my weakness I led the services the entire month of Elul, praying for mercy. You know that I did not pray for my own sake, but for the sake of Your beloved people, *Klal Yisrael*.

But now, *Ribbono shel Olam*, my fragile body cannot carry the heavy burden of praying for Your children. For the sake of Your cherished children, it is surely not too hard for You, Powerful and Almighty G-d, to utter the two words "*Salachti kidvarecha*, I have forgiven according to Your words," and forgive the sins of your people who are doing *teshuvah* today.

If You don't want to say "*Salachti kidvarecha*" because there are no *tzaddikim* in the world, what about the holy Reb Mendele over in Riminov, who is as great a *tzaddik* as all the *tzaddikim* of our generation?

And if You are reluctant to say "*Salachti kidvarecha*" because today there are no *Urim VeTumim*, what about the saintly *Chozeh* of Lublin, whose eyes shine with wisdom as brightly as the stones in the breastplate of the *Kohen Gadol*?

And should You refuse to say "*Salachti kidvarecha*" because You cannot find any true *baalei teshuvah*, I, with my frail and broken body, am ready to do *teshuvah* on behalf of the entire Jewish people. So I beg You, *Ribbono shel Olam*, please declare already, "*Salachti kidvarecha!*"

The holy Kozhnitzer Maggid cried and sobbed. Suddenly he stopped and motioned to the choir to begin chanting the familiar solemn tune. With a thunderous roar that jolted the congregation, he cried out, "*Vayomer Hashem, Salachti kidvarecha!*"

When the saintly Rizhiner was told about this, he commented, "I am firmly convinced that the Kozhnitzer Maggid actually heard Hashem uttering the words *Salachti kidvarecha*, just as Moshe heard it when Hashem said it to him."

The *Chozeh* of Lublin remarked, "That old and fragile *tzaddik* has stirred up all the higher worlds!"

(Be'eros Hamayim)

Twice Purified

The Torah says regarding Yom Kippur, "For on this day He shall provide atonement for you to cleanse you; from all your sins before Hashem shall you be cleansed."

(Vayikra 16:30)

A king had a spectacular garden, filled with fragrant flowers and exotic fruit trees. One day a stranger broke into the garden. Recklessly stepping on the flowers, breaking the branches of the tender fruit trees, he created chaos and devastation.

As he was climbing up a tree, the branch he stepped on broke, hurling the intruder to the ground. Lying there with broken limbs, writhing in agony, the man finally came to his senses.

"See what I have done with my senseless behavior!" he moaned. "I vandalized the king's garden—and I destroyed myself, shattering my bones. How will I ever be able to settle my medical bills, besides paying for the damage I caused to the king's garden?"

A close friend counseled him, "First you should approach the king, telling him you are sorry. Ask his forgiveness for ravaging his garden. When the king takes pity on you and pardons you, he will also see to it that your fractures are healed."

When a person commits a sin, he does harm to himself, as well as causing grief to Hashem. How can he repair this situation? First he must appease Hashem, expressing sincere regret for his trespasses. When Hashem forgives him, He will also heal the wounds he inflicted on himself by sinning.

"For on this day He shall provide atonement for you to cleanse you." Hashem will heal you from the sickness you inflicted on yourself through your sins, provided that "you are cleansed from all your sins before Hashem."

(Yetev Panim)

The Gemara (*Megillah* 28a) says that one may not gaze at the face of a wicked person. When is a person considered an evildoer? One who violates even a minor Rabbinical prohibition is considered a wicked person. Who, then, can say that he is free of sin? Hashem cannot look at our faces; He hides from us, and conceals His *Shechinah*.

But the Torah says, "For on this day He shall provide atonement for you, to cleanse you from all your sins." Once we are cleansed of our sins, "You are cleansed before Hashem"—Hashem will be able to look at us. And when He directs His countenance toward us, we are blessed abundantly.

(Yismach Moshe)

Broken Bottles

The Rebbe of Tartchin, son of the saintly *Chozeh* of Lublin, told the following parable during his *Kol Nidrei* sermon:

A poritz (wealthy Polish landowner) gave a lavish banquet for his friends. While the feast was in progress, he told one of his servants to go down into the wine cellar and bring up a few bottles of an exquisite wine.

Instead of bringing the bottles, the servant helped himself to a bottle of strong wine. Staggering drunk, he flung bottles to the floor and cracked open several barrels of the finest wine.

Getting impatient, the poritz went down to the cellar. Seeing the awful mess of broken bottles and wine flowing from damaged barrels, he flew into a rage.

Finding himself alone with the poritz, the drunken servant foolishly thought of seizing the opportunity to ask for a raise. "Sir, I've always served you well," he mumbled, "so I'd like to ask you for an increase in salary."

"The nerve you have!" the poritz shouted, his face flushed with anger. "You break bottles and barrels, letting wine run all over the floor, and you have the audacity to ask for a raise! Are you out of your mind?"

Continued the Rebbe: Last year on Yom Kippur we pledged to do better and improve our ways. Not only did we not observe the *mitzvos* properly, we broke "bottles" and "barrels," piling up transgressions and failings. And now we have the gall to ask the *Ribbono shel Olam* for a raise, imploring him, "*Zochreinu lechayim,* Remember us for life- grant us another year of life!"

Let us resolve to act righteously in the coming year, to avoid bringing Hashem's anger against us.

(Rabbi Yosef of Tartchin)

Seizing the Moment

This inspirational sermon was related by my grandfather, the Rav of Weitzen:

A wealthy merchant had a son who did not have a talent for business. All he knew was in which season of the year his father would buy a given product. Unable to run the business, the son lost his money and could not make ends meet. His friends advised him, "In business, proper timing is of the essence. Since you know the right time to buy commodities, you should become a financial consultant, advising people when to buy and when to sell." Following their suggestion, he soon became a rich man.

We stand empty-handed before the Heavenly tribunal on Yom Kippur. But we vividly remember how our fathers shed bitter tears on the night of *Kol Nidrei*, doing *teshuvah* with all their hearts. They knew that time is of the essence, that the night of *Kol Nidrei* is the right moment. It is the *eis ratzon,* "the favorable time" when Hashem accepts our *teshuvah.*

Said the Rav of Weitzen: I come to you acting as your investment consultant, advising you that now is the time to buy mercy and forgiveness. You will all profit abundantly by it.

"My voice is to G-d when I cry out; my voice is to G-d, that He give ear to me." (*Tehillim* 77:2) The commentators explain: All year long, when praying, we formulate our thoughts, putting them into words, because the angels that carry our prayers to Heaven do not understand thoughts. But on Yom Kippur, Hashem is with us; He knows our thoughts. We need not put them into words. On Yom Kippur, a wordless cry from the heart reaches all the way to the Gates of Heaven.

"My voice is to G-d"—on Yom Kippur Hashem is close to us, "when I cry out" to Him, "He gives ear to me"—He understands my wordless sobs, and He listens.

(Derashos Dvar Tzvi)

The Shechinah in Exile

The Satmar Rebbe gave the following Yom Kippur sermon in 1940:

"The Mishnah in *Yoma* 2a relates that seven days before Yom Kippur, the *Kohen Gadol* was removed from his house and taken to the *Palhedrin* chamber.

"Woe is to us!" the Rebbe exclaimed. "How many tens of thousands of Jews are far removed from their homes on this Yom Kippur, suffering in labor camps!

"During the seven days of isolation, the *Kohen Gadol* was watched by the guardians of the Sanhedrin. Tragically, the Jews in the labor camps are prisoners of the vicious Germans, watched by brutal guards.

"But that's not all. Hashem Himself is removed from His Heavenly abode, for He has sworn not to enter the Heavenly counterpart of the *Beis Hamikdash* until the *Beis Hamikdash* on earth has been rebuilt.

"Dear friends!" the Rebbe continued. "At the conclusion of Yom Kippur, the *Kohen Gadol* was escorted to his house accompanied by singing and dancing crowds of people. Let us all do *teshuvah*, so we will merit to go home tonight with singing and dancing, celebrating the coming of Mashiach. May we live to see the rebuilding of the *Beis Hamikdash*, when Hashem will be able to enter the *Beis Hamikdash* in Heaven and let the *Shechinah* dwell in the *Beis Hamikdash* on earth."

(Divrei Yoel)

Chapter Twenty Two

The Mitzvah of Teshuvah

The Power of Teshuvah

Teshuvah has the power to bring sinners closer to G-d. Before his *teshuvah*, the sinner was hated and despised by G-d. Now that he has repented, he is accepted as a beloved friend of G-d.

Yesterday he was separated from G-d, as it says, "Your iniquities have separated between you and your G-d." (*Yeshayah* 59:2) He cried out but was not answered, as it says, "Even if you were to intensify your prayer, I will not listen." (*Yeshayah* 1:15) If he did a *mitzvah*, it was cast aside, as it says, "Who asked this from your hand, to trample My courtyards?" (*Yeshayah* 1:12)

Yet today he is attached to the *Shechinah*, as it says, "You who cling to Hashem, your G-d." (*Devarim* 4:4) When he cries out to G-d, his prayer is answered, as it says, "It will be that before they call I will answer." (*Yeshayah* 65:24) When he does a *mitzvah* it is received with joy and delight, as it says, "For G-d has already approved your deeds." (*Koheles* 9:7)

Not Mentioned in the Torah

Teshuvah is not mentioned in the Torah as an explicit command, for if *teshuvah* would be a clear-cut positive command, one would be required to sin in order to be able to do *teshuvah*, repenting of that sin.

If *teshuvah* would be a definitive *mitzvah*, Hashem would be required to accept *teshuvah* as prescribed by law. But Hashem grants *teshuvah* and forgives sins as an act of Divine grace and kindness toward the sinner. (*Yismach Moshe*)

Seizing the Moment

If you have an impulse to do *teshuvah*, don't dismiss it. That impulse is a message from Hashem *Yisbarach*. Surely no one would disregard a message that comes directly from the King of kings! Can there be greater contempt of G-d than that?

Feelings of *teshuvah* are sparked by *yiras Hashem,* and *yiras Hashem* is G-d's most precious treasure.

(Yismach Moshe)

Sinning and Repentance

The Mishnah in *Yoma* 85b says: If one says, "I will sin and repent, sin and repent," no opportunity will be given to him to repent. Why? If he did not think that *teshuvah* wipes out his sin, he would not commit the sin at all. It is the thought of *teshuvah* that gives rise to his sin, and for this reason he is denied the opportunity of doing *teshuvah.*

(S'fas Emes)

"I will sin and repent, sin and repent." Why does the Mishnah repeat itself? The first time he says this, he might say that he sinned in order to be able to fulfill the *mitzvah* of doing *teshuvah,* because one can do *teshuvah* only if he commits a sin. But when he sinned a second time he cannot use this rationale. For he already fulfilled the *mitzvah* of *teshuvah* after his first sin. Therefore the Mishnah says, if he says: I will sin and repent, sin and repent, his *teshuvah* is not accepted.

(Meir Einei Chachamim)

The Sanzer Rav sees the Mishnah in a positive light. "If one says: I will sin and repent." If, while engaging in the sin, he intends to repent of his transgression—but he is only sinning because he is unable to control himself—then the moment his desire has dissipated, he will do *teshuvah*. "*Ein maspikin beyado laasos teshuvah*." The word "*maspikin*" can be translated as *safeik*, "doubt." Thus the phrase may be rendered: There can be *no doubt* this person will be helped from Above to do *teshuvah*.

Sincere Teshuvah

Rabbi Pinchas of Koritz said: As long as a person is in the habit of lying, the *teshuvah* he does for any sin is worthless. *Teshuvah* must be sincere, and a habitual liar's repentance is not sincere.

(Midrash Pinchas)

Torah Verses Concerning Teshuvah

- "If a man or woman sins against his fellow man, thus being untrue to Hashem, and becoming guilty of a crime, he must confess the sin that he has committed." (*Bamidbar* 5:6)

- "When you are in distress and all these things have happened to you, you will finally return to Hashem your G-d and obey Him. Hashem your G-d is a merciful Power, and He will not abandon you or destroy you; He will not forget the oath He made upholding your fathers' covenant." (*Devarim* 4:30-31)

- "There will come a time when you will experience all the words of blessing and curse that I have presented you. There, among the nations where Hashem has banished you, you will reflect on the situation. You will then return to Hashem your G-d, and you will obey Him." (*Devarim* 30:1-2)

- "You will then repent and obey Hashem." (*Devarim* 30:8)

- "When you return to Hashem your G-d with all your heart and soul." (*Devarim* 30:10)

- "This mandate that I am prescribing to you today is not mysterious or remote from you ... It is something that is very close to you. It is in your mouth and in your heart, so that you can keep it." (*Devarim* 30:11,14)

The Nevi'im Speak About Teshuvah

- The *navi* Hoshea said, "Return, Yisrael, unto Hashem your G-d, for you have stumbled in your iniquity." (*Hoshea* 14:2)

- The *navi* Yeshayah said, "If you really desire it, repent and come." (*Yeshayah* 21:12)

- The *navi* Yirmeyah said, "Return, O wayward sons, and I will heal your waywardness." (*Yirmeyah* 3:22)

- The *navi* Yechezkel, elaborating on the subject of *teshuvah*, said, "As for the wicked man, if he repents of all the sins he committed, and observes all My decrees and practices justice and righteousness, he shall surely live, he shall not die. All the transgressions that he committed will not be remembered against him; he shall live because of the righteousness he did. Do I desire at all the death of the wicked man?   Is it not rather his return from his ways, that he might live? Cast off from upon yourselves all your transgressions through which you have transgressed, and make for yourselves a new heart and a new spirit. Why should you die, O House of Yisrael? For I do not desire the death of the one who should die   Turn yourselves back and live!" (*Yechezkel* 18:21-23, 18:31-32)

All the *nevi'im* exhorted *Klal Yisrael* to do *teshuvah.* They are speaking to us today as they did to their own generation, teaching us the paths to *teshuvah,* encouraging us to return to Hashem.

(Shelah, Shaar HaTeshuvah 81:43)

The Sages Speak About Teshuvah

- Rabbi Yochanan said: *Teshuvah* is so great that it has the power to annul a person's guilty verdict. For it says, "Make fat that people's heart, stop its ears and seal its eyes, lest, seeing with its eyes, and hearing with its ears, it also grasps with its mind, and repents and is healed." (*Yeshayah* 6:10) [Which indicates that repentance has the power to heal, that is, to annul an evil edict.]

(Rosh Hashanah 17b)

- R' Chama ben Chanina said: Great is *teshuvah,* for it brings healing to the whole world, as it says, "I will heal their rebelliousness, I will love them freely." (*Hoshea* 14:5)

- R' Levi said: Great is *teshuvah,* for it reaches up to the Throne of Glory, as it says, "Return, O Yisrael, to Hashem your G-d." (*Hoshea* 14:2)

• R' Yochanan said: *Teshuvah* is so great that it brings about redemption [before the proclaimed time], for it says, "A redeemer shall come to Zion, and to those of Yaakov who regret of willful sin." (*Yeshayah* 59:20) He expounds: How is it that a redeemer shall come to Zion [prematurely]? Because of "those of Yaakov who repent of willful sin."

• Resh Lakish said: Great is *teshuvah,* for because of it, intentional sins are counted as errors. For it says, "Return, O Yisrael, to Hashem your G-d, for you have stumbled because of your sin." (*Hoshea* 14:2) ["Sin" means an intentional transgression, yet "stumbling" implies error.]

    The Gemara asks: But has not Resh Lakish said that *teshuvah* is so great that because of it, intentional sins are counted as merits, as it says, "And when a wicked man turns back from his wickedness and practices justice and charity, he shall live because of them" (*Yechezkel* 33:19)? That is no contradiction. The latter verse speaks of *teshuvah* out of love [when intentional sins convert to merits]; the first of repentance out of fear [when intentional sins are counted as errors].

• R' Meir used to say: Great is *teshuvah*, for on account of a single individual who did *teshuvah*, his sins and the sins of the whole world are forgiven, for it says, "I will heal their rebelliousness, I will love them freely, for My anger is turned away from him." (*Hoshea* 14:5) [It does not say "from them," but "from him."]

• R' Shmuel ben Nachmani said: Great is *teshuvah*, because it prolongs the life of a person, as it says, "If a wicked man turns away from his wickedness . . . he will live longer." (*Yechezkel* 33:19)

(Yoma 86a)

What Is Teshuvah?

Teshuvah means a sinner gives up his sins, erases them from his mind and resolves never to commit these transgressions again. "Let the wicked give up his ways." (*Yeshayah* 55:7)

He also regrets his past misdeeds. "Now that I have turned back, I am filled with remorse." (*Yirmeyah* 31:18)

He must reach the stage where Hashem, Who knows man's innermost thoughts, can testify that he will never relapse and sin again. "Never again will we call our handiwork our god." (*Hoshea 14:4*)

He must verbalize his confession, clearly articulating his heart's resolutions.

(Rambam, Hilchos Teshuvah 2:2)

The Essentials of Teshuvah

Teshuvah is possible only if the following seven conditions are met:

- You must clearly recognize that you did the deplorable deed. If you are not certain that you did it, or think that perhaps you did it unintentionally or inadvertently, you cannot truly regret the deed or ask forgiveness for it. "For I recognize my transgression, and my sin is before me always." (*Tehillim* 51:5)

- You must know how reprehensible your deed was. If you are not convinced that your deed was wrong, you will neither regret it nor accept upon yourself the specifics of repentance. You will be convinced that you did it by mistake, and you will come up with a valid excuse. "Who can discern mistakes? Cleanse me from unperceived faults." (*Tehillim* 19:13)

- You must understand that you deserve to be punished for your deed. Without this realization, nothing will prompt you to regret your action. If you do realize that you will be punished, you will be remorseful and ask G-d for forgiveness. "For now that I have returned I am filled with remorse, now that I am made aware [of the punishment that awaits me] I slap my thighs in anguish."(*Yirmeyah* 31:18) "My flesh shuddered from dread of You, and I feared Your judgments." (*Tehillim* 119:120)

- You must be aware that your transgression is recorded in the book of your wrongdoing; it is neither overlooked, forgotten, nor set aside. "Is it not revealed with Me, sealed in My treasuries?" (*Devarim* 32:34) "He seals a judgment with the hand of every man, so that all people He has made shall know." (*Iyov* 37:7) If a person thinks that his transgressions are unimportant, he will neither regret nor ask forgiveness for them. Since his punishment is delayed, he may come to think it has been canceled. "Because the sentence for wrongdoing is not carried out quickly—that is why men are encouraged to do evil." (*Koheles* 8:11)

- You must believe that repentance is the remedy for your disease, and that through repentance you can correct your errors and recover your losses. If you are not convinced, you will give up hope, and you will not ask the Creator for forgiveness for your past misdeeds. "Thus have you spoken, saying, 'Since our sins and iniquities are upon us, and we are wasting away because of them, how can we live?'" (*Yechezkel* 33:10) The Creator replied to this through His prophet: "'As I live!' so says Hashem. 'I swear that I do not desire the death of the wicked one, but rather the wicked one's return from his way, that he may live.'" (*Yechezkel 33:11*)

- You must give thought to the favors G-d has shown you, and how you repaid Him with disobedience rather than gratitude. Weigh the punishment you will receive for a transgression against the pleasure you derive from it. Likewise, you should balance the satisfaction you will obtain as reward for your good deed in this world and the next, against the discomfort your good deed may have entailed. As our Sages said, "Calculate the cost of a *mitzvah* against its reward, and the reward of a sin against its cost." (*Avos* 2:1)

- You must do your utmost to keep away from your accustomed vice. Resolve in your heart and make up your mind to shake it off. "Rend your hearts and not your garments." (*Yoel* 2:13)

Only once these seven points are firmly fixed in your mind is it possible for you to repent of your transgressions.

(Chovos HaLevavos, Shaar HaTeshuvah 3)

The Particulars of Remorse

There are five details of remorse:

- The fear that the Creator's punishment for your sins is fast-approaching. This fear will intensify your regret. "Give honor to Hashem your G-d before it gets dark, and before your feet stub themselves upon the mountains of the night." (*Yirmeyah* 13:16).

- To be humble before G-d because of your sins. "My people, upon whom My name is proclaimed, humble themselves." (2 *Divrei HaYomim* 7:14)

- To change your mode of clothing and jewelry, showing contrition in the way you speak, eat, and move about. "For this don sackcloth, lament and mourn." (*Yirmeyah* 4:8) "Both man and animal shall cover themselves with sackcloth." (*Yonah* 3:8)

- To weep and lament for the sins you committed. "My eyes shed streams of water because they did not keep Your Torah." (*Tehillim* 119:136) "Between the Hall and the Altar let the *Kohanim*, the ministers of Hashem, weep." (*Yoel* 2:17)

- To criticize and humiliate yourself for being careless about fulfilling your obligations to the Creator. "Rend your hearts and not your garments." (*Yoel* 2:13)

                              (Chovos HaLevavos, Shaar HaTeshuvah 5)

Actions That Preclude Teshuvah

There are twenty-four actions that stand in the way of *teshuvah*. Four of them are sins so grave that G-d does not give the one who commits them an opportunity to repent. These include:

- One who causes the masses to sin. Included in this category is one who prevents others from performing a *mitzvah*.

- One who leads his neighbor astray, for example, by persuading him [to worship idols].

- One who sees his son fall into bad ways and does not reprimand him. Since he holds sway over his son, were he to admonish him, he would stay away [from his bad ways]. Therefore, [by not admonishing him, it is] as if he made him sin. Included in this sin are those who have the opportunity to reprimand others, yet fail to do so. [Rather than admonishing them] they allow them to continue their misdeeds.

• One who says, "I will sin and then repent." Included in this category is one who says, "I will sin, and Yom Kippur will [atone my sins]."

(Rambam, Hilchos Teshuvah 4:1)

Actions that Stand in the Way of Teshuvah

There are five transgressions of which one cannot possibly repent completely. These are sins between man and his fellow where one does not know the person against whom one sinned, making it impossible to return what one owes or ask for forgiveness.

• One who curses the community without cursing a specific individual of whom he can ask forgiveness.

• One who buys stolen goods, for he does not know to whom the stolen articles belong, since he bought them from a thief who offered him items stolen from many people.

• One who finds a lost object and does not announce it right away to return it to the owner. Later on, when he wants to do *teshuvah*, he will not know to whom to return the article.

• One who eats the meat of an ox belonging to the poor, orphans, or widows. These unfortunates are not well-known or recognized people. They wander from city to city, and no one is able to identify them as the owners of the ox, so it cannot be returned to them.

- A judge who takes a bribe to render a false judgment. He does not know the consequences of his act and is unable to pay the wronged, because his flawed judgment has far-reaching ramifications.

(Rambam, Hilchos Teshuvah 4:3)

Addictive Habits

There are five habits that, once a person becomes addicted to them, are difficult to give up. A person must be wary not to indulge in them because they will turn into habits that are nearly impossible to break. They are:

- talebearing;
- slander;
- hot-temperedness;
- thinking bad thoughts;
- becoming friendly with a wicked person. He learns from his deeds, and they become rooted in his personality. Shlomo had him in mind when he said, "He who keeps company with fools comes to grief." (*Mishlei* 13:20)

(Rambam, Hilchos Teshuvah 4:5)

All of the above and similar transgressions, although they hold back *teshuvah*, do not prevent it altogether. If one repents, he is a *baal teshuvah* and has a share in the World to Come.

(Rambam, Hilchos Teshuvah 4:6)

Actions that Close the Door to Teshuvah

- One who isolates himself from the community. When they do *teshuvah* he will not be with them, nor will he share in their merit.

- One who contradicts the words of the Sages. As a result of this quarrel he cuts himself off from them, and never learns to repent.

- One who shows contempt for the *mitzvos*. Considering them pointless, he does not want to fulfill them. If he does not fulfill *mitzvos*, how can he expect to do *teshuvah*?

- One who belittles his teachers. They will then reject him, turning him away, as Elisha did to Geichazi. (*2 Melachim* 5) Once cast away, he will not find another guide to show him the path of truth.

- If one hates reprimands, his road to *teshuvah* is blocked, for reproof leads to repentance. When a person is told about his sins and feels ashamed of them, he will repent.   The Jewish people are often rebuked in the Torah. In fact, all the prophets admonished Israel until they repented. Every congregation should likewise appoint a great rabbi to reprove the congregation, inspiring them to do *teshuvah*. But a person who hates criticism will not listen to one who reprimands him. He will continue his sinful ways.

(Rambam, Hilchos Teshuvah 4:2)

Abandoning Sin

There are five parts to abandoning sin:

1. To abstain from everything forbidden by G-d, as it says, "Despise evil, and love good" (*Amos* 5:15) and "Praiseworthy is the man . . . who guards his hands against doing any evil." (*Yeshayah* 56:12)

2. To forsake permitted things that may lead to forbidden things—for example, to abstain from something when you are doubtful if it is permitted or forbidden. Devout people would abstain from seventy types of permitted things, for fear of stumbling into one forbidden thing. Being careful with precautionary measures the Sages instituted is another example, as it says, "Make a protective fence for the Torah." (*Avos* 1:1)

3. To avoid sin and restrain yourself because you fear the Creator's punishment, although you have the ability and opportunity to sin, as it says, "My flesh shuddered from dread of You, and I fear Your judgments." (*Tehillim* 119:120)

4. To avoid sinning because you are ashamed before the Creator—not because you fear or are ashamed of others, or want something from them. Do not be like those about whom it says, "Their fear of Me is like rote learning of human commands" (*Yeshayah* 29:13), or as it says, "Yehoash did what was proper in the eyes of Hashem as long as Yehoyada the Kohen was alive and guided him." (2 *Melachim* 12:3)

5. To divorce yourself completely from wrongdoing, so the thought of repeating the offense would be unthinkable, by saying in your heart and in words what the pious Elihu said: "If I have done wrong, I will not continue." (*Iyov* 34:32)

Asking Forgiveness

Asking forgiveness involves five steps:

1. To confess that you transgressed and to believe that your sins are great, as it says, "For our sins are great before You." (*Yeshayah* 59:12)

2. To always remember your transgressions and set them before you, as it says, "For I recognize my transgressions, and my sin is always before me." (*Tehillim* 51:5)

3. To fast during the day and pray at night when you are not distracted by worldly concerns, as it says, "Arise, cry out in the night!" (*Eichah* 2:19)

4. To implore G-d, praying to Him constantly to forgive your transgressions and accept your repentance, as it says, "I acknowledge my sin to You, I did not cover up my guilt; I resolved, 'I will confess my transgression to Hashem,' and You forgave the guilt of my sin. Therefore, let every devout person pray to You in a time when You may be found." (*Tehillim* 32:5-6)

5. To warn others not to stumble into sins like yours, frightening them with the punishment that is in store for sinners and encouraging them to repent of their sins. As it says, "He who knows [that he sinned] will repent, and G-d will relent" (*Yonah* 3:9) and "I will teach transgressors Your ways." (*Tehillim* 51:15)

(*Chovos HaLevavos, Shaar HaTeshuvah 5*)

Resolving Not to Backslide

The resolve not to regress and repeat one's sins depends on the following:

1. Weigh the immediate but short-lived pleasure you derive from the sin against the lasting and pure gratification that will be yours in the hereafter, as it says, "You will see and your heart will exult." (*Yeshayah* 66:14)

Weigh the passing discomfort that doing a *mitzvah* entails against the never-ending anguish in the World to Come that stems from transgression, as it says, "And they will go out and see the corpses of the men who rebelled against Me, for their decay will not cease and their fire will not be extinguished" (*Yeshayah* 66:24) and "For behold, the day is coming, burning like an oven, when all the wicked people and all the evildoers will be like straw; and that coming day will burn them up . . . But a sun of righteousness will shine for you who fear My name, with healing in its rays." (*Malachi* 3:19-20)

When you take this to heart, you will not revert to your past transgressions.

2. Think about your day of death, when your Creator will be angry with you for neglecting your duty, as it says, "Who can bear the day of His coming?" (*Malachi* 3:2) Reflecting upon this will make you aware and afraid of His punishment, and you will resolve never to sin.

3. Reflect about the length of time you have turned your back on G-d, though all that time He has been good to you. As it says, "For I [G-d] have always broken your yoke and torn off your straps, and you [Yisrael] said, 'I will not enter.'" (*Yirmeyah* 2:20) ["I will not enter" means I will not take it upon myself to serve You, and I will not enter into Your covenant.]

4. Return stolen goods, avoid immorality, and refrain from causing injury to anyone, as it says, "The wicked person returns the pledge, repays for his thefts" (*Yechezkel* 33:15) and "If there is iniquity in your hand, put it far away; and let not sin dwell in your tent. Then you would lift your face without blemish; you would be steadfast and never fear." (*Iyov* 11:14-15)

5. Contemplate the grandeur of the Creator against Whose word you rebelled by leaving His service and casting aside the teachings of His Torah. You should admonish yourself for that, as it says, "Is this the way you repay G-d?" (*Devarim* 32:6) and "Do you not fear Me? says Hashem." (*Yirmeyah* 5:22)

(Chovos HaLevavos, Shaar HaTeshuvah 5)

Do Teshuvah Now!

Teshuvah done at a young age, when a person is keen and robust, is more readily accepted than *teshuvah* done late in life, after a long existence steeped in transgression and wrongdoing. For Hashem despises the prayers and praises of the wicked.

This is evident from the Midrash on the verse, "This is the law concerning the leper" (*Vayikra* 14:2), which states: We know from the Torah, the Prophets, and the Writings that Hashem does not want to hear the praises of the wicked.

We know it from the Torah, because it says that a leper must keep his mouth covered and call out, "Unclean! Unclean!" (*Vayikra* 13:45) Keeping his mouth covered means that he may not learn Torah or praise Hashem, because he is a wicked person.

We know it from the Prophets from the encounter of Geichazi, the wicked servant of the prophet Elisha, with Naaman, the commander of the army of the king of Aram who was stricken with leprosy. (2 *Melachim* 5) The Midrash says that Geichazi told Naaman that Elisha had revived the child of the Shunammite woman. At that very moment, the Shunammite woman was standing at the door. Overhearing how Geichazi was about to mention her name, she entered and related G-d's miracle herself. On this the Sages comment: Even if the Shunammite had been at the other end of the world, Hashem would have whisked her over at that instant, to prevent the wicked Geichazi from relating His miracle and praising Him.

We know it from the Writings, for it says, "But to the wicked Hashem said, 'To what purpose do you recount My decrees and bear My covenant upon your lips?'" (*Tehillim* 50:16)

(Imrei No'am)

Complete Teshuvah

At what point does a person attain complete *teshuvah*?

When a person is faced with the same situation in which he originally sinned, with the ability and the desire to repeat the sin, yet refrains from sinning on account of his *teshuvah*—this man is considered a complete *baal teshuvah*.

(Rambam, Hilchos Teshuvah 2:1)

Three Levels of Teshuvah

"Remember your Creator in the days of your youth, before those days of sorrow come and those years when you will say, 'I have no pleasure in them.'" (*Koheles* 12:1) The greatest level of *teshuvah* is when one repents when he is in his youth—when he is still capable of sinning, yet refrains from doing so.

If one does not do *teshuvah* until he is old and lacks the ability to do what he used to do, he is still considered a *baal teshuvah,* but his repentance is not on as high a level.

Even if he transgressed his entire life, repenting only on his deathbed and dying in *teshuvah,* all his sins are forgiven, as the verse continues, "Before the sun, the light, the moon, and the stars grow dark, and the clouds come back after the rain" (*Koheles* 12:2)—which refers to the day of death. If one remembers the Creator, repenting before he dies, he is forgiven.

(Rambam, Hilchos Teshuvah 2:1)

The later authorities conclude that there are three types of *teshuvah*. The preferred *teshuvah* is that of a young person in possession of his youthful prowess, who is capable of doing the same transgression. Yet, when the opportunity presents itself, he resists temptation because of his *teshuvah*. The Rambam calls him the true *baal teshuvah*. His *teshuvah* is not only a pious resolve, but confirmed by his action of turning away from sinning.

The second type of *teshuvah* is that of a person who repents at an advanced age, when his physical strength has waned. Intellectually he is doing *teshuvah*, but the reason he refrains from sinning is not because of *teshuvah*, but because he lacks the energy to transgress. Although his *teshuvah* is not ideal, it is accepted, and he is considered a *baal teshuvah*.

The third category of *teshuvah* is that of a person lying on his deathbed. The Rambam says that Hashem forgives all his sins, and he will not be punished for his wrongdoing. However, the Rambam does not call him a *baal teshuvah*, because he does not possess the merits of a *baal teshuvah*.

The first two *baalei teshuvah* have the merit inherent in *teshuvah*—the power of bringing a person closer to Hashem, as it says, "Return, Yisrael, unto Hashem your G-d" (*Hoshea* 14:2) and "If you repent, O Yisrael—the word of Hashem—you will return to Me." (*Yirmeyah* 4:1) A person who repents on his deathbed does not have this merit, although his sins are forgiven.

(Liteshuvas Hashanah al HaRambam 2:5)

Repent One Day Before You Die

The Gemara in *Shabbos* 153b relates that R' Eliezer said: Repent one day before you die. R' Eliezer's students asked him: Does anyone know on what day he will die? How can one do *teshuvah* the day before? Replied R' Eliezer: Therefore he should repent today, since he might die tomorrow. That way he will spend his whole life in *teshuvah*.

(Shabbos 153b)

Teshuvah for the First Sin

Rabbi Elimelech of Lizhensk said: A person should do *teshuvah* for the first sin he committed as a child. For the Sages tell us that "one sin leads to another sin." (*Avos* 4:2) The sin one does today was sparked by an earlier sin, which in turn was caused by a previous sin, so all sins a person commits originated with a childhood transgression.

This thought is alluded to in the verse, "Return, Yisrael, unto Hashem your G-d, for you have stumbled in your sin." (*Hoshea* 14:2). How is it possible that *Klal Yisrael,* the children of G-d, should transgress? For they have stumbled in their very first sin as children. Though committed unintentionally, this sin led to the next and to the one after that.

(Divrei Chaim)

Required for All

Many people mistakenly think that they have no reason to repent. Considering themselves paragons of virtue and piety, they insist, "We *daven* with a *minyan* every day, put on *tefillin,* keep Shabbos, recite *birkas hamazon* after meals, give *tzedakah,* and are careful to eat only strictly kosher food; why, we are truly *tzaddikim! Teshuvah* is meant for people who desecrate the Shabbos, eat non-kosher food, and violate every command of the Torah."

Such self-righteous people don't realize that there are multitudes of sins for which one has to do *teshuvah.* When the rabbi announces a lecture of *mussar* and reproof, they don't show up; *mussar* is not for them. But they are mistaken! They perform the *mitzvos* routinely, copying the things their parents did, or doing the *mitzvos* to gain recognition and respect, but not for the sake of honoring Hashem. For that alone they should do *teshuvah.*

And what about the grave sin of *bittul Torah*, neglecting Torah study? And let's not forget the sin of *lashon hara*, talebearing, gossip and slander.

Even if one is innocent of all these sins, he still has to do *teshuvah*, as the Rambam says: Do not think that *teshuvah* applies only to sins involving actions, such as immorality, robbery, and theft. Just as one must repent of these wrongdoings, so must one identify any bad character traits he may have, repenting of such vices as anger, envy, hatred, mockery, yearning for money or honor, and so on. These negative traits require *teshuvah* too. In fact, these vices are worse than sins involving action, for it is extremely difficult for a person addicted to these bad traits to break away from them. Concerning this it says, "Let the wicked one forsake his way and the corrupt man his thoughts." (*Yeshayah* 55:7)

Who can say that he is innocent of all these negative character traits? Who can claim that only others need to repent?

(Ohr HaTeshuvah)

Overlooked Sins

It may happen that a person transgresses all the days of his life without knowing! Many are not aware of the importance of praying with concentration, and refraining from talking during services. They are unaware that one should give *tzedakah* to a deserving poor man, not harden one's heart and shut one's hand or speak harshly to the poor. No one ever told them that one should not utter G-d's name in an unclean place, or with unwashed hands. They never heard of the many details of the laws of Shabbos; and many people inadvertently stumble on these matters.

(Orechos Tzaddikim, Gate of Teshuvah)

There are five transgressions of which a person is not likely to repent, since most people regard these matters lightly:

- One who eats a meal where the host has not prepared enough food for him, but invites him because he feels uncomfortable turning him away. This is a "semblance of theft." The person who ate from this meal does not realize that he sinned, for he will tell himself, "I ate only with his permission!"

- One who makes use of a security taken from a poor man, which is usually his ax or plow. One may think that these objects do not lose their value if they are used, and rationalize, "Its value did not decrease by using it, so I have not stolen anything from him."

- One who looks at a woman who is forbidden to him. He thinks it does not matter—"Did I come in contact with her?" He does not realize that gazing at women is a great sin, for it leads to immorality, as it says, "Do not stray after your heart and eyes." (*Bamidbar* 15:39)

- One who gloats over his neighbor's shame, comparing his good deeds and wisdom to that of his neighbor. He thinks he has done nothing wrong—since his neighbor was not present, he was not humiliated.

- One who suspects an innocent person. He will think, "I have not sinned. After all, what harm have I done him?" He does not realize that it is a sin to consider an innocent person a transgressor.

(Rambam, Hilchos Teshuvah 4:4)

Six Ways to Obtain Forgiveness

The Gemara says:

- He who answers *Amein yehei shemei rabba* wholeheartedly—
  Hashem forgives all his sins.

- He who keeps the Shabbos, even if he worshipped idols, as the
  people did in the generation of Enosh—Hashem forgives him.

- If a person recites the *Shirah* (the Song of the Sea) in the daily
  tefillah with a joyous feeling, as if he himself were crossing the
  Red Sea—Hashem will forgive his transgressions.

- If a person acts with forbearance, not responding to taunts and
  insults—Hashem forgives his transgressions.

- If a person goes into seclusion, directing his thoughts to
  Hashem in an effort to come closer to Him—Hashem
  responds by coming nearer to him. *(as heard by Rabbi Dovid
  Dov Meisels from his Rebbe, the saintly Rabbi Yosef Sanis zt"l)*

- If a person listens intently to words of *mussar* and reproof,
  Hashem will overlook his failings.

(Chareidim, Mitzvas HaTeshuvah 7)

Humiliating Others

The Mishnah (*Avos* 3:11) says that one who humiliates his fellow
in public has no share in the World to Come. Comments Rabbeinu
Yonah: But when it comes to a murderer, the Sages do not say that he
forfeits his share in the World to Come. Why is this so?

Not realizing the gravity of his sin, one who humiliates his fellow
feels no remorse over his misdeed. By contrast, a murderer, aware of
the enormity of his crime, eventually will be contrite and deeply
regret his sin. For this reason, one who humiliated his fellow will not
do *teshuvah*. As a result, he will have no share in the World to Come.

How appalling! Being ignorant of the seriousness of a transgression brings in its wake the loss of one's share in the World to Come. What can be worse than that?

Tosafos in *Sotah* 11b comments that shaming one's fellow is as grave a transgression as the three cardinal sins for which one must offer his life rather than transgress—murder, idolatry, and immorality. The *P'ri Megadim* says that by humiliating one's fellow, one heaps guilt on his ancestors as far back as the generation that departed Egypt.

(P'ri Megadim, Orach Chaim, 284)

Shaming a person just once in a lifetime incurs a harsh punishment. Imagine the consequences if one humiliated another several times—not to mention if one humiliated many people several times!

With that in mind, the *navi* says, "Behold, I will bring you to judgment for saying, 'I have not sinned.'" (*Yirmeyah* 2:35)

(Ohr Yechezkel)

Yom Kippur Atones

Now that the *Beis Hamikdash* is not standing, and there is no altar for atonement, we have nothing to help us except *teshuvah*. *Teshuvah* makes amends for all our sins. In fact, no mention is made of the wickedness of a person who, though wicked his whole life, repented in his final moments. As it says, "The wickedness of the wicked will not cause him to stumble when he turns back from his wickedness." (*Yechezkel* 33:12)

The day of Yom Kippur itself atones for those who repent, as it says, "This day will bring about atonement for you." (*Vayikra* 16:30)

Although *teshuvah* makes amends for all sins and the day of Yom Kippur brings about atonement, there are different degrees of sin, and accordingly, different stages of atonement. Some sins can be rectified at once, while others need the passage of time. What are these degrees of sin?

If a person violates a positive commandment which is not punishable by *kareis*, and he repents, he is forgiven immediately.

If a person violates a negative commandment which is not punishable by *kareis* or the death penalty, and repents, the *teshuvah* allows his judgment to remain pending until Yom Kippur, and Yom Kippur itself atones for the sin.

If he violates a commandment that is punishable by *kareis* or death and repents, his judgment is left pending through Yom Kippur, and suffering is brought on him to complete the atonement. Yom Kippur is not enough for complete atonement—he will not be completely forgiven until he undergoes suffering.

This applies to transgressions which do not involve desecration of G-d's name. However, a person who desecrated G-d's name may repent, have Yom Kippur be part of his *teshuvah*, and undergo suffering, yet he will not be granted complete atonement until he dies. For it says, "The Lord of Hosts revealed Himself to my ears: 'This iniquity shall never be atoned until you die.'" (*Yeshayah* 22:14)

(Rambam, Hilchos Teshuvah 5:3-4)

Healing For Our Sins

In Castilia, Spain, a nobleman out on a fox hunt was bitten by a fox. The next morning, the seemingly harmless small wound caused the leg to swell and turn an ugly purple color. The nobleman's doctors treated the wound, prescribing the latest expensive medicines, but it was to no avail. With the infection spreading rapidly, they gave up hope.

Lying on his deathbed, surrounded by his loved ones, the nobleman was crying bitterly. An Arab servant suddenly entered the room. After surveying the tragic scene, he said, "Don't worry. I know of some herbs growing out in the woods which will cure the leg overnight."

A short time later the Arab returned with the herbs. After grinding them up, he made a poultice which he applied to the festering wound. By the next day, the nobleman felt much better, and he soon fully recovered. Amazed at the remarkable cure, the doctors praised G-d for creating such marvelous plants.

When searching for a cure, a gravely ill person will consult the greatest specialists, who often prescribe pills and medications that are extremely costly. But he overlooks the natural remedies of extracts of herbs and roots, which are perhaps more effective. Not only are they abundantly available, they are usually inexpensive—and sometimes they can be picked in the fields, free of charge!

We should likewise go out into the "field" of Torah knowledge and gather the wisdom of the Gemara, which is guaranteed to bring healing to the ailing soul. This natural remedy is readily available, highly effective, and free of charge.

(Rabbi Elazar Azkari, Chareidim)

Chapter Twenty Three

Viduy-
Confessional Prayer

Confessing One's Sins

It is a Torah command to confess one's sins, declaring one's remorse and repentance. When confessing his sins, a person must verbally articulate the transgression he committed.

The *mitzvah* of *Viduy* is applicable at all times and all places, to men, women, and children, for a person does not know the hour of his passing, as the Gemara says, "Repent today, for tomorrow you may die." (*Shabbos* 155a)

The best time for doing *teshuvah* is during the ten days between Rosh Hashanah and Yom Kippur. G-d then eagerly anticipates the *teshuvah* of *Klal Yisrael*, especially on Yom Kippur, the day selected for *teshuvah* and atonement. Failure to do *teshuvah* on Yom Kippur means neglecting a positive *mitzvah* of the Torah.

But *teshuvah* is effective only for sins against G-d, such as eating non-kosher food, desecrating the Shabbos, or neglecting to perform a positive commandment, such as putting on *tefillin* or shaking the *lulav* on Sukkos. *Teshuvah* does not atone for transgressions against another person, such as humiliating, hurting, offending him, or destroying or stealing someone's property, unless one makes restitution and appeases the person he has wronged.

(Chinuch 364)

Confessing All Sins

During the time of the Rambam, there was a distinguished person who absolutely refused to recite the *Viduy*. He insisted that he had not committed any of the sins mentioned in the confessional prayer. "How can I confess to something I did not do?" he declared. "I would be telling a lie!"

When the Rambam heard about it, he invited the man to have a talk with him.

"Every *mitzvah* has many branches and subdivisions," the Rambam explained. "Take, for example, the law of, 'Do not steal.' There are many deeds forbidden under that law. You may not take something just to tease or annoy a person, even if you fully intend to return it to him. You also may not steal back an object a thief has pilfered from you. Another subdivision of 'Do not steal' is 'stealing someone's belief,' which means deceiving him by uttering even one misleading word.

"Or take the prohibition of 'Do not lie to one another.' This includes much more than not telling a falsehood. The Gemara relates that Rav Safra had an article for sale. A buyer came and made him an offer. Since Rav Safra was reciting the *Shema*, he did not answer. Thinking that Rav Safra wanted a higher price, the buyer raised his bid. When Rav Safra ended the *Shema*, he told the buyer, 'You can have the article for your original lower bid, for I was ready to accept it.'"

Continued the Rambam, "If you reflect on the far reaching implications of every *mitzvah*, you will realize that you have violated each and every one of the sins listed in the *Viduy*.

"But let me tell you, your greatest sin is thinking that you are faultless and did not transgress at all!"

(Sefer Toledos Adam)

The Kabbalists say that a person must confess all the sins listed in the Viduy, even if he is convinced that he is not guilty of certain sins. Perhaps he committed these sins in a previous existence, and his soul was reincarnated in order to atone for those failings. In addition, since all Jews are responsible for one another, everyone is accountable for the sins of his fellow-Jew. Therefore, everyone has to confess all the sins in the Viduy, even if he himself has not transgressed all of them.

A Great Mitzvah

When visiting a gravely ill person, it is a great *mitzvah* to persuade him to recite the *Viduy*. You should tell him, "Many sick people recited the *Viduy* and recovered. They are alive and well today. In the merit of saying *Viduy* Hashem will help you get well and live to a ripe old age."

If the sick person is unable to utter the words of the *Viduy*, he should confess in his heart. The Ramban composed the following short version of the *Viduy* for the benefit of the gravely ill:

"Blessed are You Hashem, my G-d and the G-d of my forefathers. My recovery is in Your hands, and my life is in Your hands. May it be Your will to heal me and bring me complete recovery. If, G-d forbid, I should die, may my death atone for all my errors and willful sins. May You grant me a share in *Gan Eden*, permit me to enter the World to Come and share in the infinite good that is set aside for the *tzaddikim* in *Gan Eden*."

(Chinuch 364)

How Is Viduy Effective?

The Gemara in *Kiddushin* 61a says, "Words cannot annul action, [only an action can undo an action]." Asks the *Chida:* In that case, how can reciting *Viduy* annul a person's sinful actions?

Resh Lakish says, "A person does not commit a transgression unless a spirit of foolishness enters into him." (*Sotah* 3a) By doing *teshuvah,* one expels the spirit of foolishness and acquires a new personality. Acquiring a new personality is considered an action, for his body is undergoing a drastic change. This action, in conjunction with the *Viduy,* has the power to annul the sins a person has committed.

(Midbar Kedeimos, Teshuvah 21)

When a person commits a transgression, the *kedushah* that is in him departs, and the Satan gains control over him. In *Tehillim* such a person is described as a *beheimah,* an animal: "Man is glorious [if he behaves righteously], but if he does not understand, he is likened to a dumb animal." (*Tehillim* 49:21) When a person does *teshuvah* he drives away the Satan that controls him and causes *kedushah* to enter. As a result, he is transformed from a *beheimah* to an *adam* (human). The change which was brought about by *teshuvah* surely counts as an action. Consequently, the action generated by *teshuvah* has the capacity to annul the action of his sin.

(B'nei Yissoschor)

Alef-Beis Order

Asked the Gerer Rebbe: Why are the sins in the *Viduy* listed in the order of the *alef-beis?* It would take a person all day if he were to enumerate all his sins. Arranging the sins according to the *alef-beis* assures us that there is an end to them.

(Chiddushei Harim)

A queen was in the habit of gossiping and telling bad tales about her husband, the king. Angry, the king banished her from the palace, sending her into exile in a distant province to live among crude peasants. Lamenting her tragic fate, the queen deeply regretted offending the king. In an attempt to pacify him, she went to the palace, taking along her violin. Appearing before the king, she performed the songs that were played at their wedding. She cried while playing, asking him to forgive and forget, pleading with him to make up with her. Recalling the love he once had for her, the king pardoned her and reinstated her as his queen.

Hashem, our King, married *Klal Yisrael* at the Giving of the Torah. We transgressed and were sent into exile. Recalling the glorious times when the *Beis Hamikdash* was standing, we take our violin in hand and play the music that was heard at our wedding at *Har Sinai*: the symphony of the *alef-beis*, the letters with which the Torah is written.

When *Klal Yisrael* recites the *Viduy* in the order of the *alef-beis*, when they say *Al Cheit* and *Ashamnu bagadnu*, they pray that Hashem should have mercy—remember the love of our wedding day at Sinai, and redeem us from our *galus*.

(Tiferes Uziel, Yom Kippur)

Beating the Heart

When reciting the *Viduy* it is customary to beat the heart. In this way our limbs demonstrate that they do not agree with the dictates of the heart, which is trying to infuse them with improper desires.

Why do we beat with the hand? The hand is the limb that carries out most of the transgressions. It beats the heart on behalf of the other limbs, scolding it for causing them to act sinfully.

There are people who absentmindedly beat their breasts when saying the *Viduy* without internalizing what they are saying. Their prayers may be compared to a scarecrow that is meant to chase away harmful birds. Once the birds realize that the scarecrow is a just a lifeless contraption, they swoop down to feast on the seeds in the garden.

Reciting the *Viduy* is meant to drive away the *yetzer hara*. Thinking that a person is sincerely remorseful when saying the *Viduy*, the *yetzer hara* backs off. But when it sees that the breast-beating is only an empty gesture, it comes back with a vengeance, strongly enticing the person to stray and transgress.

This may be the intent of the confession, "For the sin we have sinned before You through speaking with the mouth," referring to the sin of saying *Viduy* only with our mouths, not with our hearts.

(Yismach Moshe)

Bending Over

It is customary to bend forward slightly when saying the *Viduy*. The *Shelah* explains that this custom is based on the Gemara which says that if one does not bow down when saying *Modim* in the *Shemoneh Esrei*, his spine will become curved like a snake.

When we say *Viduy*, we confess our sins which originate with the primeval Serpent—the Satan. We incline our backs like a snake, to rectify the sins that were prompted by the Serpent, Satan, and the *yetzer hara*.

(Elef Hamagein 607:8)

Lashon Hara

In the *Viduy* we ask forgiveness, "For the sin that we have sinned through evil talk."

The saintly *Chafetz Chaim* remarked, "With the approach of the *Yomim Noraim*, people resort to all kinds of expedients and practices to be inscribed for a good year. They go to *Tashlich*, they perform the *kaparos* ritual, and so on. Why don't they also think of the simple remedy of not listening to *lashon hara*, gossip and talebearing? For in return, the Heavenly Judge will turn a deaf ear to Satan's accusations and grant them a good year."

Sinning With the Lips

In the *Al Cheit* we confess "the sin we have sinned with the utterance of the lips."

> *Someone soiled the royal palace and was judged to receive a harsh punishment. Feeling sorry for him, the king was lenient and told him to just clean up the mess. If that person neglects to do so, his punishment will be all the more severe, for he was given a chance to repair the damage he had done—and he ignored it.*

Hashem offers us the opportunity to rectify our shortcomings. If we fail to take advantage of that, we will be punished, not only for our imperfections but also for disregarding the opportunity to do *teshuvah* and atone for our faults. We ask forgiveness "for the sin that we have sinned before You with the utterance of the lips"—the sin of saying the *Viduy* merely with our lips, and not with our hearts.

(Divrei Yoel, Leil Yom Kippur)

Unwarranted Hatred

In the *Viduy* we ask forgiveness "for the sin of baseless hatred."

The *Chafetz Chaim* writes: If a person is beating someone else's child for no reason, the child's father will surely be furious, and indignantly berate that person for abusing his innocent child.

The *Chafetz Chaim* continues, "I cannot understand it. Our Sages say that as punishment for baseless hatred, one's children die at a young age. Then how is it that this compassionate father could be so heartless toward his children, causing them to die, G-d forbid, by harboring baseless hatred against others?"

Sinning With the Yetzer Hara

In one of the *Al Cheit* confessions we ask G-d to pardon us "for the sin we have sinned before You with the *yetzer hara*, the evil impulse."

Said Rabbi Pinchas Horowitz, the *Baal Haflaah*: We recite a total of fifty-three *Al Cheit* confessions of various sins. Could it be that only one of these was prompted by the *yetzer hara*? What, then, provoked the other fifty-two sins?

In fact, most of our sins are induced by the *yetzer hatov*, our good inclination. How can this be? Because we do not have the slightest inkling that our evil tendency is causing our sins. Most of the time we think that our actions are virtuous, and that we are motivated by noble impulses. Our consciences our clear. It is rarely that we realize that it was our *yetzer hara* that seduced us to sin.

(Shemen Hatov)

The Sin of Light-Headedness

In the *Al Cheit* we ask forgiveness for the "sin of light-headedness."

Human nature is made up of two opposing elements. Man's intellect urges him to do G-d's will, while his base instincts drive him to fulfill his physical desires. If he allows his base instincts to gain the upper hand, he is guilty of *kalus rosh*, "light-headedness."

Light-headedness is forbidden even when doing the *mitzvah* of rejoicing with a bride and groom. Boisterousness, raucous behavior, and excessive hilarity should be avoided.

The Sages advise, "Your teeth and your mouth should not put you to shame. Your lips should not embarrass you. Don't eat while standing; don't lick your fingers; don't be boastful in front of others; don't be overly joyous; don't overindulge in pleasures; sleep in moderation; know the person with whom you converse, with whom you sit, and with whom you do business. Be refined when eating and drinking, give in to others   "

Acting contrary to these rules is a form of *kalus rosh*, lightheadedness, for which we ask G-d's forgiveness.

Kareis and Death Penalty by the Heavenly Court

In the *Al Cheit* we ask forgiveness "for the sins for which we incur the death penalty at the hands of the Heavenly Court, and for sins for which we incur *kareis* (spiritual excision, premature death) and childlessness."

The Mishnah in *meseches Kerisos* lists thirty-six transgression for which a person incurs *kareis*, including having incestuous relations, eating *chametz* on Pesach, eating or working on Yom Kippur, failing to offer the *korban Pesach*, and failing to undergo *milah*.

The difference between *kareis* and death at the hands of the Heavenly Court is that the soul of one who incurs *kareis* is punished also after his death if he did not do *teshuvah*, which is not the case with *misah bidei Shamayim*.

According to Rashi, *kareis* consists of two punishments: the sinner dies prematurely, and his children also die. With *misah bidei Shamayim*, the sinner dies, but not his children.

The Four Death Penalties

In the *Al Cheit* we ask forgiveness "for the sins for which we incur the four death penalties of the human court: Stoning, burning, beheading, and strangling." What are the sins for which the four death penalties are applied?

Stoning is the punishment for desecrating the Shabbos, cursing one's father or mother, or idol worship.

Burning is the punishment for committing incest with one's daughter.

Beheading is the punishment for committing murder.

Strangling is the punishment for a false prophet and other transgressions.

> *The Gemara says that although there is no longer a Sanhedrin, the four death penalties of the human court have not ceased. The beis din cannot enforce the death penalty; instead, G-d enforces it through comparable forms of death. For example, someone who would have been sentenced to death by stoning will either fall off a roof, or a wild beast will trample him. Someone who would have been sentenced to burning will be consumed by fire or bitten by a snake. Someone who would have been sentenced to beheading is either arrested by the Roman government and executed, or robbers attack and kill him. Someone who would have been sentenced to choking is drowned in a river or dies from the croup.*

> *(Kesubos 30b)*

Chapter Twenty Four

The Yom Kippur Service in the Beis Hamikdash

Isolation

Seven days before Yom Kippur, the *Kohen Gadol* was removed from his house and isolated in the *Palhedrin* chamber. This was done to allow him to concentrate on the service he was to perform on Yom Kippur. He was to divest himself of all mundane concerns, preparing and purifying himself for the holy task at hand.

(Yoma 2a)

Sprinkling the Kohen Gadol

Twice during these seven days—on the third and the seventh day, which is *erev* Yom Kippur—the *Kohen Gadol* was sprinkled with some of the ashes of the red cow, out of concern that he may have become defiled by unwittingly touching a corpse.

If the third or seventh day fell on a Shabbos, the sprinkling of ashes was postponed.

(Tiferes Yisrael)

Rehearsing the Avodah

Throughout these seven days, the *Kohen Gadol* was tutored in the various services, in order to familiarize him with the duties he had to perform. He threw the blood of the sacrifice on the Altar, burned the incense, prepared the lamps of the Menorah, and burned the limbs of the *tamid* offering on the Altar.

Sages of the Sanhedrin read to him and taught him the rituals of the Yom Kippur service and the order in which they had to be performed. Then they said to him, "Honorable *Kohen Gadol*, please read it out loud. Perhaps you have forgotten something, or perhaps you never learned it."

On the morning of *erev* Yom Kippur they stood with him at the Eastern Gate, where a line of bulls, rams, and sheep passed before him, making sure that he recognized them and was proficient in performing the service.

(Rambam, Avodas Yom HaKippurim)

The First and Second Beis Hamikdash

The first *Beis Hamikdash* stood for 410 years, and only eighteen *Kohanim Gedolim* officiated during that period. By contrast, during the era of the second *Beis Hamikdash*, which lasted for 420 years, there were more than three hundred *Kohanim Gedolim*. Since during this time the office of the *Kohen Gadol* became corrupt and was sold to the highest bidder, the *Kohanim Gedolim* were changed every year. To them applied the verse, "The years of the wicked will be shortened." (*Mishlei* 10:27)

(Yoma 9a)

The Garments of the Kohen Gadol

The common *kohen* wore four garments: a tunic, pants, a hat, and a belt. The four garments were made of white linen, woven of six-fold threads. Only the belt was embroidered with wool.

The *Kohen Gadol* wore eight golden garments, woven with fine golden threads. Four of these were the same as the garments of a common *kohen*. In addition, he wore the robe, the *efod*, the breastplate, and the forehead plate. The *Kohen Gadol* wore an embroidered belt, just like the common *kohen's* belt. The hat worn by the *Kohen Gadol* was the same as the hat worn by the common *kohen,* but it was wound differently: the *Kohen Gadol* wound a long scarf around his head, as one bandages an injury, while the common *kohen* wound a shorter scarf into a cone-shaped hat.

On Yom Kippur, the *Kohen Gadol* wore four white garments: the tunic, pants, belt, and the hat. All four white garments were linen, made with six-fold threads. The *Kohen Gadol* had two other tunics on Yom Kippur—one which he wore in the morning, the other in the afternoon [for the sole purpose of removing the ladle and coal shovel from the Holy of Holies]. Together, both garments were worth thirty *maneh,* paid out of the Temple treasury. If he wanted to add to them, he had to sanctify the additional material, after which he could make the tunic with it.

(Rambam, Hilchos Beis Habechirah)

Sanctified Garments

Throughout the year, the *Kohen Gadol* performed the service in the *Beis Hamikdash* wearing the eight garments. If one of the garments was missing, his service was invalid. The garments sanctified the *Kohen Gadol,* empowering him to do the *avodah.* Unless he wore all eight garments, he was not sanctified. Doing the *avodah* without wearing all eight garments made him liable to the death penalty.

(Ralbag)

Garments Bring Atonement

The Gemara says that just as sacrifices bring atonement, so do the priestly garments. The tunic gains atonement for bloodshed; the pants for incest; the hat for arrogance; the belt for sinful thoughts; the breastplate for errors in legal decisions; the *efod* for idolatry; the robe for slander; the golden forehead plate for brazen deeds.

(Arachin 16a)

Morning Incense

After the daily *tamid* offering, the *Kohen Gadol* would enter the Sanctuary to burn the daily incense of the morning on the golden Incense Altar. With a golden shovel he scooped up some coals from the top of the outer Altar. Carrying a spoonful of incense, he entered the Sanctuary, spread the coals on the Incense Altar, and then poured the incense on the burning coals. He stayed there until the Sanctuary was filled with smoke, after which he bowed down and left. Miraculously, the wind never dispersed the cloud of smoke which rose up, straight as a cedar tree.

(Yoma 52b)

The Accuser May Not Defend

The *Kohen Gadol* performed the *avodah* of Yom Kippur wearing the four white linen garments—pants, a tunic, a hat, and a belt—rather than the eight golden garments he wore all year.

Explaining why the *Kohen Gadol* did not wear the eight golden garments, the Gemara says, "An accuser may not act as a defender." Gold is considered the accuser in reference to the golden calf, which *Klal Yisroel* made in the desert. It would not be proper for the *Kohen Gadol* to enter the Holy of Holies, asking forgiveness, while wearing garments that recall the sin of the golden calf.

(Rosh Hashanah 26a)

The First Confession

The *Kohen Gadol* brought a sin offering to atone for himself and his family. He walked over to the bull, which was standing between the Entrance Hall of the Sanctuary and the Altar. Leaning both his hands on the head of the bull, he made the following confession:

"I beg of You, Hashem, forgive now the iniquities, willful sins, and errors, for I have been iniquitous, sinned willfully, and erred before You, I and my family. As is written in the Torah of Your servant Moshe, 'For on this day you shall have all your sins atoned, so that you will be cleansed. Before Hashem you will be cleansed of all your sins.'" (*Vayikra* 16:30)

Prostration

Ten times during the *Viduy*, the *Kohen Gadol* pronounced the Ineffable Name of Hashem. This corresponds with the ten *Sefiros* (Divine emanations)—the vessels that connect the loftiest level of spirituality and *kedushah* to the realm of the physical world. The *Kohen Gadol's* voice grew progressively louder with each mention of Hashem's name. By the tenth time, his voice could be heard as far away as Yericho.

(*Maharsha on Yoma 39b, s.v. uk'var amar*)

The Arizal says that the *Kohen Gadol* did not actually utter Hashem's Ineffable Name. He merely opened his mouth, and the Ineffable Name emanated from him; it was the *Shechinah* speaking through his mouth.

When all the people merited to hear the voice of the *Shechinah*, they sensed Hashem's Presence. Overcome with awe, they prostrated themselves out of deep veneration of Hashem.

(*Avodas Yisrael*)

Miracles in the Beis Hamikdash

The Mishnah (*Avos* 5:5) lists ten miracles that happened in the *Beis Hamikdash*, one of which was that the people stood crowded together, yet prostrated themselves in ample space. Though there was not even enough room to stand up, each person had ample room to prostrate himself and confess his sins on Yom Kippur. The miracle was performed so no one could hear his neighbor confess his sins.

The *Chasam Sofer* notes that a similar miracle happened in the Holy of Holies, where the Ark did not take up any space. (*Yoma* 21a) When the people found themselves crowded together, they began to wonder, "Why can't the same miracle happen to us? Evidently, we are not worthy of it, for we did not cleanse ourselves sufficiently from our sins." They wholeheartedly confessed their sins—and miraculously, there was suddenly enough room for everyone.

(Chasam Sofer)

Drawing the Lots

After the first confession, the *Kohen Gadol* proceeded to draw the lots for the two goats. The lottery box was set up on the east side of the Courtyard. The two goats were placed facing west toward the Sanctuary. The *Kohen Gadol* came with the deputy *Kohen Gadol* standing at his right, and the head of the *beis av* at his left. The two goats were standing in front of him, one at his right, the other at his left.

The two lots had to be identical. One could not be bigger than the other; neither could one be made of silver, with the other of gold. The lots were made of wood, but during the second *Beis Hamikdash*, Ben Gamla made them of gold, and the Sages praised him for it.

The lots were placed in a box that allowed no more than two hands to be inserted in its opening, to prevent the *Kohen Gadol* from taking one lot intentionally. It was considered a good omen if the lot marked "for Hashem" came up in his right hand. While the lots were identical, it was possible to discern the engraved words by touch.

(Yoma 39a, Rashi)

Tosafos Yeshanim says that in his eagerness to have the lot marked "for Hashem" come up in his right hand, the Kohen Gadol may forget to draw lots. Instead, he might simply pick up the desired lot with his right hand without inserting the two lots in the lottery box.

There is a profound lesson in this. If a person has a strong desire to do something that is forbidden, his subconscious mind will make him forget that he is doing something wrong. The Sages were not afraid that the Kohen Gadol would intentionally violate the law, omitting the drawing of the lots. They did have misgivings that his ardent wish would override his sense of duty, causing him to skip the drawing of the lots.

A strong desire to attain a goal will blind a person's eyes, making even a Kohen Gadol stray from the right path. May Hashem help us follow the path of righteousness.

(Divrei Yoel, Motza'ei Yom Kippur)

The *Kohen Gadol* hastily shook the lottery box, pulled out the two lots for the two goats and opened his hands. If the lot marked "for Hashem" came up in his right hand, the deputy *Kohen Gadol* said, "Honorable *Kohen Gadol*, please raise your right hand." If it came up in his left hand, the head of the *beis av* said, "Honorable *Kohen Gadol*, please raise your left hand." The *Kohen Gadol* then placed the lots on the two goats, the lot in his right hand on the goat on his right, calling out in a loud voice, "A sin offering for Hashem!" The lot in his left hand he placed on the goat on his left without calling out, "This one is for Azazel."

(Me'iri Yoma 31a)

During the forty years that Shimon Hatzaddik served as Kohen Gadol, whenever he drew the lots for the goat on Yom Kippur, the lot inscribed "for Hashem" always came up in his right hand. This was a sign of Hashem's favor. After his death, sometimes it would come up in the Kohen Gadol's right hand, sometimes in his left. The last forty years before the destruction of the Beis Hamikdash, the lot marked "for Hashem" never came up in the Kohen Gadol's right hand.

(Yoma 39a,b)

The Strip of Red Wool

The *Kohen Gadol* tied a strip of red wool to the head of the goat that was to be sent to Azazel. It stood at the east gate of the Courtyard, facing its destination. He then tied a strip around the neck of the goat that was to be slaughtered, to prevent any confusion between the goats.

(Ritva)

The red wool was used to allude to the verse, "If your sins are like scarlet, they will turn snow white; if they have become red as crimson, they will become white as wool." (*Yeshayah* 1:18)

(Tosafos Yeshanim, Yoma 42, s.v. beshaar)

The Gemara Yerushalmi relates that originally everyone would tie a red ribbon to the windows of their homes. Some ribbons turned white, while the ribbons in the windows of sinners remained red, which was a source of great embarrassment for them. It was then decided to tie the red ribbon to the opening of the Sanctuary. For many years, it turned white, but there were years when it remained red, to the deep sorrow of the people.

(Yerushalmi Yoma 6:5)

The strip of red wool was tied to the outside of the entrance of the *ulam*, the hall leading to the interior of the *Beis Hamikdash*. When it turned white, the people rejoiced. But if it did not turn white, the people were sad and ashamed.

The method was changed, and the thread was tied to the inside of the entrance of the *ulam*. This was to prevent the people from seeing it. But they managed to peek inside.

Finally, it was changed again. The man who led the goat into the wilderness divided the strip of red wool, tying one half to the rock, the other half between its horns.

What was the purpose of dividing the strip? If the whole strip was tied to the rock, and it turned white before the goat was hurled down, the man might be so happy with the sign of forgiveness that he would forget to push the goat down, neglecting to fulfill the *mitzvah*. Why didn't he tie the whole strip to the horns of the goat? Occasionally, when the goat fell, the position of its head would make it impossible to see the strip, and there would be no way to tell if it changed color. It was therefore divided and tied in both places. The divided thread on the rock did not change color until the goal was hurled down.

(Yoma 67a)

Satan's Gift

A king appointed a minister of justice to enforce the laws of the land. A heartless man, the minister showed mercy to no one. Once a year, on judgment day, the minister had to appear before the king to report on all the crimes and misdemeanors that had been committed over the course of the year. The king would fix the punishment to be meted out for each violation. The king also awarded generous grants to all the governors and administrators who capably ran the day-to-day affairs of the country.

One day, the king's closest friend and most trusted adviser was found to be involved in an unlawful activity. What did the king do?

He told his good friend to pay a fine to the royal treasury as punishment for his offense. On judgment day, as usual, the king distributed generous awards to all high government officials, except for the brutal minister of justice, who received nothing.

Ten days later, the king asked his discredited good friend to deliver a lavish gift to the unkind minister of justice. The king meant to appease him, so he would not denounce his good friend.

The king's friend entered the minister's office. The minister, who was aware of his wrongdoing, greeted him with a barrage of angry accusations and rebuke, showing him the indictment he had drawn up to present to the king. But when the friend handed him the king's magnificent gift, the minister's attitude underwent a profound change. When the friend told him that he had already paid a fine to the treasury, the minister smilingly tore up the indictment and withdrew the charges. Instead of harshly condemning him, he treated him kindly and graciously.

Hashem, the King of the universe, is the Master over the seventy nations of the world—the governors and administrators of the parable. The heartless minister of justice is Satan, and Judgment Day is Rosh Hashanah, when Hashem decides the fate of the nations of the world. But for His beloved Jewish people Hashem waits ten more days before passing final judgment.

What does Hashem do to prevent Satan from accusing *Klal Yisrael* on Rosh Hashanah? He grants gifts to all the nations of the world, pointedly overlooking Satan. Satan is kept waiting for ten days, until Yom Kippur.

On Yom Kippur, he receives his gift in the form of the goat that is sent to Azazel in the wilderness, the desolate home of ghosts and demons, the domain where Satan is king. This gift silences Satan. In fact, he now defends the Jews and speaks up for them, telling Hashen that the suffering they endured throughout the year is enough punishment for their failings. Listening to the good things Satan says about the Jewish people, Hashem forgives their transgressions, turning their sins into *mitzvos* and merits.

(Sefer Tz'ror Hamor)

Finding Klal Yisrael to be faultless, Satan approaches G-d and says: Ribbono shel Olam! Your nation Yisrael is like the angels in Heaven. Angels do not wear shoes; neither do the Jews on Yom Kippur. Angels do not eat or drink; neither do the Jews on Yom Kippur. Angels live in peace with each other; so do the Jews on Yom Kippur. Angels are free of sin; so are the Jews on Yom Kippur.

Listening to Satan the Accuser's defense of the Jewish people, Hashem happily forgives Klal Yisrael.

(Pirkei D'Rabbi Eliezer 46)

Slaughtering the Bull

The *Kohen Gadol* returned to the bull on which he had earlier confessed the sins of himself and his family. Now he confessed the sins of all the *kohanim*. Next, he slaughtered the bull. He received the blood in a basin and handed it to a *kohen*, who stirred it to prevent it from thickening.

(Rambam, Beis Habechirah)

The Incense Service

Having slaughtered the bull, the *Kohen Gadol* began the Incense Service by going up to the top of the Altar, where he scooped up some coals from the western side of the Altar. He descended and put the shovel down on the pavement stones of the Courtyard.

The *Kohen Gadol* was given a ladle and a vessel filled with the very finest incense. He scooped up the incense with his cupped hands—neither heaped nor leveled, but liberally measured, as much as his cupped hands would hold—and poured the incense into the ladle.

> *Carrying a sacred object in the left hand invalidates the service. Considering that the incense is the more important part of this mitzvah, why didn't the Kohen Gadol carry the coal shovel in his left hand and the ladle with the incense in his right hand? Since the shovel was heavy and hot from the burning coals, he could not carry it in his left hand all the way to the Ark. He had to hold the shovel in his stronger right hand and the lighter ladle with the incense in his left hand, as he passed through the Sanctuary to get to the Holy of Holies.*

Inside the Holy of Holies

The curtain that separated the Sanctuary from the Holy of Holies was held up by a clasp, so the *Kohen Gadol* could pass by and get to the Ark. When he reached the Ark, he placed the coal shovel between the two carrying poles of the Ark.

Since there was no Ark in the second *Beis Hamikdash* (it was hidden by King Yoshia, see *Yoma* 52b), the *Kohen Gadol* placed the shovel on the *Shesiah* stone, on the place where the Ark had stood.

(Rosh, Seder Haavodah)

After taking the incense from the ladle into his two cupped hands, he poured it onto the coals—without spilling a grain of incense. This was one of the most difficult rituals in the Sanctuary.

How did he accomplish it? With his fingertips or his teeth, the *Kohen Gadol* pushed back the ladle until the handle was secured firmly under his armpit. He tilted the ladle with his thumb, pouring all the incense into his cupped hands.

He piled the incense on the burning coals on the western side of the shovel, closer to the Ark and away from his face, so he would not get singed. He set down the coals in the Holy of Holies and *then* burned the incense, as opposed to the claim of the Sadducees that he was to put the incense on the coals outside the Holy of Holies.

The *Kohen Gadol* waited until the entire chamber was filled with smoke. Then he left, walking backward the way he came in, turning his face toward the place of the Ark as a sign of humility and fear of G-d.

The Kohen Gadol's Prayer

Standing in the Sanctuary, the *Kohen Gadol* said a short prayer. He kept his prayer short, concerned that the people would be afraid that he had died in the Holy of Holies.

"May it be Your will, Hashem our G-d, that if this year is destined to be a hot year, let it be a year rich in rain; may there not depart a ruler from Yehudah; may it be a year in which Your people Yisrael will not need to depend on one another for sustenance; and do not listen to the prayers of travelers who pray that it should not rain."

(Rambam, Avodas Yom Hakippurim)

Sprinkling the Blood

The *Kohen Gadol* took the basin with the blood of the bull which he had slaughtered earlier from the *kohen* who was stirring it to prevent it from congealing. He carried it into the Holy of Holies and sprinkled it eight times between the poles of the Ark. He then exited the Holy of Holies and put the basin down on a golden stand in the Sanctuary.

Next he left the Sanctuary and slaughtered the goat on which the lot "for Hashem" had fallen, receiving its blood in a basin. He carried it into the Holy of Holies and sprinkled the blood eight times between the poles of the Ark. He exited and placed the basin on a second golden stand in the Sanctuary.

Taking the bull's blood from the stand, the *Kohen Gadol* sprinkled it eight times at the curtain in front of the Ark. He put down the bull's blood, took the goat's blood and sprinkled it eight times at the curtain in front of the Ark.

He then emptied the remaining bull's blood into the basin with the rest of the goat's blood. He poured the mixture of blood into an empty basin, creating a perfect blend.

Sprinkling on the Golden Altar

Standing between the Golden Altar and the Menorah, the *Kohen Gadol* began to daub the mixture of blood with his finger on the corners of the Golden Altar. He started with the northeast corner, proceeded to the northwest corner, then onto the southwest corner, ending at the southeast corner. He applied the blood to each corner with an upward stroke, except for the last corner which was right in front of him. He applied the blood there from the top to the bottom to avoid soiling his garments, since an upward stroke might cause the blood to run down his hand and stain his garments.

(Rambam, Avodas Yom Hakippurim)

The *Kohen Gadol* was able to apply the blood to the four corners of the Altar without moving from his place. This was possible because the Golden Altar was only one cubit square.

(Rosh, Seder Haavodah)

He cleared away the coals and ashes of the daily incense on the Golden Altar. When its golden surface was exposed, he sprinkled the blood mixture seven times on the Altar's southeast corner, where he had applied the last daubing. He exited the Sanctuary and poured the remaining blood on the western base of the outer Altar.

(Kesef Mishneh, ch. 4)

The Goat Sent to Azazel

The *Kohen Gadol* went to the Nicanor Gate, where the goat that was to be sent away to Azazel was standing. He leaned both his hands on it and confessed:

"I beg of You, Hashem! Your nation, the family of Yisrael, has been iniquitous, sinned willfully and erred before You. I pray with Your name! Forgive now the iniquities, willful sins and errors, for Your people, the family of Yisrael, has been iniquitous and erred before You, as it says in the Torah of Your servant Moshe, 'For on this day he shall atone for you to purify you, for all your sins before Hashem will you be purified.'"

(Vayikra 16:30)

In his Viduy confession over the goat, the Kohen Gadol mentioned Hashem's name three times. In so doing he attached all the destructive and accusing angels that were created through the sins of Klal Yisrael to the goat. Eventually the goat's legs buckled under the heavy weight of all the sins, so the appointed man was forced to carry the goat on his shoulders all the way to the cliff of Azazel.

The three times the Kohen Gadol mentioned Hashem's name had a threefold effect. It gave strength to the man who carried the goat to Azazal while fasting, it helped the goat endure the pain of bearing the sins, and it helped attach all the destructive and accusing angels to the goat.

Indeed, it was for this reason that a goat and no other animal was chosen to be thrown off the cliff, because a goat has hair, which can be used to tie on the harmful angels.

(Sifsei Kohen, Acharei Mos)

The *Kohen Gadol* appointed a *kohen* who knew his way in the desert to take the goat to Azazel in the wilderness. The Mishnah in *Yoma* 6:4 says that there was an elevated walkway leading from the

Courtyard to the outskirts of the city. This walkway was made because the rough Babylonians who came to Yerushalayim for Yom Kippur used to pull at the goat's hair, shouting at the *kohen*, "Hurry up! Take [our sins] and get going! Hurry up! Take [our sins] and get going!" The Gemara says that these people were really Alexandrians, but because the Jews of Eretz Yisrael disliked the Babylonians, they used this name as a slur for anyone who behaved in an uncivilized manner.

(Yoma 66a)

> *The Satmar Rebbe explained why they went to the great expense of building a ramp, rather than deploy police to control the unruly crowd. The people who pulled at the goat's hair were religious Jews who were saddened by the sins of Klal Yisrael. Of course, pulling an animal's hair is forbidden on Yom Kippur, but since they did it because of their anguish over Klal Yisrael's sins, the police were not ordered to arrest them. You don't fight against faithful Jews who are acting for the honor of Hashem; you find peaceful ways to enforce the law. It was better to build the walkway, rather than detain and scuffle with observant Jews.*
>
> *(Chidushei Torah, Mo'adim, 1962)*

Ten booths were built along the route to Azazel at 2000 cubit intervals. In each booth, people awaited the man leading the he-goat in case he became weak and needed refreshment. The man was not exempted from fasting, but the assurance that food was ready in case of an emergency eased the fast and helped him finish. The Gemara (*Yoma* 67b) relates that it never happened that the appointed man had to eat.

The last escort would not go with him to the Azazel cliff, but stood from afar and watched.

(Yerushalmi, Yoma 6:4)

When he arrived at the mountain, the *kohen* divided the strip of red wool, tying half of it to the rock and half between the goat's horns—and then he pushed the goat backward. It tumbled down the mountain. Before it reached halfway down, it was torn to pieces. The man would say, "May the sins of *Klal Yisrael* be obliterated like this!" He would leave the mountain, returning to the last booth and sitting in the shade until it became dark.

The Gemara tells us that after the death of Shimon HaTzaddik, who served as Kohen Gadol at the beginning of the second Beis Hamikdash era, the goat never reached its destination at Azazel. Invariably it escaped into the desert, where it was hijacked by Arabs living in the wilderness. As a result, the strip of red wool did not turn white.

(Yerushalmi, Yoma 6:3)

The Message of the Goat

The goat that was sent into the wilderness teaches a profound lesson. A sinner may think that after death, once he has been punished for his misdeeds, his soul will dwell among the righteous, enjoying some of the bliss of *Gan Eden*. Seeing the ashes of the offerings piled up on the Altar in the *Beis Hamikdash*, he mistakenly thinks that the animals that are sacrificed represent the sinner. Just as the ashes of the sacrifices remain on the holy Altar for a long time, so too, after receiving its punishment, the soul of the sinner will remain in the holy environment of *Gan Eden*.

The goat that is sent to Azazel teaches the sinner otherwise. The Mishnah says that before the goat tumbled halfway down the mountain, it was torn limb from limb. This tells the evildoers that they will never see the good of *Gan Eden*. As it says, "Their worms shall not die, nor their fire be quenched." (*Yeshayah* 66:24) Just as the goat bearing the sins of *Klal Yisrael* is not sacrificed on the Altar, but is sent into the wilderness to be destroyed, so evildoers will never enter the World to Come.

(Chinuch 95)

Burning the Bull and the Goat

After sending the goat into the wilderness, the *Kohen Gadol* went to the bull and the goat whose blood he had sprinkled inside the Sanctuary. He removed their sacrificial fats, putting them on a plate to be burned on the outer Altar, and sending the remaining parts to the place of burning outside Yerushalayim.

(Tosefta Yoma 3:12)

The Torah Reading

Watchposts would signal to one another, waving cloths, to let everyone know that the goat had arrived in the wilderness. Once the *Kohen Gadol* was told that the goat had reached the wilderness, he went to the Women's Courtyard to read from the Torah the portion describing the Yom Kippur service, *Vayikra* 16.

How did he read? He would be seated facing the people. The attendant of the synagogue took a Torah scroll and handed it to the head of the synagogue; the head of the synagogue handed it to the deputy *Kohen Gadol*, and the deputy *Kohen Gadol* handed it to the *Kohen Gadol*. The *Kohen Gadol* rose, accepted the Torah scroll, and read from *parshas Acharei Mos* and the portion in *parshas Emor* that begins with, "But on the tenth." (*Vayikra* 23:26-32)

The Torah scroll was handed from one to another to honor the *Kohen Gadol*, indicating that he had many subordinates.

The *Kohen Gadol* then rolled up the Torah scroll, put it in his bosom, and said, "There is more than I have read to you written here." He recited by heart from *sefer Bamidbar, parshas Pinchas,* beginning with, "On the tenth." (*Bamidbar* 29:7-11)

Why did he read it by heart? We do not roll a *sefer* Torah in public, since it would be considered disdainful to keep the congregation waiting. When he read "But on the tenth" from *parshas Emor*, he was allowed to roll the Torah from its earlier reading in *Acharei Mos*, because the two chapters are close together and the rolling takes just a moment.

Why didn't he read from another *sefer* Torah? This is forbidden, because it would imply that this portion was missing from the first *sefer* Torah. (*Rambam, Avodas Yom HaKippurim*)

> *On Yom Kippur we do not read the chapter about Yom Kippur beginning with, "On the tenth" (Vayikra 23:26-32), which the Kohen Gadol did read in the Beis Hamikdash. Why?*
>
> *That portion mentions the gravity of doing work on Yom Kippur. "If one does any work on this day, I will destroy him [spiritually] from among his people." (Vayikra 23:30) In the avodah of Yom Kippur, the Kohen Gadol did perform a number of labors that may not be done outside the Beis Hamikdah. He read this portion to warn the people not to desecrate Yom Kippur by doing the same type of labors they had seen him do in the Beis Hamikdash. Since today we cannot see the avodah of the Kohen Gadol, we do not need this warning. Therefore we do not read this chapter in Emor.*
>
> *(Avodas Yom HaKippurim, p. 208)*

After the Torah reading, the *Kohen Gadol* sacrificed the goat of the *Mussaf* offering.

Eight Brachos

The *Kohen Gadol* recited the same *brachah* after the reading as we do in the synagogue. He then added the following seven *brachos*:

- "*Retzeih*, Be favorable," from the *Shemoneh Esrei*.

- *"Modim anachnu Lach,* We gratefully thank You."

- *"Mechol la'avonoseinu,* Forgive our sins," ending with, *"Melech mocheil vesolei'ach la'avonoseinu,* the King who pardons and forgives our sins."

- A special *brachah* for the *Beis Hamikdash,* that it should remain standing with the *Shechinah* dwelling in it. He concluded with, "Blessed are You, Hashem, who resides in Zion."

- A separate *brachah* for *Klal Yisrael,* that Hashem should save *Klal Yisrael* and the king should not be removed, concluding, *"Habocheir be'amo Yisrael,* Blessed are you Hashem, who selects Yisrael."

- A separate *brachah* for the *kohanim,* that Hashem may favor their deeds and their service, and that He should bless them, concluding, *"Mekadeish hakohanim,* Who sanctifies the *kohanim."*

- A prayer that Hashem should help each and every Jew who needs help, concluding with, *"Shome'a tefillah,* Blessed are You, Hashem, Who hears prayer."

Reading from His Own Sefer Torah

After the reading, each person would bring his own *sefer* Torah from his house and read from it to show its beauty to the crowd. One should do the *mitzvos* in the most beautiful way, such as building a beautiful *sukkah* and having a Torah scroll written by an excellent scribe, in fulfillment of the verse, "He is my G-d and I will glorify Him." (*Shemos* 15:2) Showing one's scroll to the people would be an expression of one's natural pride in that precious possession.

Rashi explains that they brought their Torah scrolls before Yom Kippur, because carrying is forbidden on Yom Kippur. Others say that there was an *eruv* in Yerushalayim, so carrying was permitted.

(Yoma 70a)

Offering the Rams

The *Kohen Gadol* offered his own ram and the ram of the people. "He is to go and sacrifice his burnt offering and the people's burnt offering." (*Vayikra* 16:24) He burned the sacrificial parts of the bull and the goat and offered the continual afternoon (*tamid*) offering.

Next he entered the Holy of Holies, taking out the ladle and shovel which he had left there while continuing with the service of the day. He entered the Sanctuary to burn the afternoon incense and light the lamps of the Menorah, as on other days.

Finally, the *Kohen Gadol* took off his golden garments, put on his personal clothing, and went home, where he made a feast to celebrate his leaving the *Beis Hamikdah* unharmed. [The Torah warns that if the *Kohen Gadol* performs any part of the service improperly, he is liable to lose his life.

(Vayikra 16:2-3)]

The Kohen Gadol Goes Home

Rabbi Yaakov Emden, in his *Siddur Beis Yaakov*, quotes a remarkable letter written by a Roman official stationed in Yerushalayim at the time the *Beis Hamikdash* was standing. He writes as follows:

At the close of the Day of Atonement, the Temple area overflowed with a huge crowd of people, all eager to pass before the High Priest. It seemed as if the entire population of Jerusalem was lining up to press the High Priest's hand. The men were wearing white robes, many of them carrying white burning torches. All the windows in the area were decorated and brightly lit up.

People told me that, due to the enormous crush, the High Priest would not be able to come home before midnight. Although everyone had been fasting for more than twenty-four hours, the people did not want to go home before greeting and thanking the High Priest.

The next morning, the High Priest served a meal to which all his relatives and close friends were invited, celebrating that he had successfully completed the service in the Holy of Holies.

Afterward, the High Priest ordered a golden plaque to be inscribed with the following text:

I, So-and-so, son of So-and-so, officiated as High Priest in the great Holy Temple, in the year so-and-so of Creation, serving the One Whose Name rests on this House. May He who granted me the privilege of completing this service permit my children to serve G-d in this House.

(Siddur Beis Yaakov by Rabbi Yaakov Emden)

Birkas Hagomeil

Birkas Hagomeil, the Thanksgiving Blessing, is recited by one who has survived a dangerous situation. A *Kohen Gadol* who did not perform the service in the Holy of Holies exactly as prescribed died there. Did the *Kohen Gadol* therefore recite *Birkas Hagomeil* after successfully performing the Yom Kippur service?

In his *sefer Machazik Brachah*, the *Chida* relates a debate between his father and Rabbi Eliezer Nachum about whether or not the *Kohen Gadol* had to say *Birkas Hagomeil* after emerging alive and well from the Holy of Holies on Yom Kippur. The *Chida* had a dream in which he asked his father: Since the *Kohen Gadol's* life was in jeopardy when he entered the Holy of Holies, did he have to say *Birkas Hagomeil* when coming out?

The *Chida's* father replied that according to *halachah*, the *Kohen Gadol* was not required to say *Birkas Hagomeil*. It was the *Kohen Gadol's* duty to follow G-d's order to enter the Holy of Holies. *Birkas Hagomeil* is said when one survives an unwanted dangerous situation, such as a person who recovered from a sickness or was released from prison. But since the *Kohen Gadol* willingly risked his life to fulfill G-d's will, he was not required to say *Hagomeil*.

The *Chida's* father continued: The same goes for Yitzchak *Avinu*, after surviving the *Akeidah*; Avraham *Avinu*, after emerging from the fiery oven; Chananiah, Mishael, and Azariah, after surviving the fiery furnace; and Daniel, after coming out alive from the lions' den. Since they willingly offered their lives, they did not have to say *Hagomeil* either.

Rabbi Eliezer Nachum replied that in his opinion, the *Kohen Gadol* did recite *Hagomeil*. Proof of this is the Mishnah that says: After emerging from the Holy of Holies, the *Kohen Gadol* recited a short prayer so as not to frighten the people who might think that he had died. No doubt the short prayer was *Birkas Hagomeil*.

(Machazik Brachah, Ohr Hachaim 219)

Chapter Twenty Five

The
Minchah Service

The Torah Reading

For *Minchah* we read the chapter of forbidden sexual relationships in *Vayikra* 18. *Tosafos* explains the reason for this seemingly strange selection for the afternoon Torah reading. The women dress up when they attend the synagogue on Yom Kippur, and this chapter is meant to warn against lustful thoughts.

(Tosafos, end of Megillah)

The *Chasam Sofer* questions this *Tosafos*. If this is the reason for the Torah reading, then the women should simply refrain from adorning themselves on Yom Kippur!

He goes on to explain that the Sages tell us that genuine *teshuvah* is when one is able to refrain from repeating his sin when confronted with the same situation that caused his original sin. Throughout the year, women stumble by dressing immodestly. Men stumble by gazing at improper sights. On Yom Kippur—the perfect day for doing *teshuvah*—the women do *teshuvah* by beautifying themselves solely in honor of Hashem, and for no other reason. Men are careful not to cast improper glances in order to avoid thinking indecent thoughts. This is genuine *teshuvah*—and we read the chapter of *Arayos* to remind us of it.

(Toras Moshe Yom Kippur)

One Yom Kippur before Minchah, the Gorlitzer Rebbe, Rabbi Baruch Halberstam, mounted the bimah to give the following inspirational address:

"Rabbosai! The month of Elul, the month of teshuvah, has gone by; the Selichos days have passed; the two days of Rosh Hashanah, the Ten Days of Teshuvah, and erev Yom Kippur have elapsed. And now the hour of Minchah of Yom Kippur is at hand. Perhaps someone may imagine that he has reached a high level of piety and devotion. To teach you otherwise, we will now read the parshah of Arayos. In this way everyone will realize how low he still ranks, and how great is the need to do teshuvah."

(Divrei Baruch, Yom Kippur)

Recurring Number Twenty-Four

It is interesting to note that in connection with *teshuvah* and forgiveness, the number 24 keeps cropping up:

- The Rambam mentions twenty-four items that preclude *teshuvah*.

- In *parshas Emor,* the concept of atonement is mentioned twenty-four times as a means of attaining forgiveness for various transgressions, including:

- The twenty-four transgressions listed in *Sefer Yechezkel*

- The twenty-four forbidden sexual relations in the chapter on *Arayos*

- Violations that are committed twenty-four hours a day.

- Transgressions against the twenty-four books of *Tanach*
                                                        (Rokeach)

The Book of Yonah

For the *Hafotarah* of *Minchah* on Yom Kippur we read the Book of Yonah, for it teaches the power of *teshuvah*. In addition, the miraculous way in which Yonah's flight was foiled shows that no one can escape from G-d.

                                                        (Levush 622)

Who Was Yonah?

The *navi* Yonah ben Amitai lived during the era of the first *Beis Hamikdash*. He was a student of Elisha Hanavi, who was a disciple of Eliyahu Hanavi. He prophesied during the reign of Yeravam ben Yoash, King of Yisrael.

The Talmud *Yerushalmi* in *Sukkah* 5a relates that Yonah was born in the town of Gas Hacheifer (*2 Melachim* 14:25) in the territory of Zevulun. His mother is identified as the poor widow of Tzorfas who offered hospitality to Eliyahu Hanavi, giving him a room in the attic of her house. The only food she had was a handful of flour and a bit of oil in a pitcher. But Eliyahu prophesied in the name of Hashem, "The jug of flour shall not run out, and the flask of oil shall not lack until the day that Hashem provides rain upon the face of the earth."

                                                        (1 Melachim 17:14)

A while later, the woman's son (Yonah) became ill and died. Eliyahu prayed for him, and he came back to life in the merit of the kindness his mother had shown to Eliyahu.

The Gemara says that Yonah would travel to Yerushalayim for the three *Yomim Tovim*, rejoicing at the *Simchas Beis Hashoevah* in the *Beis Hamikdash* on Sukkos until he reached such an exalted spiritual elevation that the *Ruach Hakodesh* descended on him. For the Sages say that the *Shechinah* comes to rest only on a person who is *besimchah*, in a joyful frame of mind.

(Yerushalmi, Sukkah 5a)

The Gemara in Sanhedrin 11b testifies that Yonah was a navi emes, "a true prophet." The Gemara in Nedarim 38a says: Yonah ben Amitai was a perfect tzaddik. He entered alive into Gan Eden.

Yonah was as great a prophet as Eliyahu Hanavi.

(Mishnas R.A. 8)

The Gemara lists Yonah Hanavi as one of the forty-eight prophets and seven prophetesses whose prophecies were recorded for the benefit of future generations.

Yonah's Mission

Hashem told Yonah to go to Nineveh, a great city, to warn its inhabitants to repent. Nineveh was an ancient city, dating back to the generation of the Dispersion, the people who built the Tower of Bavel.

But Yonah was reluctant to carry out his mission. He was afraid that if the people of Nineveh did *teshuvah*, it would reflect badly on the stubborn nation of Yisrael, who ignore prophetic calls to repent.

(Pirkei D'Rabbi Eliezer)

The Merit of Nineveh

The Midrash explains why the people of Nineveh merited to be prodded to do *teshuvah* by a prophet, while no other nation—aside from *Klal Yisrael*—was privileged to receive a similar prophetic message.

For several generations after the Flood, the people still believed in G-d and were in awe of Him. But when the wicked Nimrod appeared on the scene, the situation began to change. Nimrod incited the people to rebel against G-d and build the Tower of Bavel, with the intention of ascending to Heaven to make war against G-d.

The Torah then states, "From that land, Ashur went forth and built Nineveh." (*Bereishis* 10:11) Noting Nimrod's depraved ways, and fearing that his children would be swayed by his G-dless rantings, the righteous Ashur moved away and built the city of Nineveh. Many years later, Nineveh was saved in the merit of Ashur, the single righteous man who performed a single righteous act.

Imagine how great the Heavenly reward will be for *Klal Yisrael* for all the *mitzvos* and good deeds they perform! May Hashem help us that we may live to see the fulfillment of this promise.

(Chizkuni al Hatorah)

Yonah Runs Away

Yonah decided to flee to Tarshish, a sea outside of Eretz Yisrael (*Rashi*), so G-d would not repeat His command to go to Nineveh. Yonah knew that a *navi* is given a prophecy only while in Eretz Yisrael.

(Mechilta)

A Stormy Wind

It was a Thursday when Yonah went to the harbor of Yaffo, the ancient port city closest to Yerushalayim. He found a ship bound for Tarshish. Being a wealthy man, he paid his own fare as well as the fares of all the passengers, for a total of four thousand guilders. He did this to make sure the ship sailed right away, without waiting for more passengers.

No sooner had the ship put out to sea than G-d cast a mighty wind toward the sea. Such a great tempest came upon the sea that the ship was in danger of breaking up. In their fright, the sailors cried out, each to his own god; they flung the ship's cargo overboard to make it lighter.

Yonah Is Sound Asleep

Yonah, meanwhile, had gone down in the hold of the vessel, where he lay down and fell asleep. The captain went over to him and cried out, "How can you be sleeping so soundly? Get up, call upon your G-d! Perhaps your G-d will be kind to us all and we will not perish."

Meanwhile, there were other ships sailing the sea. Gliding smoothly over the water, these ships were not affected by the storm. Seeing that only their ship was being tossed and rocked by the pounding waves, the passengers said to one another, "Surely this storm has come upon us as punishment for a sin. Let us cast lots and find out on whose account this misfortune has come upon us."

They cast lots, and the lot fell on Yonah. They cast lots many times, to ensure that the result was correct. Every time it fell on Yonah.

The sailors said to Yonah, "Tell us, what sin caused this disaster to happen to us? What is your business? What is your country, and of what people are you?"

"I am a Hebrew," Yonah replied. "I worship Hashem, the G-d of Heaven, Who made both sea and land."

Terrified, the men asked him, "What have you done?"

Yonah told them that he was a prophet, and that he was running away to avoid being sent by G-d to Nineveh. That was his sin.

When the men found out that he was fleeing from the service of Hashem, they reproached him, "How could you dare do such a thing!" Then they asked, "What must we do to make the sea calm around us?"

"Heave me overboard," Yonah replied, "and the sea will calm down for you. For I know that this terrible storm came upon you on my account."

The sailors were reluctant to throw him overboard. They rowed hard to get back to shore, but they could not, for the sea was growing more and more stormy. They realized that they had no choice but to follow Yonah's advice.

Before casting him into the sea, they cried out, "Please Hashem, do not let us perish on account of this man's life. Do not hold us guilty of killing an innocent person! For You, O G-d, by Your will have brought this about."

Yonah Cast Into the Sea

They heaved Yonah overboard, and the sea stopped raging.

Pirkei D'Rabbi Eliezer comments that the men were reluctant to cast Yonah into the sea. They first lowered him into the water down to his knees, and the storm subsided. So they brought him back on deck—and the wind blew up with renewed force.

They next lowered him down to his neck, and the wind died down. But as soon as they pulled him up, the storm began raging again.

Convinced by now that the disaster was Yonah's fault, they flung him into the sea, and the sea stopped raging.

Witnessing the miracle, the passengers on the ship realized that G-d's Providence guides the world, and He repays everyone according to his actions. This awareness inspired them with deep awe of G-d. They pledged to bring offerings in the *Beis Hamikdash* and resolved to give *tzedakah* to the needy. They cast aside their idols and vowed to convert to Judaism.

(Pirkei D'Rabbi Eliezer)

The *Zohar* says that they all became converts and learned Torah, eventually becoming leading Torah sages.

(Zohar 2:231)

Many Miracles

The commentators remark that it took many miracles for Yonah to survive. One usually cannot survive in a fish's belly for even an hour! That he was able to survive for three days was in itself nothing short of a miracle.

(Ibn Ezra)

G-d allowed him to survive without oxygen, like an embryo in its mother's womb.

(Malbim)

G-d fed the fish *manna*, as He did with the Jews in the wilderness, to prevent the fish from digesting Yonah. Yonah, too, ate the *manna*. Another miracle was that the fish just happened to be there to swallow Yonah the moment he was tossed overboard, saving him from drowning.

The Midrash says that Yonah entered the fish's mouth with the same ease as walking into a big synagogue. The eyes of the fish were like windows, lighting up its belly with two big lamps. Rabbi Meir says that there was a luminous gem in the belly of the fish, shining like the sun at the height of summer, so Yonah could see everything happening in the depths of the sea.

Yonah asked the fish to show him everything that exists in the sea. The fish showed him the great ocean, the Red Sea, and Gehinnom. Then it showed him the *Shesiah* Stone, the foundation stone on which the world rests, and the sons of Korach as they were standing in prayer before Hashem.

Encounter With Leviasan

The Midrash says that after Yonah was swallowed by the large fish, the fish said to Yonah, "Today is the day that the Leviasan is going to eat me up. You see, every day the Leviasan consumes a large fish. Hashem decides which fish it is that he is going to eat, and the fish know when it is their turn to be devoured. I know that today is my turn."

Said Yonah, "Take me to the Leviasan. I'll make sure he doesn't eat you, so I'll save both our lives!"

The fish swam to the Leviasan, as Yonah had told him. Yonah said to the Leviasan, "I came to pay you a visit, because in the future I will tie a rope around your head and pull you out of the ocean. You will be the fish course at the banquet Hashem will prepare for the *tzaddikim*."

Terrified, the Leviasan took flight, swimming for three days without a halt. Both Yonah and the big fish were saved.

(Pirkei D'Rabbi Eliezer)

Yonah's Prayer

Seeing the sons of Korach, Yonah began to pray.

"In my trouble I called to Hashem, and He answered me, for I see that although I stayed in the belly of the fish for three days and three nights, I am still alive, which proves that Hashem does not want me to perish.

"From the belly of *sheol,* the grave, I called out, and You heard my voice. You cast me into the depths, into the heart of the sea. The floods engulfed me; all Your waves swept over me. I thought I was driven away, out of Your sight. Would I ever gaze again upon Your holy *Beis Hamikdash?*

"The water closed in over me, the deep engulfed me, weeds surrounded my head. I sank to the base of the mountains. The bars of the earth closed upon me forever, yet You brought my life up from the pit.

"When my life was ebbing away, I called Hashem to mind; and my prayer came before You, into Your holy *Beis Hamikdash.*

"They who cling to empty folly forsake their own welfare. But I, with loud thanksgiving, will sacrifice to You. What I have vowed I will perform. Deliverance is Hashem's!"

Yonah resolved that as soon as he was rescued, he would go to Nineveh and fulfill his mission to convey the prophetic message to the people of that city.

Back on Dry Land

The Midrash says: Hearing Yonah's prayer, Hashem instructed the fish to swim to the shore, where it spit up Yonah a distance of 968 miles.

The *Zohar* says: As a result of having Yonah in its belly for three days and three nights, the fish died. A swarm of small fish descended on the big fish, picking its flesh. Realizing that his life was threatened, Yonah prayed to Hashem, and Hashem brought the fish back to life. Only then did the fish spit up Yonah on the shore.

(Zohar 2:48)

Yonah in Nineveh

Hashem spoke to Yonah a second time, telling him to go at once to Nineveh and proclaim G-d's message. Yonah went to Nineveh as Hashem had told him. He proclaimed, "Forty days more, and Nineveh shall be overturned, as Sedom was destroyed!"

The Midrash says that Nineveh was an enormously large city; it took forty days to walk from one end to the other. The city had twelve wide avenues, and on each avenue there lived 120,000 people. Each avenue opened into twelve smaller streets, and in each of these streets there were twelve courts of twelve houses. Each house was occupied by twelve strong men, each of whom had twelve children.

Standing in one of the streets, Yonah warned the people to do *teshuvah*. The sound of his voice carried across the entire city.

Nineveh Repents

The people of Nineveh believed Yonah's prophetic mission, because some of the sailors who were aboard the ill-fated ship together with Yonah were living in Nineveh. These sailors confirmed that Yonah was tossed overboard and could have survived only through great miracles from G-d.

When Yonah's words of reproof reached the ear of King Asanpar of Nineveh, he rose from his royal throne, took off his royal garments and ordered that a proclamation be made in the king's name. Every citizen of Nineveh had to fast and cover himself with sackcloth, "and let them call out mightily to G-d; each person is to turn back from his evil way, and from the robbery which is in his hands."

The King ordered the men to separate from their wives; there was to be no mingling of men and women, "so that G-d will relent and turn away from His burning wrath so we do not perish."

The King held up little children toward Heaven, crying out to G-d, "Have mercy on us in the merit of the small children who have not sinned!"

The people of Nineveh repented and returned all stolen goods to their owners. The Midrash says that when they found a lost item outdoors in the fields and vineyards, they went looking for the owner and returned it to him.

If someone had stolen bricks which were then used in building the walls of the palace, the wall was torn down, and the bricks returned to their rightful owner. Garments woven with stolen threads were ripped apart and the threads returned to their owner.

The Decree Is Abolished

When G-d saw that the people of Nineveh repented and were sorry for their evil deeds, He relented and called off His decree. This displeased Yonah greatly. He knew that, unlike the people of Nineveh, the Jews would not heed the prophet's call, and eventually would be conquered by the Assyrians—of which Nineveh was the capital.

According to Rashi, Yonah said, "Now that my prophetic message failed to materialize and Nineveh was not destroyed, the nations will claim that I am a false prophet."

Yonah prayed to Hashem, "Please, Hashem, was this not my contention when I was still on my own soil? I therefore hastened to flee to Tarshish, for I knew that You are a gracious and compassionate G-d, slow to anger, abounding in kindness and relentful of punishment. I knew that if the people of Nineveh would do *teshuvah*, You would not destroy them. When they do *teshuvah*, and *Klal Yisrael* does not repent of their sins, it will reflect badly on the stubborn Jewish people.

"So now, Hashem, please take my life from me, for better is my death than my life. Please spare me the sight of the destruction [which Yonah foresaw would eventually befall Yisrael], since I was instrumental in bringing it about."

Hashem replied, "Are you that deeply grieved?" G-d asked the question but said no more, as if to imply that Yonah would yet be shown that his displeasure was improper. Is it proper for you to be grieved? Is My compassion to them deserving of your anger?

The Kikayon

Yonah left and found a place east of the city. He made a booth and sat under it in the shade, waiting to see what would happen.

Soon the booth dried up. Yonah suffered a great deal from the burning sun. While Yonah was in the belly of the fish, the heat there had caused his clothes and the hair on his head to be burned. Now, exposed to the scorching sun, Yonah was plagued by insects that stung him all over his body.

Hashem provided a *kikayon* plant which grew up over Yonah to provide shade for his head. The *kikayon* had 275 large leaves, each leaf measuring more than four cubits—enough to provide shade for four people. Yonah enjoyed the cool shade and the relief from the flies and insects.

But his happiness did not last long. The next day at dawn, G-d caused a worm to attack the plant, so it withered. When the sun rose, G-d provided a sultry wind; the sun beat down on Yonah's head, and he became faint. He begged for death: "I would rather die than live."

Then G-d said to Yonah, "Are you so deeply upset about the *kikayon*?"

"Yes," he replied, "so deeply that I want to die."

Then Hashem said, "You cared about the plant, which you did not work for and which you did not grow, which appeared overnight and perished overnight. And should I not care about Nineveh, that great city in which there are more than 120,000 people who do not know their right hand from their left—and many beasts as well?"

At this, Yonah fell to the ground. "O Hashem, guide Your world with the attribute of Mercy, as it says, 'For with Hashem, our G-d, is compassion and forgiveness.'"

Yonah lived to the ripe old age of 120 years, and he built a synagogue in the land of Ashur (Assyria).

The End of Nineveh

The *teshuvah* of Nineveh did not last for very long. Approximately one hundred years later, the people of Nineveh reverted to their corrupt ways. In the days of King Menasheh, the *navi* Nachum prophesied that Nineveh would be destroyed, saying, "Whoever will hear that Nineveh was destroyed will clap his hand with joy."

Nineteen years before the destruction of the first *Beis Hamikdash*, Nevuchadnetzar, King of Babylonia, conquered the kingdom of Ashur and destroyed the city of Nineveh.

Special Merit

Why is it that people will spend large sums of money to be called up to the Torah for *maftir Yonah*? Because this *haftarah* tells us two important facts: the population of an entire city, Nineveh, sinned against Hashem, and they did *teshuvah*. *Maftir Yonah* is therefore a very vivid reminder to do *teshuvah*.

(Zechuso D'Avraham)

In the morning we read in *parshas Acharei Mos* about the death of Aharon's two sons, so their deaths should be an atonement for our transgressions. The same idea is expressed in the story of Yonah.

The crew members asked Yonah, "Tell us now, because of whom has this calamity befallen us?" (*Yonah* 1:8) This is difficult to understand. They had already cast lots, and the lot fell on Yonah. Wasn't it obvious that it happened because of Yonah?

They cast lots not just to know whom to throw overboard. They wanted to know why the lot had fallen on Yonah. Was he being punished because of his own sins, or was he made to suffer because of their shortcomings? So they asked him whether he could pinpoint a transgression he had committed. If so, the misfortune came on his account. On the other hand, if he was free of any wrongdoing, they would know that it was their sins that had brought on the storm.

This dialogue tells us that the death of *tzaddikim* atones for the sins of others. And this is why we read *maftir Yonah* on Yom Kippur.

(Chochmas Shlomo, Orach Chaim 622)

The Primary Message

Rabbi Meir of Premyshlan once asked a wealthy person why, year after year, he bought *maftir Yonah* for a large sum of money. "Tell me, why is *maftir Yonah* so important to you?" he inquired.

"Because of the verse in the *haftarah*, 'Every man shall turn back from his evil way, and from the robbery that is in his hands' (*Yonah* 3:8)," the rich man replied.

Retorted Rabbi Meir, "No, the essential message of *sefer Yonah* is, 'The ship's captain approached him, and said to him, "How can you sleep so soundly? Arise! Call to your G-d!"'"

(Divrei Meir)

Chapter Twenty Six

Neilah

Moshe Originated Neilah

From the day Moshe was told that he would not be allowed to enter Eretz Yisrael, he inserted a special prayer during *Shacharis, Minchah* and *Maariv*, asking to have this decree reversed—a total of 515 prayers.

The *Chasam Sofer* calculates how to arrive at the total of 515 prayers. Moshe was told the decree at the end of the seven days of mourning over the death of Miriam, which was on the 16th of Nissan. At *Maariv* that night he began his prayers, which ended with *Minchah* on Yom Kippur, 171 days later. 3 x 171 = 513, plus the first and the final *Neilah* prayer equals 515 prayers. The final prayer, the *Neilah* prayer—which was the 515th prayer—was thus instituted by Moshe. This is why Moshe said, "I implored Hashem at that time" (*Devarim* 3:23), referring to *Neilah*.

(Derashos Chasam Sofer, p. 334)

The Name Neilah

According to Rav, the term Neilah, "closing," refers to the closing of the gates of Heaven. Rabbi Yochanan disagrees, stating that Neilah refers to the closing of the gates of the Sanctuary, which took place after the Menorah was lit in the afternoon. In deference to Rabbi Yochanan's view, we begin Neilah before sunset.

(Shulchan Aruch, Orach Chaim 623)

Rabbi Tzvi Hirsch of Riminov explains that the tefillah is called Neilah, "Closing Prayer," because at that hour the tzaddikim are closeted with Hakadosh Baruch Hu in a secluded Heavenly chamber, which is closed off and inaccessible to Satan and his accusing angels.

(Be'eros Hamayim)

Atonement at Day's End

The Gemara *(Avodah Zarah 8a)* describes how Adam reacted when he first saw the setting sun, on the day he was created. "Woe is me!" he exclaimed. "Perhaps because of my sin the world is growing dark and returning to its primordial emptiness and formlessness. This must be the death I have been sentenced to!"

He stayed up all night fasting, crying, and doing teshuvah—and his teshuvah was accepted.

This was a portent for all future generations. We close the Neilah service with the Viduy confession, because on Yom Kipper, atonement is granted in the final hour of the day.

(Machzor Chasam Sofer)

The Special Niggun

In a *piyut* authored by Rabbeinu Gershon, *Me'or Hagolah*, we say during *Neilah*, "Look—our devout ones are lost, they are no longer with us. We have no one to pray for us!" By singing ancient traditional *niggunim*, we recall the great *tzaddikim* of a bygone age.

A story is told about the cantonists, the young Jewish children who were torn from their families and forcibly inducted into the czarist Russian army. After many years of hardship, living among coarse Russian soldiers, they forgot how to daven.

Once—after several years of army service—a group of boys somehow discovered that that day was Yom Kippur. "We have to daven to Hashem," they lamented, "but we don't know how!"

"I still remember the melody we sang in shul," one boy said.

"Me too, me too!" the others shouted.

Together they chanted the wordless niggun they all still remembered, repeating the tune over and over again.

The tzaddikim commented, "The singing of these unfortunate children lifted the Yom Kippur tefillos of the entire Klal Yisrael straight to Heaven."

(Igra DeTzvi 326:5)

Servants of Hashem

The good-hearted master of a large mansion treated his staff with great kindness. He once had to travel overseas for a year, so he leased the mansion to a manager. The manager, a vicious scoundrel, made the workers labor for long hours while cutting their wages.

When the year was over, the workers heard that their generous master was coming back. So they planned to petition him not to lease the mansion for another year to the evil manager.

> *On the day of the master's return, the manager, aware of what was afoot, put the staff to work in the distant fields, preventing them from getting in touch with the master. The workers out in the field hoped to have an opportunity to see the master in the evening after work.*
>
> *When they arrived at twilight, they found the master's coach ready to leave. In desperation, they threw themselves in front of the horses, preventing the master's departure. Then they all cried out, telling their master about the hardship they had to endure. "Dear master," they cried, "please help us!"*

Klal Yisrael are G-d's servants. Because of our sins, G-d departed, saying, "I will go, I will return to My place until they will acknowledge their guilt and seek My face." (*Hoshea* 5:15) Instead, G-d allows a ruthless slave to reign over us—the Satan. "Because of three things the earth trembles   because of a slave who reigns." (*Mishlei* 30:21)

During the Ten Days of *Teshuvah*, when Hashem comes close to us, the Satan tries to confuse us, keeping us from praying the Master of the universe. *Neilah* is our last opportunity to pray to Hashem, before He returns to His Heavenly abode—for if He leaves the world to the Satan for another year, how are we going to survive?

In this final hour of Yom Kippur, let us pour out our hearts to Hashem that He should not destroy His nation, letting the Satan rule over us. Instead He should be our Ruler, as we pray, "You, Hashem, will reign over all Your works."

The Sin of Stealing

The tractate *Bava Kamma* ends with a discussion of the laws of stealing, evidence of the severity of this sin.

The year culminates in the *Yomim Tovim*. The crowning point of the *Yomim Tovim* is Yom Kippur, and the climax of Yom Kippur is

Neilah. What do we pray in the *Shemoneh Esrei* of *Neilah*? That "we may withdraw our hands from inflicting injustice on others," meaning robbing and stealing.

The dreadful fate of the generation of the Flood was sealed only because they were guilty of robbing and stealing. It was the sin of stealing that tipped the scale. At *Neilah*, when our lot for the coming year is sealed, we *daven* that we should not harm our neighbors through theft and robbery.

(Maharam Schiff)

Last Call for Forgiveness

In *Neilah* we pray, "Forgive us, please, for the day is waning."

After misbehaving and skipping school, a young boy ran away from home and boarded a ship, sailing the seven seas. During a fierce storm the ship ran aground on a remote island populated by savages. Learning of the shipwreck, the father set out to search for his son, and after many month of arduous travel, finally located him.

In an effort to test the boy to see if he had mended his ways, the father told him, "I'm sorry, but I cannot ransom you. Your captors are demanding too high a price."

The son did not respond, merely shrugging his unconcern.

As the sun was about to set, the father went through the motions of preparing to leave. Suddenly the son cried out, "Father, please don't leave! I promise I'll behave from now on. Please pay the ransom and set me free!"

And so we cry out, "Forgive us, please, for the day is waning!"

(Yismach Moshe, Yom HaKippurim, p. 82)

Hashem, He Is the G-d

Rav Yehuda'i says: Immediately following *Neilah*, before beginning *Maariv*, the *chazzan* and the community should recite, "Hashem, He is the G-d!" seven times, escorting the *Shechinah* to the seventh Heaven.

(Ba'er Hetev 623)

Chapter Twenty Seven

Conclusion of Yom Kippur

The Shofar Blast

It is customary to blow the *shofar* immediately after *Neilah*, symbolizing that the *Shechinah*, which dwelled among us throughout Yom Kippur, is now leaving to return to its Heavenly abode. "G-d has ascended with the blast; Hashem with the sound of the *shofar*." (*Tehillim* 47:6)

(*Turei Zahav*)

The blast of the *shofar* announces that it is nightfall, time to prepare the meal for the hungry family after the fast.

(*Tosafos Shabbos 114b, s.v. ve'amai*)

Throughout Yom Kippur, the *yetzer hara* was powerless. Now that Yom Kippur is over, he is returning full force. So we confuse him with the *shofar* blast, reminding him of the coming final redemption when "a great *shofar* will be sounded" (*Yeshayah* 27:13)—and the *yetzer hara* will die.

(*Levush 623*)

253

The blowing of the *shofar* is symbolic of freedom, for on Yom Kippur the soul has been freed from its sins, and the body has been liberated from punishment.

(Levush 623)

A Single Tekiah

On *motzei* Yom Kippur we blow only one *tekiah* sound, because the *tekiah* alludes to Avraham *Avinu*. The first *brachah* of *Shemoneh Esrei* mentions Avraham, Yitzchak, and Yaakov, but it ends only with "*magein Avraham*," as Rashi says: "*Becha chosemin*, with your name will the prayer be concluded." Avraham is symbolic of *chesed*, kindness. We end Yom Kippur with a *tekiah*, providing an aura of *chesed*, so we may be sealed for a good year.

(Zera Avraham)

The Gemara in *Rosh Hashanah* says that when we blow the *shofar* on Rosh Hashanah, G-d rises from His Throne of Justice and moves to His Throne of Mercy. At the conclusion of Yom Kippur, when G-d in His Mercy judged us favorably, we take along the *shofar* which defended us and pleaded on our behalf.

(Sefer HaTanya 426:2)

The straight sound of the *tekiah* symbolizes the *tzaddik*, while the broken, wavering sound of *shevarim-teruah* represents the wicked. On Rosh Hashanah, when the *tzaddikim* have been inscribed for life, there are still those who are "in-between"—people whose decrees are still pending—as well as evildoers who are inscribed for death. Therefore we blow both *tekiah* and *shevarim-teruah*.

But on Yom Kippur we are confident that the "in-between" people have been judged favorably. Now all are *tzaddikim*. We therefore blow only a *tekiah*, the straight sound of the *tzaddik*.

(Chochmas Shlomo, Orach Chaim 623:6)

Forgive Us

Immediately following *Neilah* we *daven Maariv*. As always during the weekday *Maariv*, we say in *Shemoneh Esrei,* "Forgive us, our Father, for we have sinned."

But we have just been forgiven for all our sins! Why are we again asking for forgiveness?

It is of paramount importance that we firmly believe that Hashem has pardoned all our sins. Harboring the slightest doubt about G-d's forgiveness is a grave transgression. It is because of this lack of unconditional faith that we pray, "Forgive us, our Father, for we have sinned"—for not firmly and irrevocably believing that You have pardoned our sins.

(Chiddushei HaRim)

Havdalah

Unlike on other *Yomim Tovim*, the *brachah* of *Borei meorei ha'eish* is said even when Yom Kippur falls on a weekday. The source of the flame must be a fire that had been kindled before Yom Kippur, known as *ner sheshavas*. Why is this unnecessary for *havdalah* after every Shabbos?

On *motzei* Shabbos we thank Hashem for teaching Adam how to create fire, which took place on the first *motzei* Shabbos. Since that fire was newly made, the *havdalah* flame, too, may be new.

But on *motzei* Yom Kippur the *brachah* highlights the difference between Yom Kippur, when it is forbidden to use fire for kindling, and other *Yomim Tovim*, when we are permitted to use fire for cooking. Since the *brachah* demonstrates that that only now has the fire been rendered permissible for use, it must be recited only over a flame that burned on Yom Kippur—which has now become permissible.

(Kol Bo)

Hamavdil

In the *Hamavdil* hymn which we sing after *havdalah* we say, "May He forgive our sins." Why do we say this right after Yom Kippur, minutes after Hashem has forgiven all our sins?

The Gemara says that there is one sin which is not forgiven on Yom Kippur—that of *chillul* Hashem, desecration of Hashem's name. However, we read in *Shaarei Teshuvah* (1:47) that by fulfilling the *mitzvah* of *kiddush* Hashem, sanctifying Hashem's name, one can rectify the sin of *chillul* Hashem.

If a father teaches Torah to his children, raising them to observe the *mitzvos* proudly and publicly for everyone to see, he performs a great *kiddush* Hashem—for he thereby spreads the knowledge of Hashem throughout the world. In this way he repairs the sin of *chillul* Hashem.

In *Hamavdil* the words, "May He forgive our sins," are followed by, "May He increase our offspring like dust." May Hashem forgive us if we committed the sin of *chillul* Hashem, for we raise our offspring in the spirit of Torah and *mitzvos*—which brings about a great *kiddush* Hashem.

(Rabbi Yissachar Dov of Belz)

No Brachah over Besamim

In the *Havdalah* on *motzei* Yom Kippur we do not say the *brachah* of *Borei minei vesamim*, as we do on *motzei* Shabbos. This is because on *motzei* Shabbos, the *neshamah yeseirah*, the "additional soul" we receive on Shabbos, leaves us. To alleviate the distress we feel over the loss of the *neshamah yeseirah*, we inhale the pleasant fragrance of the *besamim* spices. Since on Yom Kippur we do not receive a *neshamah yeseirah*, there is no need to smell *besamim*.

Motzei Yom Kippur-A Yom Tov

The Mishnah in *Yoma* 8:4 says that on *motzei* Yom Kippur, the *Kohen Gadol* made a feast for his friends for having completed the *avodah* and left the *Beis Hamikdash* safely.

Midrash Rabbah (*Koheles* 9) says that on *motzei* Yom Kippur, a Heavenly Voice goes forth and says, "Go eat your bread with joy, and drink your wine with a merry heart, for Hashem has already accepted your deeds favorably."

The custom of eating an elaborate meal on *motzei* Yom Kippur is a celebration of the fact that Hashem has forgiven our transgressions. We consider it a *Yom Tov* meal, just as one would make a party for friends and relatives if he came into an unexpected windfall. The message of the Heavenly Voice is indeed a cause for rejoicing.

(Toras Emes LeMotzei Yom Kippur)

The Seudah of Motzei Yom Kippur

The Sages tell us that when we eat on *erev* Yom Kippur, it is considered as if we fasted both on *erev* Yom Kippur and Yom Kippur. This is because the festive meal of *erev* Yom Kippur has the aura of the solemn spirit of Yom Kippur. The same holds true for *motzei* Yom Kippur.

The verse tells us to observe Yom Kippur "from evening to evening." (*Vayikra* 23:32) Do we fast on *motzei* Yom Kippur? Not at all—we only fast during the day of Yom Kippur, not in the evening! A possible answer is that the spirit of Yom Kippur extends into *motzei* Yom Kippur. So it is that when you eat a festive meal on *motzei* Yom Kippur, it counts as if you fasted for two days.

(S'fas Emes, Yom Kippur, 1892)

May You Add Days

David Hamelech said in *Tehillim* (61:7), "May You add days unto the days of the king, may his years be like all generations." The following fascinating calculation sheds a new light on this passage:

The punishment of the spies for maligning Eretz Yisrael was, "Like the number of days that you spied out the land, forty days, a day for a year, a day for a year, shall you bear your iniquities—forty years." (*Bamidbar* 14:34) They explored the Land for forty days; as punishment, *Klal Yisrael* had to wander in the wilderness for forty years.

The Gemara says that the reward for a good deed is five hundred times as great as the punishment for a wrong deed. (*Sotah* 11a) Since Hashem punished the spies one year for each day of wrongdoing, His reward is 500 years for each day of good deeds.

There are the Ten Days of *Teshuvah* between Rosh Hashanah and Yom Kippur, during which all our sins are converted into merits. In addition, there is *erev* Rosh Hashanah, which is also a special day of *teshuvah* when many people fast, and there is the day after Yom Kippur, which is an extension of the atonement and forgiveness of Yom Kippur. Accordingly, we have a total of twelve days of *teshuvah* and forgiveness. The reward for those twelve days of virtue is 12x500=6000 years—the length of time the world will exist.

The Ten Days of *Teshuvah* are called "the days of the King," because Hashem judges the world on those days. By adding two days—*erev* Rosh Hashanah and the day after Yom Kippur—"to the days of the King," the six thousand years the world exists will be filled with *teshuvah* and good deeds.

(Toras Moshe, Naso, s.v. yevarechecha)

Yom Kippur with the Berditchever

The holy Berditchever—also known as the *Kedushas Levi*, the title of his work—once spent Yom Kippur in a small town where the father-in-law of the *Yeshuas Yaakov* officiated as Rav. At that time *chassidus* was still in its infancy, meeting widespread opposition from devout and learned Jews who had serious misgivings about the new movement. The *Yeshuas Yaakov*, an illustrious *gaon* who served as the *rav* of Lemberg, shared these doubts about the *chassidim*.

The *baal tefillah* was not feeling well that year, and he told the Rav that he was unable to *daven Kol Nidrei*. "I notice that we have a guest in town who seems to be a *talmid chacham*," the Rav said. "He sits in the *beis midrash* learning all day, and he has a beautiful voice. Let's ask him to lead us in *Kol Nidrei*."

When the *shamash* invited the Berditchever to be the *baal tefillah*, he immediately accepted. Running to the *shul*, he eagerly approached the *amud*, leading the *davening* with a fiery devotion that enthralled the entire congregation. The sweetness and warmth with which he *davened* the *Kol Nidrei* and the *piyutim* transported the people to a higher world; never before had they heard a *baal tefillah* like that.

The moment the Berditchever intoned the *Kol Nidrei*, the *Yeshuas Yaakov* jumped from his seat and ran to the *amud*, where he stood watching the venerable *baal tefillah* with utter fascination.

The young *gaon* thought to himself, "This *baal tefillah* who *davens* with such fervor and *kavanah* must be one of the *chassidim*. If all *chassidim* are like this *baal tefillah*, they must be the most wonderful people!"

At the end of *davening*, the Berditchever gave a *shiur* in *meseches Yoma*, expounding the *sugya* with an amazing breadth and depth of knowledge. The *Yeshuas Yaakov*, himself an eminent Talmudic scholar, listened with rapt attention to the Berditchever's brilliant discourse.

After several hours of intensive study, the *Yeshuas Yaakov* became tired and went home. To his utter amazement, the next morning he found the Berditchever standing at his *shtender*, still learning with undiminished fervor.

The Berditchever then continued as *baal tefillah* for *Shacharis*, *krias haTorah*, and *Mussaf*, with a depth of feeling that inspired everyone to do *teshuvah*. *Mussaf* was followed by *Minchah*. Listening to the Berditchver's *Neilah*, the congregation reached an emotional climax.

After *Maariv*, the *Yeshuas Yaakov* and his father-in-law, the Rav, escorted the Berditchever to the Rav's house, where a sumptuous meal awaited the hungry family. The Berditchever did not touch the food. Instead, he said to his *shamash*, "Chaykel, please bring me my delicacy."

Everyone thought that the Berditchever was asking for a very special kind of pastry or fancy dish. How surprised they were when the *shamash* brought a Gemara *Sukkah*! That was the Berditchever's delicacy. All night long, the Berditchever learned without taking a single bite of food. Only when he finished his "delicacy" did he break the fast, after which he departed.

In later years, the *Yeshuas Yaakov* often would reminisce about the Yom Kippur when he heard the awesome *davening* of the saintly Berditchever Rav, *zechuso yagein aleinu*, "May his merit shield and protect us."

Beneficial Prayers

When Yom Kippur is over, people wish each other "*Zolst hobn als guts oisgebeten*," which roughly translates as, "May your prayers for good things be fulfilled." What is the underlying idea behind this statement?

Who can say that he *davened* properly, that he prayed with the necessary concentration? So we say to each other, "Even if your prayers were not said with the right intention, I wish that, nevertheless, Hashem will accept your pleas with favor."

(Divrei Yechezkel)

Chovos HaLevavos (*Gate of Introspection*, 18) describes how a certain *tzaddik* added the following prayer to his *Shemoneh Esrei*: "I let You know my needs. It is not because I want to persuade you to fulfill them. After all, You know what is best for me. I only express my needs to remind myself of my dependence on You. If, in my ignorance, I have asked You for something that is not good and beneficial for me, please do not fulfill my request, but do what You judge to be best for me—because what Your exalted choice sets aside for me is better than what I would choose for myself. I leave all my concerns to Your immutable decision and Your sublime guidance."

It is with this thought in mind that we wish one another, "*Du zolst hobn als guts oisgebeten*—May the things you prayed for be good and beneficial for you."

(Yismach Yisrael 5)

Various sybolic foods are eaten at the festive meal on the first night of Rosh Hashanah (some also eat them on the second night) and a short prayer alluding to the symbolism is recited for each food. Many communities have developed interesting customs based on the names of foods. Some of these foods taste sweet and symbolize a sweet year, while others grow abundantly and indicate an abundance of merits (*Rashi*).

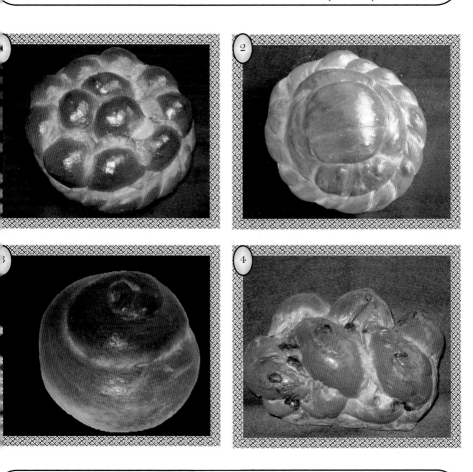

1, 2- The round challah for Rosh Hashanah, *erev* Yom Kippur, and Hoshanah Rabah symbolizes that Hashem will reign alone over the entire universe. People from the far ends of the world will hear it and come to present Hashem with the crown of kingship. Another reason: Like a circle which has no beginning or end, the round challah symbolizes the Oneness of Hashem. 3- Round challah named *Rudish*. 4- Challah with raisins.

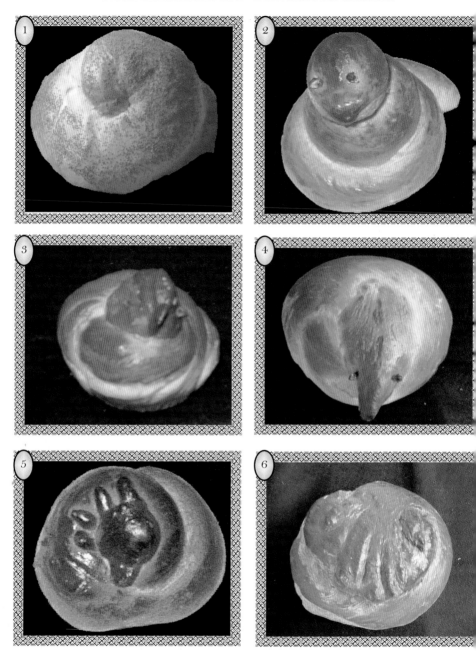

1, 2, 3, 4- "Bird Challah" alludes to the verse, *"Like flying birds, so will Hashem, Master of legions, descend to do battle upon Mount Zion and upon its hill"* (Yeshayah 31:5).

5, 6- Round challah with hand on top alludes to Hashem's hand which is open to accept penitents.

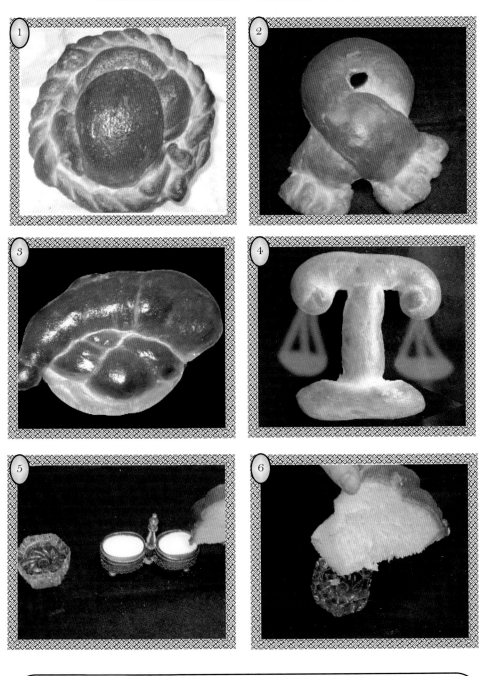

1- Round challah with hand on top alludes to Hashem's hand which is open to accept penitents. 2- Challah formed as a priestly blessing. 3- Shofar challah. 4- Challah in the shape of a scale, the sign of the zodiac (libra) of the month of Tishrei. 5, 6- Dipping one side of te *Hamotzi* piece of the challah into salt, the other side into honey.

1- Dipping one side of te *Hamotzi* piece of the challah into salt, the other side into honey. 2- Many have the custom of dipping the top end into salt and the bottom end into sugar. 3, 4- On the first night of Rosh Hashanah we eat an apple dipped in honey, to symbolize that Hashem should grant us a sweet new year.
5, 6- Some eat an apple baked in honey or dipped in sugar.

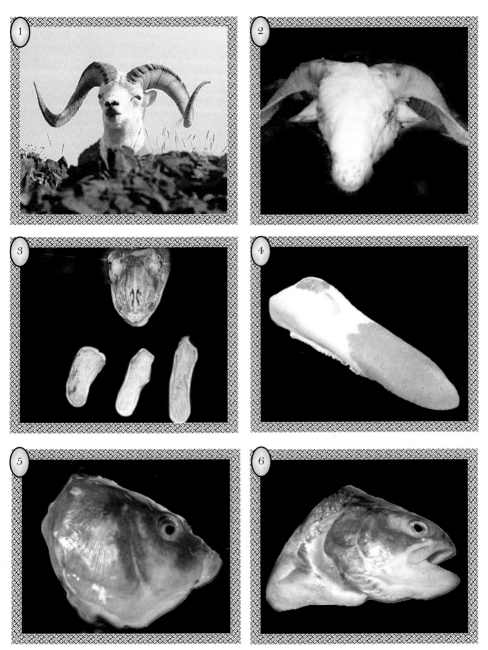

1, 2- A sheep's head is eaten because it serves as a reminder of the merit of the *Akeidah*, the binding of Yitzchak, at which the ram replaced Yitzchak on the altar. 3, 4- Many have a custom to eat also the sheep's tongue, that their tongues may not blunder. 5, 6- Head of a fish when a sheep's head is not available.

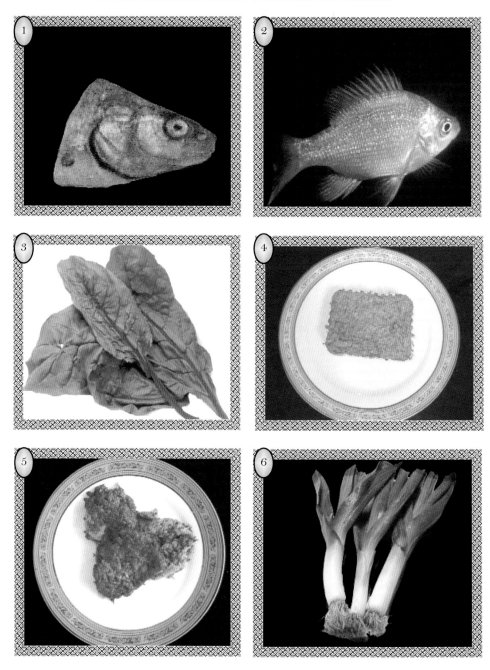

1- Head of a fish, when a sheep's head is not available.
2- Some have the minhag to eat sun fish on Rosh Hashanah and *erev* Yom Kippur. The Yiddish name of sunfish is *Karasel* fish, to indicate that we should be saved from *Kareis*. (*Belz, Skvere*) 3, 4, 5- *Silka*, Swiss chard. 6- *Karti*, Leek. The word *karti* implies that our enemy, the Satan, be decimated.

1, 2- Cooked leek. 3, 4- *Kara*, snake squash, raw and cooked. 5, 6- Black eye peas, its Aramaic name is *rubia*, a word that also implies increase and abundance.

1- Carrots, the Yiddish word for carrots is *meren*, which means "increase, multiply". 2- Pears, *baren*. The Yiddish word for "pear fruit" is *fruchtbaren* which also means to be fruitful and multiply. 3- Sardines. The word sardine sounds like *Sar Din*, "the bad verdict has been removed". 4- Watermelon, which is cold in the heat of the sun symbolizes the "cooling off" of strict Justice. (*Imrei Pinchas*)
5- Hungarian plums are harbingers of *simcha*. To show that we should do *teshuvah mitoch simcha*. (the *Rebbe* of Lublin) 6- Cooked plums, *eingemachts*.

1- Chicken liver. The Yiddish word for liver, *Leb-Erlach* sounds like *leb erlich*, "live honestly". 2- Pomegranate. Our merits should increase as the seeds of a pomegranate. 3- *Farfel*, the Yiddish word *farfel* sounds like *farfallen* (wiped out), that all our sins should be wiped out. 4- *Kreplach*, eaten on erev Yom Kippur. 5, 6- Olive oil, helpful for remembering the Torah. (*Imrei Pinchas*)

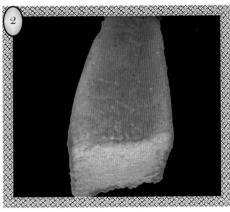

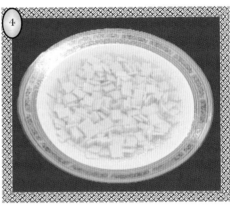

1- Raw honey from honeycomb. (*Haga'os Osheri*)
2- Honey cake and pastry baked in honey. 3- New fruits at the second night's meal. Thus, the *Shehecheyanu* of the *Kiddush* will apply to the new fruits as well. 4- Soup with square *lokshen* (noodles), so that we do not have to cut the noodles that hang down from the spoon that the coming year may not be cut short.

Another reason: We do not use thin (*dinne*) *lokshen*, so as not to mention the word *din* (verdict).

Another reason: The four sided square *lokshen* indicate that Hashem rules over the four corners of the world.

1- It is customary to sharpen a new knife for Rosh Hashanah as a good omen for *parnassah* (sustenance). 2- Some have the custom not to eat the tail of a fish, others do not eat fish at all because *dag* (fish) sounds like *daagah* (worry). Our *minhag* is to eat fish to sybolize that we may multiply like fish. (*Matteh Efraim, Ketzei Hamatteh*) 3- On Rosh Hashanah it is customary not to eat nuts, because the Hebrew word for nuts - *egoz* (17) - has the same numeric value as *cheit* (sin, omitting the final *alef*). 4- It is customary not to eat grapes on Rosh Hashanah (Gra). 5- Long wax candles for Yom Kippur symbolize our prayer that Hashem may hear our outcry (*tishma shavaseinu*). The Hebrew word *shava* "wax" souds like *shavaseinu*. 6- *Ner neshamah* candle for Yom Kippur.

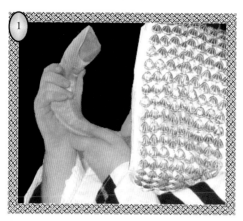

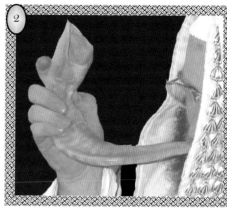

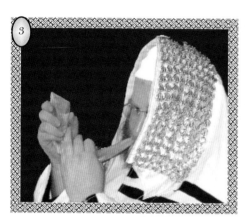

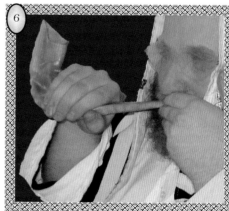

Various customs of Holding the Shofar. The Shofar should be long enough that when it is held, it should be visible on both sides of the hand.

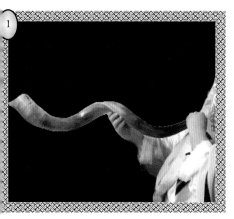

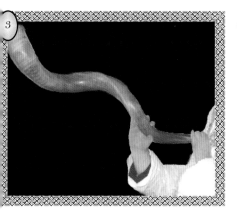

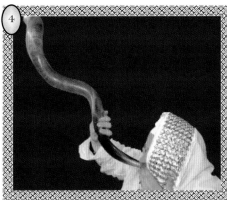

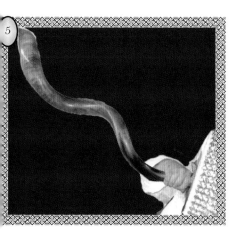

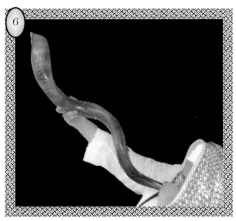

Various customs of holding the Yemenite Shofar.

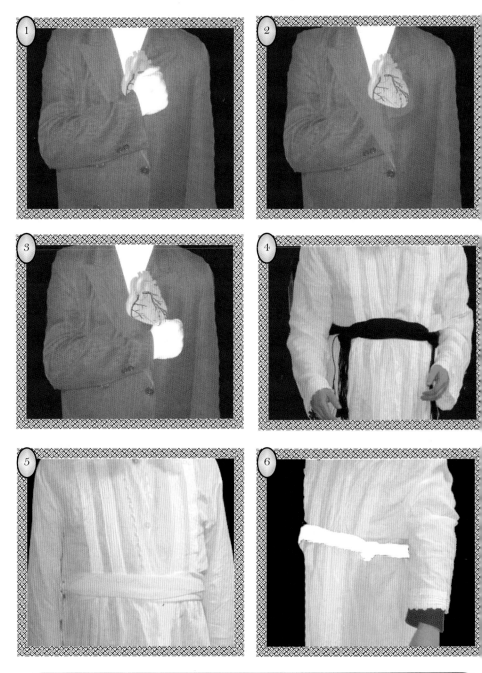

1, 2- One strikes the heart, as if to say "you are te one that made me sin". *(Magen Avraham 607:4)* 3- One should not strike below the heart. 4, 5- Some are careful not to wear a black *gartel* on the white *kittel*, for this is the vestment of gentile clergy. 6- The *kitte* should be worn on top of one's Yom Tov suit, in honor of the Yom Tov. *(Shabbos 119a)*

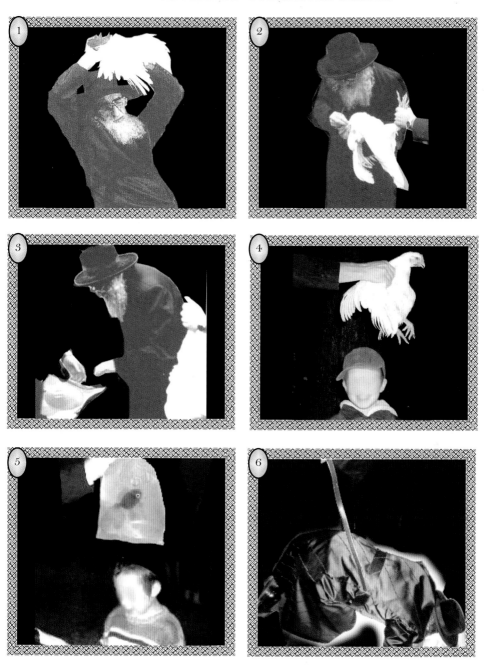

1- Revolving the chicken around the head three times.
2, 3- The Rivnitzer Rebbe shechts the *kapparah* and covers the blood. 4- Revolving the chicken around a child's head. 5- If a chicken is not available a fish or money is used. 6- Some follow the custom of having symbolic *malkus* (stripes) geven to them (*Matteh Efraim*).

SIGNIFICANT OMENS

A small piece of the apple is eaten and the following prayer is recited before the apple is finished.

יְהִי רָצוֹן מִלְפָנֶיךָ שֶׁתְּחַדֵּשׁ עָלֵינוּ שָׁנָה טוֹבָה וּמְתוּקָה:

Head of a sheep (or fish):

יְהִי רָצוֹן מִלְפָנֵי אָבִינוּ שֶׁבַּשָׁמַיִם, שֶׁנִּהְיֶה לְרֹאשׁ וְלֹא
לְזָנָב:

Dates:

יְהִי רָצוֹן מִלְפָנֵי אָבִינוּ שֶׁבַּשָׁמַיִם שֶׁיִּתַּמּוּ שׂוֹנְאֵינוּ
וְאוֹיְבֵינוּ:

Pomegranate:

יְהִי רָצוֹן מִלְפָנֶיךָ, שֶׁתַּרְבֶּה זְכֻיּוֹתֵינוּ כְּרִמּוֹן:

Rubia - Black eye peas:

יְהִי רָצוֹן מִלְפָנֵי אָבִינוּ שֶׁבַּשָׁמַיִם, שֶׁיִּרְבּוּ זְכֻיּוֹתֵנוּ:

Karti - Leek:

יְהִי רָצוֹן מִלְפָנֵי אָבִינוּ שֶׁבַּשָׁמַיִם, שֶׁיִּכָּרְתוּ שׂוֹנְאֵינוּ:

Kara - Snake squash:

יְהִי רָצוֹן מִלְפָנֵי אָבִינוּ שֶׁבַּשָׁמַיִם, שֶׁתִּקְרַע רוֹעַ גְּזַר
דִּינֵנוּ, וְיִקָּרְאוּ לְפָנֶיךָ זְכֻיּוֹתֵנוּ:

Silka - Swiss chard:

יְהִי רָצוֹן מִלְפָנֵי אָבִינוּ שֶׁבַּשָׁמַיִם, שֶׁיִּסְתַּלְּקוּ אוֹיְבֵינוּ
וּמַשְׂטִינֵנוּ:

Fish:

יְהִי רָצוֹן מִלְפָנֵי אָבִינוּ שֶׁבַּשָׁמַיִם, שֶׁנִּפְרֶה וְנִרְבֶּה
כַּדָּגִים: